THE FORT
COOKBOOK

THE FORT COOKBOOK

New Foods of the Old West from the Famous Denver Restaurant

SAMUEL P. ARNOLD

HarperCollins*Publishers*

HarperCollins books may be purchased for educational, business, or sales promotional use. For information please write: Special Markets Department, HarperCollins Publishers, Inc., 10 East 53rd Street, New York, NY 10022.

FIRST EDITION

Designed by Joseph Rutt
Hand-drawn ornaments by Carrie F. Arnold

Library of Congress Cataloging-in-Publication Data

Arnold, Samuel P., 1926–
    The Fort cookbook : new foods of the Old West from the famous
Denver restaurant / Samuel P. Arnold. — 1st ed.
        p.   cm.
    Includes bibliographical references and index.
    ISBN 0-06-017567-2
    1. Cookery, American—Western style. 2. Fort (Restaurant)—History.
I. Title.
TX715.2.W47A7623   1997
641.5978—dc21   97-35766

97 98 99 00 01 ❖/RRD 10 9 8 7 6 5 4 3 2 1

Contents

Acknowledgments

I must first extend a thank-you—and a hearty "Waugh!"—to all my employees at The Fort for their unwavering dedication and the undaunted sense of humor necessary in this business; also, to our guests, who appreciate our efforts and keep coming back for more.

Thank you, Carrie, for everything everything everything; Suzanne (Suzie) Roser, for spending a summer in my home kitchen making sure each dish was as good as it could possibly be.

After a rocky beginning with us (see page 146), Betsy Andrews became invaluable to this project. She patiently listened to my endless stories, coordinated recipe testing, organized the text, made sure everything was done on time, and edited. Mostly, though, I thank her for her dauntless approach in helping me fit my life between the covers of a book. It's difficult to face the challenge of setting down on paper the story of one's life work, to see it finite and definitive in 310 pages, when so much must go untold, and when every moment, at least to the author, seems important.

Thank you, too, to my family, Holly, Mary, and Keith, for their input; also to my patient book agent Jody Rein, who has explained New York to me; and of course a roasted buff hump rib for my editor (the best in America), Susan Friedland, at HarperCollins.

I raise a glass to those who have shared my table through the years, with a special thanks to the hapless victims who accepted invitations to lunch this past summer in pursuit of the best recipes and that lovely warm feeling that only comes when you're sitting around a plundered table with friends, leaning back in your chair with a napkin crumpled in your lap. We swigged the dregs of our iced tea and oh, how we wished to close the office for the afternoon! And, lest we forget, I must mention our German shepherd Razor, who enthusiastically finished the leftovers (there were never very many), and who once ate Santa Fe Pork Chops complete with hot red chile sauce and stuck very close to his water dish for the rest of the day.

"A tune with yer supper?" Sam Arnold and his mandola in the Tower Room.

Foreword

When I was nine, my father told me that we were moving from our comfortable home in Denver to a new home in the foothills called The Fort. I had no idea that our new home would change my life forever. As a small girl it was fascinating for me to watch the New Mexican workers construct more than eighty thousand adobe bricks. They mixed the mud of the red sandstone and clay earth with just the right amount of straw, then poured the mud into wooden forms to mold the building bricks. The bricks baked in the hot, dry sun for six weeks under the blue Colorado skies. I would sit beside the adobe workers and pretend I was an Indian, making clay pots in the mud as best as a nine-year-old could make.

Our new home was a replica of Bent's Fort, a fur trading fort of the 1840s. It, too, was adobe. Not only did our home become a living replica of that era, but so did our hearts, minds, and souls.

The Fort is nestled against a beautiful ancient red sandstone rock over eighty feet high. It is a magical place. As a child I was told that the Woodland Indians, the ancient forerunners of the Plains Indians, called our rock "Signal Rock." The Woodlands used to send smoke signals to others from our rock. I found arrowheads and could hear the ghosts of the Indians whispering to me in the Wind Cave, just on the northern side of the rock. At night the wind howled and the stars twinkled brightly. Many a night my brother and I slept out on our rock under the stars, listening to the coyotes in the distance, dreaming that we were new incarnations of the Woodlands.

After I turned ten, I asked my father for an allowance since my school friends were given allowances by their parents. "Allowance!" my father said. "With the restaurant below, you can make more money than your school friends!" So I soon found a job as tortilla maker, making fresh tortillas in the front room where the customers could watch. Then I was a salad girl, bus girl, and courtyard raker.

My very favorite dishes in the early days of The Fort were Bee-nanas and Lobster and Shrimp Swiss Enchilada. The Bee-nanas are bananas injected with honey and cooked in their own skins on the grill. When finished, they are black, and then you peel back their

roasted skin to reveal the soft, honey golden fruit, with wisps of steam. The Lobster and Shrimp Swiss Enchilada is baked like a casserole in a *cazuela* dish or on individual plates. I often asked the chef to make me an enchilada, and then I'd hike up to the top of the rock with my dinner and eat overlooking the twinkling lights of Denver.

When I was eleven, I inadvertently invented a new dessert—a brick of vanilla ice cream sprinkled with cocoa mix and a dash of cinnamon. As the ice cream melted, the powdered mix became a chocolate syrup. The resulting brown brick looked just like our adobes, and the Adobe Sundae was born.

Soon we had a new member of our family: a Canadian black bear cub named Sissy. Through unusual circumstances my father adopted Sissy at the tender age of four months. She had been abused and we had plenty of room, so we gave her a home. Our German shepherd, Lobo, became her best friend. When I came home from school, I took naps with her. As she grew, she became almost the size of a person, and we would let her upstairs, where she'd sit on the couch with her legs crossed like a proper lady.

Our neighbors down the valley were of Swedish heritage. The grandmother taught me to make a flour porridge with cinnamon and lots of butter and sugar. Of course, this became Sissy's and my favorite treat after school. After making the porridge, I gave Sissy a bowl, and we sat across from each other eating our snack. It was so funny to watch her lap up the sticky porridge with her long tongue!

As my father researched the history of Bent's Fort, he found that a prairie grizzly had lived at the original fort. It was interesting that fate brought Sissy to us, as fate had brought a bear to Bent's Fort. Sissy lived a happy and healthy life for nineteen years, and her spirit still lives in each of our hearts.

Re-creating life in the 1840s, researching foods of all cultures, having a passion for trying new things (have you ever tasted moose nose?), and touching our ancient past has enriched this little girl's life. Thank you, Daddy.

Holly Arnold Kinney

Introduction

When I think back over the past third of a century to the beginnings of The Fort, a myriad of images float back into view: Sissy bear's long muzzle, little beady eyes, and the long pink narrow tongue flicking away at an ice-cream cone. The broad Alfred E. Newman smile on the well-driller's face as he assured me that the two wells he'd drilled had been fully cased to the bottom.

I remember old Lakota Indian Charlie Randall and his birdlike wife, Belle, who lived with us for several years. It was Charlie who explained to me that modern-day names of "chiefs" were often just inside jokes—"Chief Big Turnip," "Chief Long Carrot," and his own, "Chief Big Cloud." And Belle, looking the part of everyone's prototypical aunt with her hair tightly braided into a bun; she walked me out into the countryside around The Fort to see the medicinal herbs growing there. To my amazement, nearly every weed and flower had some special use. It was God's drugstore, she'd say. It's all around us if we only will learn and remember.

Well, in the past thirty-four years at The Fort, I have learned an awful lot. I'd like to think Belle would be proud of me. Writing this book has been great fun. It's given me the opportunity to reminisce and call it work.

My cooking career began early. As a teenager I took with me to boarding school a little frying pan and a Sterno stove. I had the local dairy deliver eggs, bacon, chocolate milk, and bread, right to my room and became well known for my bacon and egg sandwiches. It made for a lot of friendships. But I was still a long way from becoming a food historian and restaurateur. That started in 1959 on a vacation to the mountains.

HOW WOULD YOU LIKE TO LIVE IN A PLACE LIKE *THAT*?

My first wife, Betty, and I were returning to our home in Denver after a weekend trip. As we drove down through the foothills on Highway 285 just southwest of Denver, and could at last see the eastern plains before us, the road turned and went by a huge red rock. At the road's edge stood a large sign.

FOR SALE
Ideal Motel site, 7½ acres

"What a beautiful spot," said Betty. And it was! A giant sandstone monolith, multilayered in shades of red and tilted on its side, rose over ninety feet in the air, covering an acre and a half of the land. The field below it sloped downhill toward the east and overlooked a vast panorama of the plains. The lights of Denver and Englewood in the distance nine hundred feet below were just beginning to twinkle in the dusk.

The owner of the land was going through a divorce and needed to cash out fast, so we bought the property for a good price with the intent of building a home where our two children, Keith and Holly, could grow up out in the country. We currently lived in Park Hill, an older section of east Denver, where the houses stood shoulder to shoulder.

We discovered on the land an artesian well 703 feet deep. Water originated from high in the mountains, and we joked that it must run through some dinosaur bones on its way to us, for it was highly mineralized. Older people from Golden came bearing empty jugs to fill with this highly valued water. Thinking that perhaps a shallower well with less mineralized water would be easier to live with, I considered drilling a well or two and consulted a friend about how to "witch" a well.

Per instructions, I procured two welding rods bent in the middle at right angles. Holding one loosely in each hand, bent ends like gun barrels pointing forward, I slowly walked over the land. Suddenly, the rods moved toward each other, without any conscious effort on my part. As I retreated from the area, the rods moved apart. I approached the spot from another direction, and the rods waited until I crossed the exact same spot and then moved together again. It was uncanny, and we decided to believe.

I hired a local well driller to drill in two places, and we found sweet water in both, in less than seventy-five feet. Unfortunately, I wasn't as good at witching well drillers, because not long after he was paid, the new pumps sanded in, and we discovered neither of them had been fully cased to the bottom.

Two years later we were in the midst of designing a Spanish colonial–style home for the site. Then one day when we were at the

Denver Public Library, we opened up a book to a drawing done in 1845. It was by Lieutenant James W. Abert, who I later learned was a West Point–educated topographical engineer for the U.S. Army. He had fallen ill while on a military reconnaissance mission and spent several days recovering at Bent's Fort on the Arkansas River in southeastern Colorado. During his stay, he drew several pictures of the adobe fur trade fort, and here they were, reproduced in a library book. "How would you like to live in something like that?" asked my wife.

"Um, I think . . ." I said, and so the planning began.

I set out to learn as much as possible about the history of Bent's Fort. It was a huge adobe structure originally built by the Bent brothers, William and Charles, in 1833, on the plains of Colorado near modern-day La Junta. It served as the hub of a vast fur trade empire and freighting business into New Mexico along the Santa Fe Trail. In 1849 it burned to the ground. Some say Indians did it; others maintain that William himself torched his property as the only alternative to handing it over the United States government.

THE FIRST MEAL AT THE FORT

As the plans for our fort moved forward, it became apparent that the building as a home would be much too expensive, so we decided we'd start a restaurant as well. Financing the project was nearly impossible. It obviously would take more money than I had, and bank after bank turned me down. I, an advertising agency man with no restaurant experience, wanted to build a three-hundred-seat restaurant nearly an hour out of Denver (at that time), out of sun-dried adobe bricks? The tight-fisted bankers would sooner have financed a mud pie in a rainstorm.

Finally, a savings and loan bank in Golden suggested that if I could get the Small Business Administration to guarantee the loan, they might participate. And so it happened. And while the SBA required that I match dollars with them, they lent me part of the construction money.

Soon after construction began, we used the backhoe on the site to carve out a ten-inch-deep, five-foot-long fire pit on the east terrace. We filled it with charcoal and covered it with a sheet of heavy wire cloth. Then we barbecued baby pork backribs, slathered these with Walter Jetton's Barbecue Sauce (page 65), and washed them down with Bent's Fort Hailstorm Juleps (page 284). Between the barbecued ribs and the

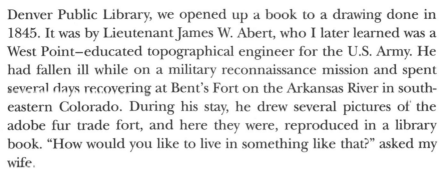

Introduction

3

Hailstorms with bourbon, the SBA officers and the bankers enjoyed the very first meal ever at The Fort when only foundations were being laid. We learned how good good food is for laying good foundations!

The next spring we hired architect William Lumpkins, a New Mexican native who was known as the dean of Spanish Colonial adobe architecture. From the 1845 drawing by Abert, Lumpkins drew the elevations and wonderful details for the building. One of his rules was that the contractor not use any plumb lines but build with line of sight. It made for a building with some charming irregularity but true to 1833 building standards of the early West.

In the early summer of 1962 we brought twenty-two men from Taos to build the citadel. Some eighty thousand adobe bricks were made, using a window frame–like mold with four openings. Mud with straw was pushed into the mold. The resulting bricks, each 14 by 10 by 4 inches, allowed us to build 24-inch-thick walls. Each brick weighed forty-five pounds, and 180 tons of earth was used. While the original Bent's Fort formed a completely enclosed quadrangle around a courtyard, we constructed our building with three sides around a courtyard, the fourth side bounded by the towering red rock.

Snow fell early in November 1962 while we were still awaiting the arrival of our doors. Plastic sheeting riffled in the arctic winds, and the

The Fort in winter clothing.

plasterers working indoors couldn't do their work for fear it would freeze.

But we were determined to move in by January, and the opening date we aimed for was February 1. The doors were installed at last, and we finally moved into the upstairs "officer's quarters" of the building. Temperatures were below zero as we moved all our belongings, including a piano, up the narrow, snow-covered stairs leading from the courtyard to the second level.

DEAR MARY

Open we did, on February 1, and one day about a month later I received a call from the county commissioners' office. "We need to talk privately with you," the commissioner's secretary advised. I drove right over. Her office door closed behind me. A guest had reported that gambling was going on at my establishment, I was told. He had seen a group of men with cards in their hands standing around a man at a table with money in his hands. Was I aware of this?

It took me a moment to figure out what had been going on, but then it hit me. Of course! On Sunday afternoons the early shift of waiters checked out their dinner tickets and turned their cash tips in to Luis Bonachea, our manager, who sat in a small room off the dining room. Someone must have seen them through a cracked open door and presumed the worst.

But in spite of false accusations and a lot of very real problems, our spirits were high. When going through volumes of old menus, business correspondence, purchase orders, and letters recently to write this book, I found this early letter to my sister that tells it like it was.

September 1963
Dear Mary,

The Fort has been a real challenge—not only all the mess of building it, but by the time we were ready to get into operation in February, we were so tight for money that we could barely stock the bar. But a newspaper story blasted us off. . . . This was fine, except that then we were completely demoralized by too many people, inexperience, and ill-trained help. But suffer through we did, and gradually straightened out most of the problems one by one. We had a good spring . . . and it's what we bargained for, so no real squawks.

Now for the fun: For some weeks we've had a wrestling black bear in the plaza. He's muzzled, of course, and "wrestles" with whoever dares—strong men, police officers, children. After each match he gets a bottle of pop or Kool-Aid. Victor is his name, and his owner, Tuffy, is very kind to him.

We've obtained three cannon—two half-pounders and one large six-pounder—the barrel alone weighs one thousand pounds. It can shoot a large juice can filled with cement some two miles. We bang them off with black powder almost every evening, to the dismay of the Bible camp two miles away.

We were given a young descented skunk about a month ago. We gave it a rabies shot and keep it as a pet. However, one night it disappeared. It had been gone for a week—taken up with a wild skunk that lives in the big rock and raids our garbage nightly. Well, last Saturday the cook shouted, "There goes Flower!" So the folk singer in the cantina and his audience all rushed out to trap the pet skunk in a drain pipe running under the building. They hosed water in from one end, and the folk singer seized the skunk as it came out the other. *Psssst!* It shot him in the chest with its juice, turned, and bit him . . . it was NOT Flower but her husband with a full load. Everyone howled with amusement except the folk singer who, with girlfriend in tow, went off to the hospital with a bitten hand. He's

Six-pounder Napoleon cannon "Bertha"
overlooking the fields to the east.

started the fourteen-day rabies series. That'll teach folk singers to squirt water at skunks!

Sunday will be a day of joviality. We're holding the first Fort Rendezvous dinner, on the anniversary of the appointment of Charles Bent as first governor of New Mexico. We've invited direct descendants of those who lived and worked at Bent's . . . namely Kit Carson III, Carson's great-granddaughter, Uncle Dick Wootton's grandnephew, and a bunch of others. We'll be serving buffalo and elk at the party, and a menu tailored from research on what Charles Bent would have eaten with it . . . rice, beans, apple pie, and Hailstorm juleps. It should be a fun, fun party.

WHAT SHALL WE SERVE?
OR, THE DISCOVERY OF ARNOLD'S LAW

While the construction team was still at work, we decided we'd better figure out just what kind of a restaurant they were building. What to serve? Our original idea was one we'd heard had been used success-fully in Australia: Each guest would cook his own steak.

To test it, we invited dinner guests to our home one Sunday evening. We offered them trays of steaks, chicken, fish, and shrimp. Choose what you want and cook it yourself, we said. Disaster ensued. Most of the men didn't have a clue as to how to cook their various foods. Chicken ended up burned black or raw inside, or both; the shrimp was shriveled and the fish immolated.

On to the next plan, which we knew was a winner. Our success would lie in serving dishes we had discovered in different parts of the world and particularly enjoyed. So upon opening we offered smoked trout and wild mushrooms from the mountains around Aspen; great golden rounds of Swedish pancakes with purple puddles of lin-gonberries poured on top; elk sausage; and even a dish called "Country Captain," a historic chicken curry supposedly brought from India to Maryland in the early nineteenth century.

These were all splendid dishes, but the public did not appreciate them. The Cuban black beans ended up in the disposal; the charbroiled bananas were eaten by only half the guests; and we learned to our sur-prise and dismay that our tastes were not that of the general public.

Several years later I took a summer vacation to Europe, where I and my motorcycle tooled through the small villages of Germany,

Introduction

Switzerland, and Spain. I soon noticed that in each village virtually all the restaurants had similar if not identical menus. In Barcelona it looked as if the fish menus from the waterfront restaurants were all printed by the same printer, with only a name change at the top of each card.

Gradually, I realized a truth: People in each region supported the restaurants that served the kind of food they liked to eat. How did this apply to me? People in Denver like to eat beef steaks and roasts. To be successful in Colorado a restaurant *must* serve those items. Eureka! Arnold's Law!

So when I returned home, I threw out all the odd and esoteric, and began serving top sirloin steaks with a wide variety of toppings: a garlic steak, a Texas barbecued steak, a steak with green chile, beefsteak with oysters in lemon butter sauce, steak basted with beer, and plain steak topped with brown butter. Immediately, guests flowed in and our fortunes changed. And while we experimented with new and different flavorings, sauces, and toppings, we still basically served beef steak.

Arnold's Law still holds true more than thirty years later, although today, public taste has become ever so much more sophisticated, which makes cooking more fun. I've learned to familiarize my waitstaff with the menu, too. Whenever we introduce a new dish, I make sure the entire dining room staff has tasted it and knows how delicious and healthful it is.

While The Fort serves five or six fresh fish options nightly, plus several interesting game birds, red meat is still our hottest item. In spite of today's emphasis on low-fat, low-cholesterol, and low-calorie foods, most people when eating out in Denver want red meat. In the 1980s, fish, birds, and vegetarian foods found a wider audience, and we expanded our menu. We enjoy preparing ostrich, quail, guinea fowl, salmon, and trout, but they account for less than one-third of our business.

We are fortunate that half the red meat we serve *is* low fat, low cholesterol, and low calorie—in the form of bison. But that's another story!

THE FIRST THANKSGIVING

Our first chef was an older Greek man named Nick. A small man with a tall toque, Nick enjoyed mingling with the guests in the dining room while his assistants toiled away back in the kitchen. "Never touch my

toque," he always warned. "Only my employer and I may touch my hat. I, when I quit, or he, when I'm fired."

A month before our first Thanksgiving in 1963, Nick exchanged our beautiful new double-oven Garland range for a used but much larger single-oven Vulcan range. The great big oven didn't have a thermostat that worked. "Never mind," Nick assured us. "I can tell the temperature by just putting my arm in the oven!"

Ten days before Thanksgiving, we finally agreed on the menu: roast prime rib of both buffalo and beef, and roast tom turkey with pine nut stuffing. On the Monday before the big day, we had over five hundred reservations and more coming in.

"Nick," I asked, "how many reservations can we take? And should you begin cooking? There are roasts, turkeys, bread, and pumpkin pies to be made, and you have but one oven."

"Have no fear, big Nick is here!" the diminutive figure replied. "I've been a member of the chefs de cuisine for thirty-seven years. You bring the guests, and I'll feed 'em."

On Tuesday evening, we were up to over 750 reservations. Nick confidently told us that he was doing the prep work and that I should continue taking reservations.

At noon on Thursday we opened our doors. Eight hundred fifty people were planning to dine at The Fort before 8 P.M. I started to relax after an hour. All was going wonderfully well. Then food seemed to be taking longer to come from the kitchen. Guests began approaching the hostess, saying they'd been waiting an hour. I went back into the kitchen to find Nick leaning against the coffee urn. "Get me a drink," he moaned. "I think I'm having a heart attack."

"Nick!" I cried. "Where's the food, Nick. Where's the food?"

Inside the walk-in cooler was bread dough bubbling up out of boxes, two dozen uncooked twenty-five-pound turkeys, six uncooked fourteen-pound buffalo roasts, eight uncooked beef roasts, and dozens of pumpkin pies, the uncooked filling sitting in unbaked pastry shells.

"It just didn't work out the way I planned it," wailed Nick. "We're out of turkey, roast beef, buffalo, and pumpkin pie."

Gently I lifted his toque. Then I made my way out to face three hundred dinner guests. I apologized profusely and told them I was lighting up the grill. Anyone who cared to stay would get a big steak dinner for the same cost as the turkey. About half the guests left, cursing us. The others stayed, also cursing us but wisely realizing that in midafternoon on Thanksgiving Day they'd never find a seat in another restaurant.

That was the moment I decided that I'd never be caught that way again. I had to learn to be a restaurant chef. From that day on it's been a continuing learning process for me. I've been to cooking schools all over the world, have read thousands of nineteenth-century journals, and have compiled a wonderful library of western history and cookbooks that contains over five thousand volumes. Reading recipes, discovering new foodstuffs, and experimenting in the kitchen are fascinating to me.

One word of advice before you strike out to discover the new foods of the Old West: Remember that recipes are only like road signs. How you travel and where you arrive depends on you. If you're like me, you'll add your own little personal touch to whatever you cook. That's the fun of the art.

TOUR OF THE FORT

The Fort's nine dining rooms are built around a central courtyard. In summer months a typical Plains Indian tipi stands in the courtyard and may be booked for special private dinners. It can accommodate up to twelve people, and shoes must be removed within. Since servers must work on their knees, they get an extra twenty-five dollars.

Bent's Quarters, a private dining room, recreates much of the feel of the 1840s. A collection of medicinal herbs of New Mexico and various items of the fur trade period line the shelves: knives, beads, buckles, musket caps, tobacco twists and "segars," tea bricks, loaf sugar, Florida water, lucifers, and much more.

On the east wall of "Bent's" hangs a wonderful oil painting of the *Western Engineer*, the 1819 flagship of Major Stephen Long and his army on their reconnaissance expedition up the Missouri River. The primitive steamboat had a sea serpent head that belched steam and a serpentlike waterline to throw fear into the Indians observing from the riverbank. The painting was done for The Fort's thirtieth anniversary by Gary Lucie, an artist well known for his intricately detailed and accurate renderings of steamboats and historic American waterways.

The St. Vrain Bar, on the west side of the courtyard, is named for Ceran St. Vrain, partner of the Bents. A French aristocrat from St. Louis, he brought fine wines, crystal glasses, and damask tablecloths to

Horno oven, tomahawk target, trade tent,
and tepee in the courtyard.

the remote West. Set in a niche in the wall of the bar is an adobe brick from the original Bent's Fort. The herringbone planed ceiling with its decorative bead is typical of the earliest New Mexican planked ceilings.

The St. Vrain Council Room angles off the St. Vrain bar and accommodates private parties and music evenings. It features artwork by my wife and others, a corner fireplace, and French doors out to the courtyard. After dark, the small fire in the courtyard glows orange through the panes.

Adjoining the Tower Room is the East Terrace, from which can be seen the magnificent panorama of red rocks and Pike's Peak to the south and Denver and its suburbs to the east.

The Main Dining Room, with its fireplace and view of the foothills and the lights of Denver and the plains beyond, features a beamed ceiling, artwork, and authentic mid-nineteenth-century artifacts. Throughout the building, the *vigas* (log beams) were stripped by drawknife, and *zapatas* (footed supports) were rough cut and then finished with a foot adz. All wood surfaces were hand-planed to remove machine saw marks.

Overlooking the Main Dining Room, The Grill is lovely for semi-private parties, with French doors out to the garden and a view of the

Introduction

11

St. Vrain Bar.

Denver skyline. The fountain to the north is carved of pink Mexican limestone.

Two round bastions stand at the northeast and southwest corners of The Fort. With their two-feet-thick adobe walls, these were used for defense in the original fort. We use the northeast bastion as a wine cellar, while the southwest tower accommodates an intimate dining room with a fireplace and a lovely view of the city lights. The Tower Room is furnished with portraits of mountain men, William and Charles Bent, Uncle Dick Wootton, Kit Carson, and Henry Clay.

The Ordinary is inhabited in winter by the trade lodge, where all manner of interesting goods can be found, from silver jewelry and beadwork to knives, tinware, and books.

The Outdoor Patio is delightful during warm weather and a good place to gather when the cannon are shot. What would a fort be without cannon?

Bertha, a six-pounder Napoleon on a sledge, with a two-mile range, overlooks the fields beyond The Fort. Unfortunately, some time ago it became inoperable because a careless gunner used too much modern powder and blew out the touchhole.

We also have a one-third-scale twelve-pounder, "Sweetlips," on a naval carriage, such as was used by famous keelboat captain Mike Fink on the Missouri River keelboats. Its barrel weighs about eighty

pounds, so "Sweetlips" requires a lot of lifting and preparation. It is fired only by trained employees. It's a real weapon, with a loud, booming voice. We also have a "thundermug" cannon, a type of mortar, which is fired on special days, and a smaller half-pounder, which is very deadly at one hundred yards. The cannon are fired on the Fourth of July, during the Fall Rendezvous, and on other special occasions that require a lot of noise, such as historic military brass band concerts and New Year's Eve.

The yucca outside Bent's Quarters provides salad blossoms in spring.

The Fort has grown in the past thirty years. Carrie, my second wife, partner, and best friend of over twenty-five years, is a meticulous historian and talented artist, and has assured that The Fort remain as authentic as possible in the face of additions and renovation. The glassed-in patio and outdoor garden facing east added in the 1980s are of traditional adobe and wood architecture. Each spring, the adobe walls on the southwest face are refaced after bearing the brunt of winter storms.

In the 1970s when the Park Service built a replication of Bent's Fort near the original site in La Junta, Colorado, Carrie and I acted as consultants because at the time, ours was the only existing replica of Bent's Fort. We think of ourselves as caretakers of the adobe building, which truly has a life of its own. For many, it's much more than a restaurant, it is a way of life. Many of our employees practice the arts and skills of the nineteenth century. Hundreds of mountain men, reenactors, and specialty tradespeople flock to the Fall Rendezvous every year; in fact, *buckskinning*, practicing the survival skills of mountain men, is the fastest growing outdoor sport in the nation. The food has grown along with everything else, constantly changing and developing as we find ourselves every day on a new frontier.

Introduction

Appetizers

———◆———

OUR APPETIZERS HAVE CHANGED OVER THE YEARS—PARTLY BECAUSE OF the popularity of certain items, and partly because our menu has evolved as we draw on the possibilities of new ingredients and historic recipes newly discovered. Appetizers are fun because they encourage experimentation. They allow us to serve unusual foods that guests might never order as an entree.

Our appetizer menu inspired the chapter organization of this book. Each chapter is divided into two parts. The first section contains recipes that we hope will appeal to everyone. The second section, "For the More Adventurous Palate," features dishes with unusual ingredients or uncommon food combinations.

Sometimes the most historically intriguing and strangest sounding dishes—such as Marrow Bones—are simple ones with surprisingly familiar flavors. Marrow bones taste like Yorkshire pudding. Other recipes, such as Cold Rattlesnake Cocktail, aren't the sort of thing your butcher will be able to help you with. Still, they're no less tasty for their oddness. With the exception of Supper for a Bear, which I included because it was served nightly at The Fort for almost twenty years (to our resident black bear), all of our dishes are delicious to humans. And home cooks with adventurous palates will find some wonderful surprises.

Fort Guacamole

I ate my first salsa cruda years ago at Sanborn's in Mexico City. It was simply tomato, onion, and serrano chile finely diced, with a dash of salt, a squeeze of lime juice, and whole-leaf cilantro. My belief is that guacamole originated when someone purposely (or otherwise) dropped some ripe avocado in a bowl of salsa and mixed it up. The basic recipe for guacamole in Mexico is just that: a combination of salsa cruda with avocado.

This recipe has been chosen by the local press as "Denver's Best Guacamole." The truth is that it is the uncomplicated, basic recipe from Old Mexico, with none of the garlic that many Gringos use!

Serves 6

3 ripe avocados, pitted and peeled
3 whole serrano chiles, finely minced
½ teaspoon salt
¼ cup freshly squeezed lime juice
2 large tomatoes, finely diced
1 large onion, finely diced
¼ cup whole fresh cilantro leaves (no stems)

Combine the ingredients in a large bowl, mashing the avocado with a fork or potato masher and leaving small lumps in the mixture. Don't use a food processor to dice the tomato and onion, because the texture of your guacamole will be much better if not too finely chopped. It's also necessary to use serrano chiles instead of jalapeños.

Taste for sufficient lime juice and add more if desired. The guacamole should be pepper-hot, so add more serranos as your taste dictates. Serve with freshly fried corn tortilla chips.

Regarding Cilantro

Many people recommend mincing cilantro. I find that the good coriander flavor disappears when it's chopped, so I always pull the leaves off the stems and use them whole. I think it makes for better flavor. But cilantro is a strong flavor and is an acquired taste for many people, so it has the ability to ruin an otherwise completely palatable dish for those who don't like it.

I think that, in a perfect world, cilantro would be as common in this country as lettuce.

Salsa Cruda

This salsa cruda most likely originated in Mexico, then migrated to San Antonio, Texas, which is where I first tasted it, made with jalapeños. I've adapted it for use with serrano chiles.

Makes 3½ cups

3 large, firm tomatoes, diced very small
6 serrano chiles, finely minced; for less pepper hotness, remove seeds and ribs before mincing
¼ large onion, finely diced
6 sprigs cilantro, coarsely chopped
¾ teaspoon salt
Juice of 1 lime

Combine all the ingredients and marinate in the refrigerator for 24 hours to let the flavors mingle and mellow. Serve cold with Finger Fajitas with Beef or Buffalo (page 28) or warm corn tortilla chips.

NOTES: If an onion seems very strong or bitter, place it in a small bowl, pour hot water over it, and drain. This will remove some of the oils.

To get the most juice from lemons or limes, heat the whole fruit in the microwave on high for one minute, then roll it on the counter before squeezing.

Jalapeños

Some people like the back-of-the-mouth hotness of jalapeños. I think they're like a lighted charcoal briquette in the throat. I love pickled jalapeño chiles, but in salsa cruda, I prefer the slim green serrano's taste and "bee-bite," front-of-the-mouth hotness.

Hot Sausage Bean Dip

Fritz Covillo made this at his fishing lodge when a group of chefs spent the weekend fishing the nearby streams. Later, I cooked it all over the country for many years while working for Coors Brewing Company. It has long been a staple at The Fort, served with fresh yellow and blue tortilla chips.

Serves 10

- 2 pounds refried beans
- 8 ounces dark beer (which leaves some of a 12-ounce bottle for the cook)
- ¾ pound bulk hot Italian sausage
- ½ small white onion, finely chopped
- 3 to 5 serrano chiles, finely minced
- 6 to 8 ounces cheddar cheese, grated (1½ to 2 cups)

Heat the beans and beer in a double boiler to prevent burning.

Meanwhile, heat a large sauté pan and brown the sausage with the onion, breaking the sausage into small pieces as it cooks. Pour off the fat and add the chiles. Sauté a few minutes longer. Combine with the bean and beer mixture and stir well. At the last minute, stir in the cheese, which will melt nicely into the warm dip. Serve with fresh corn tortilla chips.

Appetizers

Mountain Man Boudies

During the fur trade period, the American West was populated by many French-Canadian voyageurs making their living as beaver trappers. One favorite food was "boudin," or any type of sausage, preferably those similar to the blood sausage of France. The English word "pudding" originates from the French word *boudin,* and the recipe for boudin generally consisted of meat and some form of cereal cooked together and pushed into intestine casings. The English-speaking mountain men couldn't pronounce "dem furrin languidges," so they simply called boudin "dem boudies."

Early journals tell of dicing prime parts of buffalo, salting and peppering them, adding a little onion and cornmeal, and likely some red chile pepper, and then stuffing them into a piece of buffalo gut that had been cleaned and turned inside out so that any fat was on the outside. The sausages were tied off with a whang (a short length of rawhide), then either broiled over the fire or boiled. Boiling is more often spoken of in 1830 references.

To make a good sausage it is important to grind the meat coarsely. Thus, we put it twice through the "chili plate," which has larger holes than the standard hamburger meat grinder.

Makes 24 sausages

2	cups raw or roasted sunflower seed hearts
6	pounds buffalo meat (round, brisket, or plate), ground through the chili plate of the grinder twice; or substitute 6½ pounds beef and don't add the extra fat
½	pound ground buffalo, beef, or pork fat (the fat around the kidneys is the purest)
2	cups uncooked instant oatmeal
4	onions, finely minced
3	tablespoons coarsely ground black pepper
2	tablespoons medium red chile caribe (coarsely ground chile)
2	cups bread crumbs
2	tablespoons ground sage
1	tablespoon dried thyme
1	tablespoon dried leaf oregano
3	tablespoons whole cumin seed
18	feet large pork casings (optional)

If you cannot find roasted sunflower seed hearts, you can easily toast your own in a small skillet over medium heat, stirring until lightly browned, approximately 3 to 5 minutes.

The traditional way of making these boudies is to mix all the ingredients except the casings together thoroughly and, with a sausage stuffer, fill the pork casings to make individual boudies twisted off every 6 inches. But if you don't want to bother with stuffing sausage casings, simply shape the mix into patties. To cook, place over a medium-heat charcoal grill and cook to medium or medium-well. They can also be cooked on a griddle or a greased pan. If you are doing historic reenacting, the boudies would typically be boiled and served hot.

After they're boiled, boudies in sausage casings keep very well in the freezer. When you want to use them, defrost the boudies in the refrigerator and grill them or cook them on a griddle as indicated above. If you make patties, freeze them raw and then defrost and cook them in the same way as you would the boiled boudies.

Mountain man goods trader Don Erickson plies his wares at a Fort Rendezvous.

Scorpions

This fun appetizer combines a cheese-stuffed jalapeño with a shrimp in a lovely, crispy crust. The shrimp's tail curves up to form the scorpion's stinger, and the mild pepper-hotness does the stinging. Most of the work on these can be done several hours ahead so you don't have to disappear into the kitchen just as guests arrive.

We serve these at the reception for the Western Art Rendezvous. Held each year in early summer, the juried art exhibition is hosted by The Fort in cooperation with the Foothills Center for the Arts. The walls of every dining room are hung with about one hundred paintings and photographs selected from over five hundred pieces. We enjoy showing off art by contemporary Colorado artists and helping Colorado artists.

Makes 24 "scorpions"

24 large pickled jalapeno peppers (see page 24)
24 uncooked white shrimp, size 16 to 20 per pound
24 pieces Monterey jack cheese (about ¾ cup total), cut in rectangles to fit inside the jalapeño peppers, leaving room for the shrimp
 1 egg
½ cup all-purpose flour
½ teaspoon salt
¾ cup skim milk or water
   Canola or peanut oil for frying

The jalapeños can be stuffed earlier in the day and refrigerated until about 20 minutes before you're ready to batter and fry them.

Slit the peppers lengthwise from stem to stern, but don't cut all the way through the peppers; they should look like little boats. Remove the seeds under running water.

Peel the shrimp, leaving the tail section intact. Insert a piece of cheese into each jalapeño, then insert the large end of the shrimp on top of the cheese so that the tail curls upward outside the jalapeño at the stem end.

With a whisk, beat the egg, flour, salt, and half the milk to make a batter the consistency of a heavy pancake batter. Add the remaining milk a little at a time as needed; you may not use all the liquid. Set the batter aside while you prepare the jalapeños, or, if you've stuffed the

jalapeños ahead of time, let the batter sit at room temperature for about 30 minutes before using so that the gluten develops. The batter will have better consistency and cling well to the peppers.

In a deep skillet or deep-fat fryer, heat the oil to 380°F. (It must be hot enough—use a thermometer.) Stir the batter once more and dip each "scorpion" into it. Fry until crisp and light—they should crisp instantly. Drain on a paper towel and serve immediately.

Jalapeños Stuffed with Peanut Butter

Lucy Delgado, well known in the 1960s as a traditionalist New Mexican cook, taught me to stuff peanut butter into peppers. "These are the best appetizers I know," she told me during one of our recipe swaps. "But if I show you how to make them, you have to promise to try them." Peanut butter–stuffed jalapeños! I vowed I would taste them even though they sounded stranger than a five-legged buffalo. She prepared some and said, as a last word of instruction, "Pop the entire pepper into your mouth so you're not left with a mouthful of hot jalapeño and too little peanut butter." I gamely took the little morsel by the stem, and in it went. Miracle! Delicious!

Fearful of serving them to guests but eager to try them out on friends, I made them for my own parties until they became so popular that I put them on the menu. When NBC's *Today* show came to Denver, Bryant Gumbel ate eight of them in a row. (Jane Pauley would have none of it.)

Serves 10 (2 per person, usually)

   1 12-ounce can pickled jalapeño peppers
1½ cups peanut butter (smooth or chunky)

Slice the pickled jalapeños in half lengthwise not quite all the way through, leaving the 2 halves attached at the stem end. Using a knife or spoon, remove the seeds and ribs under running water. Pack the halves with peanut butter, press together, and arrange on a serving plate. Be sure to warn guests to put the whole pepper (except the stem) in the mouth before chewing, to get 70 percent peanut butter and 30 percent jalapeño. A nibbler squeezes out the peanut butter, changing the percentages and making it very hot indeed.

A fun variation is to mix Major Grey's chutney with the peanut butter. It gives a nice fruity sweetness that also buffers the burn.

Appetizers

Buffalo Eggs

One morning watching NBC's *Today* show, I saw Willard Scott, the weatherman, eating "Scotch Eggs"—hard-boiled chicken eggs wrapped in sausage and deep-fried. They are good to eat but difficult to handle. It occurred to me that pickled quail eggs were a much smaller bite. So we tried wrapping low-fat buffalo sausage around the tiny eggs and deep-frying them in canola oil. The result was a wonderfully tasty, crisp, bite-sized treat. Much later, when the *Today* show came to Denver, Jane Pauley, who had disdained the Jalapeños Stuffed with Peanut Butter (page 23), thoroughly approved of our American West version of Scotch Eggs.

Serves 12

    1½ quarts canola oil
     2 dozen pickled quail eggs (not canned quail eggs; if you can't
        find them in a jar, use 1 dozen small hard-cooked hen's eggs
        instead)
    2¼ pounds buffalo sausage or bulk hot Italian sausage
     1 cup flour
     1 cup milk
     3 cups crushed white or yellow corn tortilla chips

In a deep fryer, heat the oil to 350°F. Rinse the eggs and pat them dry. If you are using hen's eggs, cut them in half, either lengthwise or crosswise.

Divide the sausage in half and roll or pat it out on a floured surface to a ⅜-inch thickness. (If you have enough counter space, don't bother dividing it.) Wrap each egg with about 2 level tablespoons of sausage, then roll it in flour, dip in milk, and roll in tortilla crumbs. Fry several at a time for 4 to 6 minutes and drain. Allow the heat to return to 350°F between batches. Serve warm or cool with Buffalo Eggs Sauce (recipe follows).

Buffalo Eggs Sauce

Makes 4½ cups

2 cups red chile sauce (the commercial variety, such as Heinz, can be found in the ketchup aisle)
2 cups hot mango chutney, such as Major Grey's
¼ cup yellow mustard seed

Mix all the ingredients and chill for at least several hours to give the flavors a chance to mellow and mingle. This sauce is also good with Rocky Mountain Oysters (page 40) and Comanche-Style Buffalo Heart Skewers (page 32).

Spring buffalo drive in the San Luis Valley.

Appetizers

25

Fort Cheese Tostados

When I first opened The Fort, I found that people arrived hungry, and by the time they were seated, they'd enthusiastically eat anything that came to the table. We offered a splendid apple nut bread from Glenwood Springs, and our guests would fill up on it so quickly that by the time the waiter came for the order, their hunger was sated.

An experienced restaurateur, Ray Zipprich, who ran El Rancho, a popular large mountain restaurant, gave me some fatherly advice: "Give your guests something that takes a little time to eat while you prepare their dinners." So we invented Fort Cheese Tostados and served them for many years. We made a fresh salsa cruda from tomatoes, onions, serranos, cilantro, salt, and lime juice, and spread it over grated cheese on crisp corn tortilla rounds. Broiled to bubbling, one was brought to every guest to take the edge off his hunger. Bread came to the table later, with the salads.

Makes 4 dozen pieces

12 corn tortillas
   Canola oil
 6 ounces longhorn cheddar cheese, grated (1½ cups)
 6 ounces Monterey jack cheese, grated (1½ cups)
 ⅔ cup Salsa Cruda (page 18), drained of liquid
   Toasted canola or black sesame seeds

In an inch of hot oil, quickly fry the tortillas into flat crisp rounds. Preheat the oven to 400°F.

Mix the longhorn cheddar cheese and Monterey jack cheese together and sprinkle about 2 tablespoons of the mixture on each fried tortilla. Spread a heaping tablespoon of salsa cruda on top. Before baking, sprinkle a few canola or black sesame seeds on top, for both appearance and taste. Place on baking sheets and bake for 3 minutes, just until the cheese is melted. Don't overbake! Cut them into quarters to serve.

Broiled Asadero Cheese

Asadero is Spanish for "roaster;" *asadero* cheese is by definition any cheese whose taste, texture, and composition make it conducive to roasting Wonderful asadero cheese is made by Mennonite cheese factories in Mexico and is available there and in American border states. It has very little taste when cold, but when broiled or roasted, this white cheese develops a savory flavor almost like meat and is extraordinarily delicious.

Because it is difficult to obtain consistently high quality asadero cheese from Mexico, we use another cheese at The Fort that is similar and equally delicious. It is a moderately salted cheese with mint flakes called *halloumi,* and it comes from the Mediterranean island of Cyprus. It does not run when heated but becomes wonderfully golden crusted. We often prepare it at home on a charcoal grill, as we first ate it on Cyprus. There, the cheese was grilled along with pieces of lamb, fish, chicken, and beef. A bite of crisped halloumi cheese with a bite of crisp broiled lamb is a taste delight.

Serves 4

  1 **pound halloumi cheese**
  8 **slices toasted Herb Bread (page 214)**

To prepare the cheese for broiling, cut the slab in two lengthwise. Soak it in cool water for 4 hours, changing the water several times to desalinate the cheese. Dry it and place it in a greased pan under the broiler. When the cheese has turned golden brown, turn it over and repeat the process to brown both sides. Place the cheese on a serving plate and surround with toast. The cheese will cool and harden fairly quickly, so serve immediately.

Finger Fajitas with Beef or Buffalo

These are a very popular appetizer and not difficult to produce, although they are labor-intensive when you have to make one thousand or more!

Makes 48 pieces

8 small flour tortillas
½ cup sour cream
Cold buffalo or beef prime rib, medium-rare, cut into very thin
    3-inch strips
1 cup Fort Guacamole (page 17)
Red Chile Sauce (page 84), Salsa Cruda (page 18), or
    Tamarind-Chile Sauce (page 107)

Cut each tortilla into 6 wedges. Using a pastry brush, paint sour cream lightly over each piece. Place 1 or 2 strips of meat and a teaspoon of guacamole across the wide end of each wedge. Roll up the wedge; the sour cream will hold it together. Arrange on a serving plate with a dipping sauce.

NOTE: If you divide the preparation among three people, with one applying the sour cream, one adding the meat and guacamole, and one rolling up, you can make lots of these in very little time.

Blue Corn Meal Chips

When summer humidity sets in and your corn chips lose their crispness within twenty-four hours, take fifteen minutes out of your day to make your own—not quite from scratch but from fresh store-bought blue corn tortillas. They can be hard to find, but yellow or white (or even red!) tortillas are delicious, too.

> **Fresh blue corn tortillas**
> **Peanut or canola oil**
> **Kosher or sea salt**
> **Red chile powder, jalapeño pepper powder (usually found in the Mexican food aisle or in a specialty store), or cayenne to taste (optional)**

In a fairly deep pan, heat the oil to about 380°F. If the tortillas are straight from the refrigerator, they will lower the oil temperature dramatically. Best leave them out at room temperature for 1 hour before you use them. If ice crystals have formed on them, be sure to pat the tortillas dry with a paper towel before frying. With a heavy knife or Chinese cleaver, cut the stack in half, then into thirds, for 6 pieces per tortilla.

Piece by piece, place the tortilla chips in the oil until the bottom of the pan is covered. Watch them carefully so that they don't burn, and lift out with a slotted spatula when ever so slightly browned. Drain and lightly salt. If you wish, sprinkle a little finely powdered red chile, jalapeño, or cayenne onto the chips. Plan to serve them soon, for they are best within a few hours after cooking.

To reconstitute old chips, spread them on a baking sheet and place in a 400°F oven for 3 or 4 minutes.

Shrimp and Avocado Cocktail

In 1952 in Morelia, Mexico, I was served a tall glass filled with shrimp and avocado in a cocktail sauce of tomato and lime juices, cilantro, and serrano chile, all favorites of mine. It was so good that, after finishing off the shrimp and avocado, I added a double shot of white tequila to the remaining sauce and enjoyed a second cocktail as a noble completion to the dish. While I don't recommend the tequila necessarily, this wonderful combination of flavors and textures is not to be missed.

Serves 6

1 pound cooked and peeled small Icelandic or Bay shrimp, rinsed in cold water
1 cup diced celery (use a potato peeler to remove the tough outer strings)
2 avocados, peeled, pitted, and chopped into 1-inch cubes

Shrimp and Avocado Sauce:
½ cup mayonnaise
1¼ cups tomato juice
1 tablespoon plus 1 teaspoon ketchup
2 teaspoons horseradish
½ serrano chile, minced
6 to 8 cilantro leaves
Juice of 1 lime
Dash of Worcestershire sauce

6 tablespoons small capers (optional)
6 sprigs cilantro
6 slices lime

Combine the shrimp and celery; this can be done well ahead of time. Add the avocado at the last minute to keep it from becoming brown.

Mix the sauce ingredients together well in a blender or food processor, making sure the mayonnaise is fully incorporated. When ready to serve, toss the sauce with the shrimp, celery, and avocado. Pour into tall glasses and garnish each with 1 tablespoon of capers, a sprig of cilantro, and a slice of fresh lime.

Skull Cracker Soup

Originally a Mexican soup, its name and heritage may perhaps be attributed to the Tlaxcalan Indians, who were Hernán Cortés's allies in the overthrow of Montezuma. They later accompanied the Spanish when they settled Santa Fe in 1607. The city state of Tlaxcala was never ruled by the Aztec Empire. Its people were never enslaved or taxed by the Spaniards after they helped Cortés. According to Cortés's letters to the King of Spain, in the Tlaxcala city plaza stood a skull rack boasting more than 600,000 enemy skulls. Just as on the Day of the Dead in Mexico, when sugar skulls are eaten, so "Skull Cracker Soup" may be enjoyed with just a hint of spicy mysticism. When you serve it, deny that the tamale represents the brain.

Serves 18 as an appetizer or 12 as an entree

- 6 to 8 large buffalo or beef bones
- 2 large onions, chopped
- 2 cloves garlic
- 1 teaspoon cracked black pepper
- 2 bay leaves
- 2 teaspoons salt
- 8 quarts water
- 3 tablespoons Worcestershire sauce
- ½ fresh or frozen tamale per person (1 tamale if serving as an entree)
- Fresh cilantro to taste

Preheat the oven to 400°F.

Spread the bones in a roasting pan and roast for 2 hours, until the bones are brown.

Place the bones, onions, garlic, pepper, bay leaves, and salt in the water and simmer overnight or until reduced to 3 quarts. Add the Worcestershire sauce. Strain and discard the bones, reserving the broth. Freeze any broth you won't be serving immediately. Since it's a long project to reduce it, it's lovely to have a reserve of this good broth on hand.

Heat the remaining broth to serving temperature. Warm the tamales in a microwave oven or steamer. Cut into 1-inch pieces. Divide among the soup dishes and flood with the broth. Garnish with a sprig of cilantro.

Comanche-Style Buffalo Heart Skewers

The *ciboleros* were Hispanic and Native American buffalo hunters, and for several hundred years, buffalo hides were a major item of trade from Santa Fe to Old Mexico. The Comanches, who were also great hunters, relished the fresh heart immediately after a kill; this meat becomes very tough almost immediately and requires a marinade to tenderize it. I found this recipe in Peru, where beef and lamb heart are sold broiled and skewered as *anticuchos*. Any acidic marinade may be used—wine, yogurt, beer, vinegar, or citrus juices.

We serve these with a small dish of sweet red chile sauce. They are wonderful, too, as a dinner, wrapped up in hot flour tortillas with a sprinkle of salt and chile.

Serves 6 as an appetizer

1   **pound buffalo or beef heart (your butcher may be able to procure buffalo heart for you)**
½   **bottle (750 ml) red wine**
¼   **cup vinegar**
1½ **teaspoons mustard seed**
1½ **teaspoons black peppercorns**
2   **tablespoons coarsely ground hot red chile caribe**
1   **bay leaf**
2   **tablespoons salt**
¼   **cup cooking oil**
    Sweet red chile sauce such as Peanut Red Chilli Sauce (page 82), Buffalo Eggs Sauce (page 25), or your favorite commercial variety

Place the heart in a glass or other nonreactive container. Combine the wine, vinegar, mustard seed, peppercorns, chile caribe, bay leaf, and salt. Add this mixture to the container and marinate the heart for 5 days.

When you're ready to grill it, cut the heart into 4-inch strips that are ½ inch thick and ¾ inch wide; discard the veins and arteries. Preheat a grill to high or an oven to broil. Thread the meat onto skewers. Brush with oil and cook until the edges are browned and a little crisp. Serve with the sweet chile sauce.

Broiled Buffalo Marrow Bones

Nothing equals the wonderful flavor of broiled buffalo marrow. It tastes just like the beef drippings used to make Yorkshire pudding. In fact, it's so surprisingly delicious that The Fort serves more than two tons of buffalo marrow bones annually. The mountain men called this unusual delicacy "prairie butter," which speaks to its savory richness. The name is misleading, though, because the marrow is 10 percent fat and 90 percent incomplete protein. The Italians have known the secret of delicious marrow for years, and this dish is actually very similar to the veal shank marrow so prized in osso bucco.

We serve this dish with Tabasco's new Green Sauce. Many hesitant guests are persuaded to try it when they discover that Julia Child, while dining at The Fort, asked for a second helping.

Serves 4

2 buffalo femurs (leg bones)
Salt and pepper to taste
Toasted Herb Bread (page 214)

Ask your butcher to obtain buffalo femurs and cut off the knobs with a saw, then split the bones lengthwise in two, being careful to wipe away any bone dust.

Broil the bones facedown on a baking sheet for 6 minutes on the top rack of the oven, then turn them marrow-side up and broil for another 4 to 5 minutes. The marrow should be golden brown but not completely liquefied. Dust with salt and pepper and transfer to a serving plate.

Use a marrow scoop or butter knife to remove the marrow as needed, spreading it like butter over the herb toast.

Native American Use of Marrow Butter

Plains Indians often made marrow butter by boiling cracked bones. Allowed to cool, the marrow and fat rose to the surface. It was carefully scooped off and served as butter, or it was mixed with pounded jerky and mashed chokecherries and eaten as pemmican.

Appetizers

Cold Rattlesnake Cocktail

"Let them eat snake!" exclaimed the host of a small dinner party one night, much to his own amusement, when this dish was brought to the table. His guests chuckled uneasily. But cold rattlesnake cocktail has been the single most popular appetizer at The Fort. It resembles rich chicken and is delicious with a sweet red chile sauce such as the one from Heinz.

Serves 4 to 8

1   4-pound rattlesnake (see Note)
½   cup minced onion
Bay leaf
½   teaspoon black peppercorns
Bibb lettuce
2   tablespoons sweet red chile sauce per person

The longest rattler skin I've seen was 76 inches long, but there are stories in New Mexico of much, much larger rattlesnakes. The larger, the better, of course, for it will feed and impress more guests. If you've caught a rattler and want to prepare it for cooking, first cool it in the refrigerator or freezer. It will go to sleep and will be safe to handle. Using a cleaver or hatchet, cut off the head low enough down on the neck so that it may be freeze-dried and made into a hat ornament.

Next, stretch it out on a table and, using a razor blade, an X-Acto knife, or a very sharp skinning knife, slice the skin of the belly lengthwise, starting at the neck and continuing down the length of the snake. Remove the organs and wash well under running water. Use a pair of pliers to pull off the skin. It should be easy to remove since there is some fat between the skin and the muscle. Try not to damage the skin, for it may be rubbed on the underside with a little salt and then stretched onto a board and tacked down to dry for display as a monument to your bravery and culinary skills.

Once the snake is cleaned and skinned, braise it in a pot with the onion, bay leaf, and peppercorns. After 90 minutes of gentle boiling, the snake is done. Allow to cool, then strip the meat from the bones by hand. Arrange atop a bed of the lettuce on a serving plate or in cocktail glasses, and serve with sweet red chile sauce.

NOTE: Like chicken, raw rattlesnake is a carrier of salmonella. Disinfect your hands, cutting board, and tools after handling raw snake. See Suppliers (page 303).

Rattlesnake!

I first cooked rattlesnake in 1975 at a Historic Denver festival. Somehow my wife nodded "yes" at the wrong moment when the chairman was looking for food booth operators, and I ended up preparing 4,000 buffalo burgers, 300 pounds of Rocky Mountain Oysters, and 120 pounds of rattlesnake left over from a fiesta in San Antonio. After breaking the blades of a couple of French knives on the bones, I learned to use a cleaver to hack the snakes into pieces of fryable size. We dipped the chunks of snake in a tempura batter—delicious!

The Fort gets snakes from "rattlesnake roundups" in west Texas, during which individuals capture the snakes alive, and prizes are given to the longest, heaviest, and so forth. They come to us frozen in big, cylindrical coils and unwind in boiling water when the muscles flex. When we first started cooking them, young kitchen helpers panicked, thinking the snakes had somehow come alive.

In the spring of 1996, rattlesnake suddenly became as rare as it had been during the last Chinese Year of the Snake when Chinese and Japanese bought everything there was. Their numbers are again increasing, a fact for which I'm thankful, because rattlers, for all their bad reputation, are a necessary part of the West's food chain.

Buffalo Tongue with Caper Sauce

Buffalo tongue was thought by many to be the greatest gourmet delicacy of the American nineteenth century. Considered holy meat by Native Americans, it has a delicate flavor and fine texture and is far superior to beef tongue, which has a coarser quality.

The demand for buffalo tongue was a major reason for the wholesale slaughter of the bison. Tragically, whole herds were killed for their hides and tongues, which were smoked, salted, or pickled and sent east in fully loaded railroad cars. Such fine restaurants as Delmonico's in New York City reportedly served it to the likes of President Ulysses S. Grant and singer Jenny Lind, the Swedish Nightingale. Today, in limited numbers, buffalo tongues are once again gracing gourmet palates, for in addition to the herds that still roam on federally protected land, bison are thriving on ranches in all fifty states.

Serves 16 to 24 as an appetizer
or 8 to 12 as an entree

1 small onion, coarsely chopped
1 bay leaf (laurel)
1 tablespoon freshly ground black pepper
3 to 4 pounds buffalo tongue or beef tongue

Caper Sauce:
1 cup mayonnaise
1 rounded tablespoon capers
1 tablespoon prepared horseradish
Pinch of dried oregano
1½ teaspoons freshly ground black pepper

Parsley for garnish

Bring a large pan of water to a boil along with the onion, bay leaf, and pepper. Add the tongue and boil gently for 2 ½ to 3 hours.

Combine all the ingredients for the sauce, blend well, and chill.

When the tongue has cooked, remove from the water and allow to cool slightly. While still warm, peel off the light outer skin with a knife.

Preheat the broiler. Slice the tongue into ½-inch-thick pieces across the grain. Assemble on an ovenproof platter and heat briefly under the broiler. Place a bowl of the caper sauce on the platter and garnish with parsley.

Variation

Buffalo Tongue Canapés

This is an excellent way to use cold tongue. Cut the tongue into ¼-inch slices and cut out interestingly shaped pieces with a small vegetable cutter—round, serrated, or oval. Spread a cracker lightly with Caper Sauce and lay a piece of tongue on it. Shake a very little dried dill on each. Lay 2 shreds of beni-shoga (kizami-shoga) red pickled ginger on top.

Variation

Buffalo Tongue en Gelée

Serves 16

2 recipes of Buffalo Tongue with Caper Sauce (page 36)
2 tablespoons gelatin
Cold water
Red bell pepper, cut horizontally into decorative rings
Whole leaves of cilantro
Boston lettuce

After braising the tongues, set them aside and reduce the broth to about 2 cups. Add the gelatin, softened first in cold water following the directions on the package.

Peel the tongues and lay them side by side in opposite directions in a small oval dish or terrine. Arrange the rings of red bell pepper upright around the tongues, along with the cilantro. Pour the broth over the tongues and chill until the broth is firm. Remove from the dish by dipping the dish into hot water to loosen, then turn it out onto a cold platter. Slice and serve on a bed of Boston lettuce, with a spoonful of caper sauce on each slice.

Appetizers

Rocky Mountain Oysters

One of our goals at The Fort is to serve the most traditional foods of the early West. A strong abiding tradition in the 1840s among the Bents' cattle operations in the Arkansas River Valley was cooking and eating calf testicles at roundup time. Impaled on sticks, they were roasted over the fire. The cowboys called them "Rocky Mountain oysters" or "prairie oysters." Mexican shepherds in the San Luis Valley also served lamb testicles, called *criadillas,* campfire-cooked in the same way.

The eating of testicles is a tradition that goes back to ancient Rome, as documented by Apicius, a famous Roman cookbook writer. Some believe that eating "parts" imbues the eater with the power of those parts. There may be some truth to that since they do contain testosterone. The generative glands from beef, lamb, pork, rooster, and turkey are commonly eaten in ranch country even today. At The Fort we also serve bison testicles.

In 1963, not knowing better, we bought bull fries, which are large bull testicles. They came frozen and varied from grapefruit size to lemon size. To prepare them we first dipped them in hot water to thaw the skin, cut a ring around their middles with a sharp knife, and pulled off the skin like an orange peel. While they were still partially frozen, we sliced them ⅜ to ½ inch thick, brushed them with oil, and laid them over the charcoal grill, or we dusted them with seasoned flour and deep-fried them. Frankly, they weren't terribly good, with a texture not unlike overcooked liver.

We did have fun with them, though. With every order the grill-man sounded a loud and plaintive "moo!" on a horn normally used by ranchers to call in their cows. Eventually that got old and we stopped. But we never stopped serving mountain oysters, although we no longer offer bull fries. Instead, more than three thousand calf fries a week come from our kitchen.

I discovered calf fries during the early 1980s when I was working as a media spokesman for Coors Brewing Company, promoting their beer throughout the country as a cooking ingredient. At the Texas State Fair in Dallas I set up a mountain oyster booth and

bought product locally. For the first time I was able to obtain calf fries. They were much smaller than bull fries, about the size of an English walnut. Cut in half and dipped in a light tempura-style beer batter, they were wonderfully delicious.

In a taste test by eight food experts held recently at The Fort, beef calf testicles won but were virtually tied with turkey fries. Use whatever you can easily obtain from your butcher, and if you follow any of these recipes, they should turn out ultradelicious.

Maybe the faint at heart will be more inspired by the words of a thirteen-year-old than the pronouncement of a food expert. Colin St. John, the son of a friend of ours, wrote an essay for school entitled "My Favorite Food: Rocky Mountain Oysters." Here is an excerpt.

> Rocky Mountain Oysters are my favorite food. They are the testes of any kind of male animal. My favorite kind of Rocky Mountain oysters are a buffalo's testes. I am not joking, Rocky Mountain oysters are testes, not oysters. . . . The process of making Rocky Mountain oysters is rather disgusting, so if you happen to be easily sickened, I recommend that you do not read this portion of the paper . . .
>
> "Just try one," [said Dad.] I did.
>
> "Wow! These are good! What are they?"
>
> "Well, um, they're buffalo testes."
>
> . . . I thought that I was going to throw up, but I said to myself, "Hey, I like them, so who cares?" I finished off the plate and I've loved them ever since. . . . So, if you have the guts, bon appetit!

Rocky Mountain Oysters Fort Style

This is how we serve mountain oysters at The Fort.

Serves 6 as an appetizer or 2 as an entree

12 calf or veal testicles (or turkey fries may be substituted)
1 quart peanut oil
1½ cups all-purpose flour
2 teaspoons black pepper
½ teaspoon cayenne
1 teaspoon seasoned salt
Sweet chile sauce such as Buffalo Eggs Sauce (page 25) or
    Alligator Pear Sauce (page 151)
Several other sauces for dipping such as honey mustard,
    barbecue, or sweet-and-sour sauce (optional)

With a sharp paring knife, cut and peel the skin away from the testicles. They will peel and slice much more easily if they are slightly frozen.

Heat the oil to 375°F and preheat the oven to 200°F.

Cut the fries into 1-inch pieces. Combine the flour, black pepper, cayenne, and seasoned salt, and roll the pieces in this mixture. If you slice them ahead of time, pat them dry with paper towels before rolling them in flour. Fry for 3 minutes, until a light crust forms. Dredge on a paper towel and keep warm in the oven. If you are serving them as an appetizer, skewer each one on a toothpick. Serve with sweet chile sauce on the side. It's nice to fill several ramekins with your favorite sauces for a variety of flavors.

Variation

Rocky Mountain Oysters in Beer Batter

Prepare and serve the calf fries as in Rocky Mountain Oysters Fort Style but dredge them in this batter before frying. Serve them to your trembling date with a gleam in your eye.

1 egg
1 cup all-purpose flour
Approximately ¾ cup beer
½ teaspoon salt
Freshly ground black pepper

Beat the egg together with the flour, beer, and salt. Add black pepper to taste.

Variation

Rocky Mountain Oysters with Panko

Panko is a light, feathery Japanese bread crumb used in Japanese restaurants for breading pork cutlet (*tonkatsu*). It's available in most groceries or in Asian markets.

Simply peel, slice, fry, and serve the calf fries as in Rocky Mountain Oysters Fort Style, but roll them in Panko with salt and pepper instead of seasoned flour.

Appetizers

41

Rocky Mountain Oysters Santa Fe

Serves 6 as an appetizer or 2 as an entree

12 calf or veal testicles (turkey fries may be substituted)
½ cup flour
3 tablespoons peanut oil or other vegetable oil
2 scallions, including greens, finely sliced on the diagonal
1 fresh serrano chile, minced (or more, if desired)
¼ teaspoon black or yellow mustard seed
8 leaves fresh cilantro
½ teaspoon salt
3 pieces of toasted bread, sliced in half diagonally
Cilantro for garnish
Dash of paprika for garnish

With a sharp paring knife, cut and peel the skin away from the testicles. (If they are frozen, they will peel and slice much more easily.)

Cut the fries into 1-inch pieces and roll in the flour. If you slice them ahead of time, pat them dry with paper towels first. Heat the oil in a sauté pan and add all the ingredients except the bread and garnishes. Sauté for about 5 minutes or until the fries are slightly browned. Serve over the toast garnished with sprigs of cilantro and a sprinkle of paprika.

Rocky Mountain Oysters Rockefeller

A trip to New Orleans provided the incentive for this dish. It is a delicious western variation of the famed Oysters Rockefeller, created in 1899 by Monsieur Antoine Alciatore, proprietor of the famed New Orleans restaurant Antoine's. According to legend, the recipe was named when one of Antoine's customers tasted the dish and exclaimed, "Why, this is as rich as Rockefeller!"

It's important that you ask your butcher for calf fries and not bull fries. Calf fries are much more tender than the larger testicles of bulls. Turkey fries are excellent, too. Keep in mind that the taste and texture of fries is very similar to sea scallops.

Serves 6

24 calf or veal fries (or substitute turkey fries)
 1 quart peanut oil or other oil for deep frying
 2 cups all-purpose flour
 1 teaspoon freshly ground black pepper
¼ teaspoon cayenne
 2 tablespoons seasoned salt
 8 ounces bacon, finely chopped
 4 cloves garlic, finely minced
 4 tablespoons butter
 1 cup finely chopped shallots
¾ cup mayonnaise
 1 cup dried bread crumbs
 1 cup finely chopped parsley
 6 tablespoons Pernod or Ricard anisette or other anise-flavored
   liquor
 1 teaspoon celery salt
Salt
 4 cups finely chopped fresh or frozen spinach, squeezed of
   excess water
24 cleaned medium-sized oyster shells or 6 3- to 4-inch-diameter
   ceramic scallop shells, found in some gourmet groceries, or
   use individual ramekins
 1 quart rock salt (only if using oyster shells)
Spanish paprika for garnish

Appetizers

43

Prepare the calf fries as in Rocky Mountain Oysters Fort Style (page 40), using the calf fries, peanut oil, flour, black pepper, cayenne, and seasoned salt.

Brown the bacon and garlic together in a saucepan. Add the butter and shallots. Sauté over medium heat, stirring, for a few minutes, then add all the other ingredients except the oyster shells, rock salt, and paprika. Cook for another minute, stirring constantly; the bread crumbs will thicken the sauce. Lower the heat and simmer about 3 more minutes. Set aside.

If you are using oyster shells, fill 6 disposable pie plates or other ovenproof dishes with rock salt. Arrange 4 oyster shells in each pan.

Divide the mountain oysters among the shells or ramekins and cover with the spinach mixture. These may be baked immediately or refrigerated until ready to serve.

Preheat the oven to broil and place a rack 6 inches from the top of the oven. Place the pans or ramekins under the broiler until heated thoroughly and browned on top, about 3 to 5 minutes. Sprinkle with the Spanish paprika and serve piping hot.

Girl of the Golden West Opera
Colorado Benefit

This dinner was held as a benefit for Opera Colorado.

Bent's Fort Hailstorm Julep
Buffalo Eggs
Buffalo Tongue Canapés
Mountain Man Boudies

Tossed Green Sallet with Charlotte's Ranch Dressing
Steamboat Roast of Buffalo with Garden Vegetables and San Luis
Valley Colorado Potatoes
Bleasdale Petite Syrah as Carried by the HMS *Beagle*

Blue Corn Blueberry Muffins
Pumpkin Walnut Muffins
Broiled Buffalo Marrow Bones with Fruit and Wafers

Bobbie's Cheesecake
(This could get a lass into trouble but what bliss!)
French Champagne Opened by Tomahawk
Coffee and Tea

Appetizers

From the Fields and Forests:
Beef, Buffalo, Elk, and Lamb

—◦—

DEER, ELK, BEAR, AND COUGAR APPEARED ON THE TABLE AT BENT'S Fort, but more than any other, "buffler," as it was called in the early West, was the meat of choice. It would be thirty years until cattle roamed the fenced-in ranches of the cowboy West.

At our Fort, in addition to beef, buffalo, and cervina (New Zealand elk), the menu includes Arctic musk ox, ostrich, and caribou. Our most popular entrees are various combination platters of game meats.

Occasionally when I'm experimenting with a potential menu item, I try it out at Music Evenings, my best-loved tradition at The Fort. Two or three times a year a group of about thirty folk and bluegrass musicians gather in the St. Vrain room by the large open fireplace. In winter the fire gives a cozy warmth and cheerful light as the pine logs burn, scenting the air. It's a night for old folkies, mostly professional musicians who like to get together for music-making just for themselves and their peers. I play my mandolin or musical saw, and others bring guitars, banjos, basses, fiddles, Dobros, hammered dulcimers, autoharps, a few more mandolins, even sandpaper pads and a limberjack, a jointed little figure on a long stick that dances to the thumps of his master's hands.

We play the old traditionals: "Shenandoah," "Down in the Valley," "Goodnight Irene," and more modern folk songs such as Ian Tyson's "Four Strong Winds" and Bob Dylan's "Hey Mr. Tambourine Man." Someone starts a song, and the whole group chimes in, taking turns at solos and playing different parts. There's no structure or plan, and the music miracle happens that is every musician's narcotic.

After a couple of hours we break for a dinner of buffalo ribs, stuffed guinea hen breast, or whatever I've been thinking of putting on the menu. Then, back we go to play until past 11 P.M. Dinner guests are welcome to sit nearby and listen, providing they're quiet. Magical moments and shinin' times!

World's Best Beef or Buffalo Prime Rib Roast

On Sundays as a small boy, I delighted in watching my dad cut me a nice slab of medium-rare beef prime rib. Served with green peas and mashed potatoes filled with a well of beef juice gravy, it was as good as it gets!

Over thirty years of preparing both beef and buffalo roasts has led to much experimentation with rubs and marinades. The wonderful flavor of this roast is the trick of a Texas barbecue cook who "learnt me" that any meat can benefit from a little burned onion smoke.

We prepare a dozen or more beef and buffalo rib roasts a day. Here's how it's done.

Serves 6

> 5- to 6-pound beef or buffalo prime standing rib roast
>   or 4- to 5-pound boneless prime rib roast
> ½ cup beef base concentrate (available at meat markets or in specialty stores)
> ¼ cup (approximately 2 heads) freshly pureed garlic
> ½ cup dried rosemary
> Coarsely ground black pepper
> ¼ cup vegetable oil
> Outer peels of 4 large onions

Rub the roast with the beef base concentrate and then the garlic. Sprinkle the rosemary and pepper over all, letting it stick to the beef base. Wipe the oil on your hands and gently rub the herbs into the roast.

Let stand 1 hour at room temperature.

Preheat the oven to 500°F. Place the roast on a foil-covered roasting pan. Arrange the onion peels around the base of the roast and place in the oven. Roast for 8 minutes, so that the onion peels burn and the smoke lightly penetrates the meat, then lower the heat to 250°F. Roast for 18 minutes per pound, or until a meat thermometer reads 125°F for rare or 138°F for medium-rare. The low temperature will keep the roast tender. Don't cook buffalo any longer; because of its leanness, it will be tough if cooked more than medium-rare.

Remove the roast from the oven and allow it to rest for 15 to 20 minutes before carving. The temperature will rise about 10°F while resting, bringing the meat to the correct serving temperature.

Buffalo

Early writers tell us that Boston's crooked streets leading down to the Charles River were originally buffalo trails. But the last bison east of the Appalachians was killed in about 1830. The great herds of the Plains were hardly touched by the relatively few Native Americans in the West. Colorado, for example, was believed to be home to fewer than eight thousand Indians, and these were in small bands of Cheyenne, Arapaho, Lakota, and Ute—just a few people in a territory the size of New Zealand, and fewer than go to a shopping mall on Saturday. The bison were far from endangered, and the Native American took what he needed.

He used every part of the carcass: Tongues, hearts, livers, kidneys, and testicles were removed for choice eating, and the rest of the meat was sliced with the grain in thin sheets for jerky.

Drying racks in Indian camps were always filled with meat being prepared for storage. The jerked meats went into the winter stews with dried squashes, cattails, prairie potatoes, wild onions and garlic, and dried maize. This stew was called *washtunkala* by the Sioux and is still eaten today. It's pretty good!

When the "white eyes," as the Indians called the white mountain men, went west, they learned Indian ways of cooking. Pieces of buffalo meat skewered on wood sticks, called *buffalo en appolas,* was broiled over open fires. Jerked buffalo meat was commonplace. Pounded along with chokecherries and mixed with melted kidney fat, it formed a pasty mixture called *pemmican* and was the iron ration of both Native Americans and mountain men.

The ultimate in historic buffalo delicacies was the tongue, which has a smooth, fine grain and delicate flavor; it was served by the train-car-ful at the finest restaurants in the nation. I've looked high and low for a nineteenth-century buffalo or bison cookbook but can find none, although many letters and journals make references to eating it.

As trains began crisscrossing the nation, tourist trains advertised, "Bag a buffalo, and we'll even clean and dress it for you." They'd drive the locomotives into the middle of buffalo herds cross-

From the Fields and Forests

51

ing the lines, and guests would shoot from the train windows. Not quite the same sport as riding bareback into the center of a herd with bow and arrow, pumping hunting arrows into fat young cows surrounded by mean old bulls! Low-paid buffalo skinners would run and dress the kill on the spot, salting the hide to preserve it until you returned to St. Louis, where it was transformed into a buffalo robe for wintertime sleigh riding comfort.

It was little wonder that by 1910 reports indicated that only 254 buffalo existed worldwide, including a bison in a zoo in Calcutta, India. By the time James Fraser designed the Indian head buffalo nickel, minted from 1913 to 1938, the white men had effectively wiped out the animals. In so doing, they stripped Native Americans of food, clothing, and shelter, efficiently destroying their way of life and forcing them to join the white man's world.

In the first half of the century, bison became largely mythical creatures not only of the West but of the past. Small herds were seen by lucky travelers to national parks such as Yellowstone in Wyoming.

I knew little about these animals in 1963 when I opened The Fort, but when I set out to learn all I could about the original Bent's Fort, I found that Kit Carson had had a contract with the Bent St. Vrain Company to bring in one thousand pounds of meat a day, and most of it was buffalo. So I looked into serving buffalo. There were several ranches in the western states, and instead of being extinct, the herds were steadily increasing.

When we began offering buffalo that year, we had a hard time getting people to try it. "I'm not a tourist, I'm from around here and I've tasted buffalo," they'd say. "No, thanks. I'll stick to beef!" The attitude was understandable, because quality was spotty and sometimes just plain bad. Once in a while we'd get tough meat that had to have been from an old cow. But I quickly got to know my purveyors and have been insistent on getting nothing but the best meat from young bulls that are eighteen to twenty-six months old.

Today we serve buffalo tenderloin steaks, New York strip steaks, sirloin on a skewer, roast prime rib, even succulent "hump,"

the meat surrounding the dorsal-like bones forming the hump on the bison's shoulders. Appetizer plates include broiled split buffalo marrow bones, tongue, heart, homemade sausages called "boudies," and testicles, or Rocky Mountain oysters.

As we approach the turn of the century, buffalo number well over 250,000 in this country, and herds are increasing quickly in size and number, with buffalo ranches in all fifty states, including Rhode Island. Even Germany and Switzerland boast a few herds. The renaissance of the American bison is an important trend in food history. It's an essential part of our New World American heritage, truly a new food of the Old West.

Cooking Bison

Hardly any other meat or cut compares with a good "buff tender," as we call tenderloins. The texture of buffalo is similar to beef except that it is less fatty. Its taste is slightly sweeter and has been likened to beef injected with extra beef flavoring.

Since the best meat comes from young bulls between eighteen and twenty-six months, the body weight of a dressed carcass runs between 550 and 650 pounds. Most of it is bone and lesser cuts. Picture the buffalo on the Indian head buffalo nickel. The head and shoulders are mammoth, but the hind end is small and scrawny. Since the steaks come from the small end, this translates into about 11 to 12 pounds of tenderloin from a 550-pound carcass—not very much, which means it is costly to produce.

Ten years ago the cost for tenderloin was $12 per pound. It peaked at $20 per pound in 1995, and in 1997, as this is being written, the wholesale price of buffalo tenderloins varies between $17 and $20 per pound. Another restaurant in Denver runs a small delicatessen operation that sells uncooked meat; recently, it sold buffalo tenderloin anywhere from $28 to $37 per pound (depending on market price), compared to $14 per pound for beef tenderloin. The roast meats are significantly less, with buffalo prime rib roast retailing at around $15 to $17 per pound, compared to $7 for beef.

Cooking buffalo is much like cooking beef, except that it is extremely low in fat and therefore should be kept rare or medium-rare to avoid toughening when grilling. Slow oven-roasting is best for prime ribs and most hump meat, because the low temperatures will not drive off all the serum, blood, and fat. When wet-cooking, treat buffalo as if it were beef, marinating and stewing in liquids of an acidic nature: wine, beer, vinegar, yogurt, or citrus juices. These tenderize the meat by softening the collagens in the cells.

Bison Nutrition Information

mg/100 grams

	Protein	Fat	Calories	Cholesterol
bison rib eye	22.2	2.2	148	61
beef choice rib eye	22	6.5	180	72
skinless chicken breast	23.6	0.7	167	62
pork rib eye	22.3	4.9	165	71

(Source: National Bison Association. M. J. Marchello, Animal and Range Sciences Department, North Dakota State University in Fargo, North Dakota, 1996.)

New York Strip Loin Strindberg

Siggy Krauss, chef at the Briarhurst Manor in Manitou Springs, south of Denver, Colorado, taught me this wonderful dish. My impression was that Strindberg was a famous Swedish diplomat. We don't know if Strindberg created the dish himself or if it was simply named for him. Either way, it's a dramatic way to serve a whole sirloin strip. Carving it before your guests will make their mouths water!

Serves 12 to 14 (about 9 ounces per person, untrimmed)

1 8- to 9-pound boneless New York steak strip loin
4 tablespoons Coleman's English dry mustard
4 tablespoons Dijon-style mustard
3 tablespoons butter or margarine
3 cups diagonally sliced green onions
2 cloves garlic, minced
1 sweet red pepper or pimento, finely chopped
1 tablespoon whole canola seed or mustard seed (see page 246)
2 teaspoons seasoned salt
2 serrano chiles, minced (optional)
1 slice fresh garlic butter toast per person (optional)

Preheat the oven to 425°F.

Trim all the fat and silver skin from the beef, or else the topping will flavor the fat instead of the meat. In a large, wide pan, sear the

From the Fields and Forests

meat to brown the entire surface. Combine the mustards and coat the top of the loin. Let it rest while you prepare the topping.

Heat the butter in a large sauté pan. Add the remaining ingredients, except the toast, and combine. Sauté for 4 minutes, then spread over the mustard-topped strip loin. Roast for 20 to 25 minutes, then lower the heat to 350°F and continue cooking for another 20 to 25 minutes, to desired doneness. Check the internal temperature with a meat thermometer. A medium-rare roast will be 140°F.

Serve on a large platter, slicing off individual steaks to desired thickness and placing them on the garlic toast. Be sure to include a spoonful of topping with each slice.

Broiled Buffalo Tenderloin

At Bent's Fort in the 1830s and '40s, "buffler," as it was called, was the mainstay. Hunters including Kit Carson were contracted by the fort to bring in one thousand pounds of buffalo a day. Alexander Barclay, their English bookkeeper in 1839, complained in a letter that they invariably fried the meat. At our Fort we avoid such complaints by cooking buffalo steaks over mesquite charcoal.

Not long ago I was called over to a dining table where a lone man sat. "I'm from Paris, France," he said, "and all of my life I've thought that the Chateaubriand cut of beef was the *ne plus ultra* of meats. Now I must go back to France and tell my friends that Chateaubriand, it is garbage. The best meat in the world is this buffalo tenderloin steak."

There's a tough strap of meat that runs along a tenderloin, so make sure that your butcher cuts it away. The cut tenderloins will be almost square, and a thick 1-inch to 1 ½-inch piece is best. An 8-ounce portion is plenty, but let your purse rule your hunger!

Per serving:
½ **teaspoon fine sea salt**
⅛ **teaspoon lemon crystals (citric acid or sour salt)**
¾ **teaspoon medium-ground black pepper**
1 **8-ounce buffalo tenderloin steak (see Suppliers, page 303)**
Canola or peanut oil
2 **teaspoons butter or Herb Butter (page 62; optional)**
1 **teaspoon minced parsley (optional)**

Preheat the broiler or heat a grill to high.

Combine the sea salt, lemon crystals, and pepper. Dust each steak with the mixture, coating liberally on both sides, then brush lightly with oil. (The order is important here—no oiling before seasoning.)

Place the steaks about 6 inches from a medium-hot fire. Cook for 11 to 18 minutes (depending on thickness), or until the meat is medium-rare. Turn every 4 minutes. Because bison is so lean, it tends to be tough when cooked more than medium-rare, so it's important not to overcook.

Sprinkle with the parsley. A disk of herb butter gives this steak even greater magnificence. This is not precisely what the doctor ordered, but if your weight and cholesterol are fine, go for it every

From the Fields and Forests

blue moon. It's worth a lot of penance. The smell of the butter melting on a hot steak is intoxicating.

NOTE: This recipe works beautifully for beef T-bones, too. When cooking T-bones, I recommend splurging and buying the highest quality beef you can afford—USDA prime, if possible, or a good-looking USDA choice. But T-bones cut 1½ inches thick may be more than the usual serving size of 10 to 12 ounces. This makes a great sandwich the day after, but if you don't want any left over, use thinner steaks and watch them *very* carefully so that they don't overcook, or cut the meat away from the bone before serving.

I also find that a porterhouse steak, which is the same cut as the T-bone except that it has a larger eye, or tenderloin works beautifully for two servings. Simply cut the meat away from the bone before serving. Cut the tenderloin into two equal portions and slice the strip side crosswise into an even number of pieces, then divide the meat between two plates.

Green River Knives

The back of our menu offers Green River skinning knives for sale at The Fort trade lodge. These knives, manufactured by Russell-Harrington Cutlery Company in Massachusetts since 1834, were used by hunters and trappers, and are known to have been carried by Kit Carson. They're still made today, and purchasers of a knife become card-carrying members of the Green River Scalping and Joy Society. I founded the GRSJS many years ago to raise money to buy a new tombstone for Ceran St. Vrain, the Bent brothers' partner in Bent's Fort. Members receive invitations to special dinners and events held from time to time.

Gonzales Steak

On April 1, 1964, Elidio Gonzales, the gifted Taos *madero* (woodcrafts-man) who hand-carved The Fort's Spanish Colonial–style doors and Padre Martinez chairs, came to Denver to give wood-carving demon-strations. When he called me from town for help, hopelessly lost among Denver's one-way streets, I was tempted to repeat to him what he'd told me in late October when, after a heavy snowfall, I'd harangued him for being three months late finishing all of The Fort's doors: "People in Hell are always wanting ice water!" The old adage about always wanting what you couldn't have had taken all the wind out of my sails, and we'd waited another month for the doors to arrive. Now Elidio needed *my* help. I drove to town and led him back to The Fort, pondering how I could teach him a little April Fool's Day lesson. The solution came to me when he asked for a steak with chiles.

"This is no Mexican restaurant!" I thundered. "We don't have any chile here," I fibbed, as I cut a pocket into a thick sirloin and stuffed it with chopped green chiles.

"Oh, you damned gringos, you don't know what's good," he replied. "All you eat is meat and potatoes!"

I grilled the steak, placed it before a grumbling Elidio, and watched him take a bite. "April Fool, Elidio!" I shouted.

"April Fool to you, too!" he replied. "You're the biggest fool for not having this on your menu! Here, try it!"

I did, and the Gonzales Steak has been one of our most popular dishes ever since. Elidio passed away a few years ago, but his furniture and his steak live on.

Per person:

3   green Anaheim chiles, roasted and peeled (canned will do, but
      fresh are best; see page 140 for instructions on roasting)
Salt
1   clove garlic, chopped
Pinch of Mexican leaf oregano
10- to 12-ounce thick-cut New York strip, top sirloin, or tenderloin
      of beef or buffalo steak
½   teaspoon salad oil
Freshly ground black pepper
1   teaspoon butter (optional)

Slit the chiles to remove the seeds, and chop 2 into fine dice and mix with the salt, garlic, and oregano. (New Mexicans traditionally like to leave a few of the seeds in the dish. The seeds give it life, they say.)

With a very sharp knife, cut a horizontal pocket into the steak. Stuff the chopped chiles into the pocket. Brush the meat and the remaining chile with salad oil. Grill the steak on both sides to the desired doneness. If using buffalo, watch carefully so as not to over-cook! Because it contains less fat than chicken, bison cooks much faster than beef and is best medium-rare.

Salt and pepper the meat. Grill the remaining whole-roasted chile to get a nice patterning of grid burn on it. Lay it across the steak as a garnish.

A teaspoon of brown butter on the steak as a special treat is heaven. To make brown butter, simply place the butter in a sauté pan over medium-high heat and allow it to melt and turn golden brown.

Grading Meat

Years back, beef grading was very strict. To qualify as USDA "prime," meat had to have a great deal of marbling, with 28 to 34 percent fat, the result of long feed lot fattening. Lower in fat came USDA "choice," then "select," and then lesser grades.

Today, only about 2 percent of meat is graded USDA prime, so it's very difficult to find. There are four or five levels of choice, graded according to the age of the animal and the fat marbling. Poorer grades, which used to be classified as "select," make up the lower levels of choice—which they shouldn't! So for the best, look for the actual inked-mark "USDA prime" on the strip loin that your New York steak is cut from. It's best to find an ethical butcher and stick with him.

Steak à la Pittsburgh

When I was a teenager attending school in Andover, Massachusetts, I was taken to a wonderful restaurant called Locke-Ober's in nearby Boston, on Winter Place, a narrow alley just down from Boston Common. Two Germans, Mr. Locke and Mr. Ober, ran competing restaurants side by side in the 1800s, until 1875 when the enterprises merged.

When the maitre d' learned that I was from Pittsburgh, he told me about a fellow in the steel business who came to Boston from time to time. Two weeks before each visit, the industrialist sent a telegram from Pittsburgh or telephoned the restaurant long distance (quite an extravagance in the 1930s) to give the chef ample time to prepare his steak. The maitre d' told me how it was made, and this garlic steak went on our menu in 1966.

Serves 8

Garlic butter:
½ **pound (2 sticks) lightly salted butter**
4 **cloves garlic**
½ **cup chopped parsley leaves (no stems)**

1 **tablespoon plus 1 teaspoon fine sea salt**
1 **teaspoon lemon crystals (citric acid or sour salt)**
2 **tablespoons medium-ground black pepper**
8 **12-ounce New York strip steaks**
Canola or vegetable oil
Coarsely chopped parsley leaves (no stems)
Coarsely ground black pepper

Two weeks before serving (see Note), slice the garlic into slivers and insert them into the butter. Press the parsley into all sides of the butter to cover. Wrap it tightly in aluminum foil or plastic wrap, then place in an airtight bag and refrigerate. The garlic oils will permeate the butter.

When ready to prepare the steaks, preheat the broiler or heat a grill to high. Combine the sea salt, lemon crystals, and pepper, and rub each steak with the mixture, then brush with oil. Place the steaks about 6 inches from the heat source. Before turning, swab the tops

From the Fields and Forests

61

with oil again. Broil the steaks to the desired doneness. Top with 2 tablespoons of garlic butter. Place the steaks briefly under the heat once more until the butter and garlic turn golden brown. Serve with lots of parsley and pepper, and sleep alone.

NOTE: It's very important to allow the flavors to mingle for two weeks, but the butter must be placed in an airtight container to keep it from absorbing refrigerator odors. To be ready for last-minute garlic steaks, prepare the garlic butter and allow it to mellow in the refrigerator for two weeks, then freeze and use as needed.

Variation

Steaks with Herb Butter

Steak coming off the grill at over 500°F will provide enough heat to elicit flavor from dried herbs. These disks of herb butter are great to make ahead of time and keep in the freezer to use with meats.

If you have a microwave, the disks can be quickly melted and spread on breads before broiling for quick herb/garlic bread.

½ **pound (2 sticks) lightly salted butter**
1 **large or 2 small cloves garlic**
½ **teaspoon finely chopped fresh tarragon**
½ **teaspoon dried thyme**
½ **teaspoon finely chopped fresh parsley leaves (no stems)**
Your favorite steaks, cooked to your liking

Thoroughly blend the butter and garlic together in a food processor. Quickly blend in the herbs. Spoon into a cylinder mold. A small frozen juice can works well. Fill the can with the butter, cover, and refrigerate. When the butter has hardened, use a can opener to remove the bottom, and push out the butter. Cut off ¼-inch-thick disks as needed. Seal the extra in plastic wrap and an airtight plastic bag, and store in the freezer.

Place 1 or 2 tablespoons on each steak just before serving.

Steaks Blackfoot Style

When I was five years old, my parents took me to Estes Park, Colorado, for a summer holiday. Just south of Estes was another village called Allens Park, and it was there that the Perkins Trading Post sold fine Indian goods to tourists and collectors. Mr. Perkins, from Omaha, Nebraska, spent the fall, winter, and spring traveling and buying the crème de la crème to sell at his famous store.

In the summer of 1931 a handsome young man named Charlie Eagle Plume worked there. Charlie boasted Blackfoot Indian blood and was a master entertainer. He'd dress in costume and give lectures and dances at the nearby lodges. As time went on, Charlie took over the trading post and took great care of Mrs. Perkins, seeing that she wanted for nothing. He changed the name of the trading post to Charles Eagle Plume Trading Post. He taught me early on that everything you buy is more interesting when it has a story—which is why I'm telling you this story.

Charlie told me that the best steak in the world was done over aspen coals with some fresh green aspen for smoke. He called this method of cooking "Blackfoot Style." When we opened The Fort, I used aspen logs on the charcoal grills to gently smoke the meats as they cooked.

A note of precaution: One day I roasted beef and buffalo rounds for many hours with several aspen logs. It penetrated the meat, making it red almost a half-inch deep, and the outside was very black and almost inedible. So one learns once again that moderation is the key to success, and a few short twigs of fresh aspen on your charcoal briquettes is quite enough to give the meat a lovely "Blackfoot" taste.

Fort Beer Steak

After returning from Europe in 1968, I put into practice the truth that I had discovered in village after village, country after country: Successful restaurants served what people in the region liked to eat. I changed the menu radically and specialized in all manner of beef-steaks. We developed the Old-Fashioned Texas Barbecued Steak (page 65); Steak à la Pittsburgh (page 61), a garlic steak; Beefsteak and Oysters Palace Hotel (page 66); and Fort Beer Steak. This last dish mated our best cuts of beef with Killian's Red Ale made by Coors, our neighbor in Golden. The natural sweetness of caramelized malt gives steaks a delightful taste. Any brew with a heavy sweet malt and not too much bitterness from hops makes a dandy beer steak.

Your favorite steak (as done below)

Per steak:

½ **teaspoon fine sea salt**

⅛ **teaspoon lemon crystals (citric acid or sour salt)**

¾ **teaspoon medium-ground black pepper**

Canola or vegetable oil

Coors' Killian's Red or other high-malt, low-hops beer

Use a thick cut (at least 1½ inches) of the best meat possible, either New York strip, tenderloin, or a T-bone. Thin steaks will broil too quickly to allow a coating to build up on them. An hour before cooking, combine the sea salt, lemon crystals, and pepper, and rub each steak on both sides with the mixture. Brush with oil and then with beer (a natural tenderizer) on both sides

Preheat the oven to broil or heat a grill to high. Place the steaks about 6 inches from the heat source. Brush the steaks once more before placing on the grill. Baste the top several more times as the meat cooks to create a thin coating on the steaks. Turn and continue on the other side until done to your taste.

Old-Fashioned Texas Barbecued Steak

At a Western History Association conference, a group of us historians were taken to President Lyndon B. Johnson's ranch on the Pedernales River. I'm not sure what the others learned there, but the most remarkable thing I discovered was that Johnson had a wonderful caterer named Walter Jetton. *Walter Jetton's LBJ Barbecue Cook Book* has the best barbecue sauce I know. After his book was published in 1965, I modified his recipe slightly and began using it at The Fort for topping broiled T-bones and New York strips.

> Walter Jetton's Barbecue Sauce (recipe below)
> Your favorite steaks

Prepare the steaks on the grill or under the broiler (see Broiled Buffalo Tenderloin, page 57). Don't cook the steaks in the sauce, for the tomato and sugar would burn. Just brush it across the finished steak on both sides before serving.

> *Walter Jetton's Barbecue Sauce*
> *Makes about 1½ cups*
>
> 1 cup ketchup
> ½ cup cider vinegar
> 1 teaspoon sugar
> 1 teaspoon pure New Mexican red chile powder
> ⅛ teaspoon salt
> ½ cup water
> 3 stalks celery, chopped
> 3 bay leaves
> 1 clove garlic
> 2 tablespoons chopped onion
> 4 tablespoons butter
> 4 tablespoons Worcestershire sauce
> 1 teaspoon paprika
> Dash of black pepper

Combine all the sauce ingredients in a pan, cover, and bring to a boil. Simmer until reduced by half. Remove from heat and strain.

From the Fields and Forests

Beefsteak and Oysters Palace Hotel

When we were closing my childhood home in Pittsburgh, I came upon a wonderful cookbook. Written in 1887 by Mrs. Gillette, *The American Cook Book* had a superb recipe for beefsteak and oysters credited to the Palace Hotel in San Francisco. Mrs. Gillette begins, "Broil the steak the usual way," and goes on to describe a simple preparation "upon the fire."

I found that adding a nice squeeze of fresh lemon juice and freshly ground black pepper improves the dish immensely, and finely minced parsley sprinkled over the top made it menu-worthy. For many years this was a favorite among our oyster fans. One thinks of the old Palace and imagines opera singer Enrico Caruso escaping during the earthquake of 1906, wearing only a bath towel!

Serves 6

    6 10-ounce or larger New York strip, filet, or rib eye steaks, the
       best quality possible
    6 tablespoons butter
    ¼ cup flour
    1 pint freshly shucked oysters ("East coast selects" are used at
       The Fort)
    Juice of half a lemon
    ½ to 1 cup water
    2 tablespoons chopped parsley leaves (no stems)
    Salt
    Freshly ground black pepper
    Dash of red Tabasco sauce

In a large sauté pan, heat the butter and flour, stirring well to form a roux. Cook briefly but don't allow the roux to brown.

Add the drained oysters and lemon juice, stirring gently so that the oysters maintain their shape. Add water to thin the sauce to a thick, chowderlike consistency. Boil for 2 minutes, then add the parsley, salt, pepper, and Tabasco.

Broil the sirloins "the usual way" and serve the sauce over the steaks.

Green Chile Steak Bowl

So fast and easy to make! And delicious! This is just steak and green chile in a savory gravy that I made often for my family before putting it on the menu.

One night back in 1968 a waiter told me that his customer was very insistent that his dinner be *really hot!* A friend had just brought me some fiery little pili-pili chiles from the African Congo. I added a tablespoon of those to the dish and sent the poor man into orbit. "But delicious!" he said, wiping his brow.

I believe that green chile is best if it has more flavor than fiery hot. Using poblano or Anaheim chiles with a high-quality beef or buffalo sirloin makes this a tasty dish that won't burn your mouth.

Serves 4

12 to 16 ounces top sirloin or other high-quality steak
6 tablespoons butter
¼ cup flour
¼ teaspoon Mexican leaf oregano
2 cloves garlic, finely chopped
Salt
4 cups beef stock or water
2 cups green chile strips, cut into small pieces
Parsley for garnish
Warm flour tortillas (optional)
Green salad (optional)

Cut the meat into bite-size pieces. Sauté quickly in a hot, dry skillet. The meat should be browned on the outside and rare on the inside. Remove the meat to a separate bowl for reheating later.

Over medium-high heat, melt the butter in the skillet. Add the flour, oregano, and garlic, mixing thoroughly. (Sautéing herbs brings out their flavor.) Don't let the mixture brown. Add the salt and beef stock or water, keeping some aside. Stir well to make a moderately thick gravy, being sure to incorporate all the brown bits on the pan bottom. Add green chiles and boil for 1 minute.

Don't return the meat to the gravy until you're ready to serve. At that time, thin the gravy if necessary with the extra beef stock and add the meat to reheat it quickly. Serve in individual bowls garnished with parsley and accompanied by warm flour tortillas and a salad.

From the Fields and Forests

67

How to Quench a Mouthful of Fire

A wonderful old restaurant called Tia Sofia's still stands on San Francisco Street in Santa Fe. Their chile is on the very upper level of hot, and the menu warns you to eat with care. One day when I had a mouthful of fire, I poured the cinnamon sugar used for sopaipillas from a shaker on the table into a glassful of milk. A swig of this cut through the hot chile burn like a knife through butter.

Potted Beef and Buffalo in Caramelized Onions

For many years we've served wonderful prime rib of buffalo and beef. Since most people prefer it medium-rare, we are often left with the well-done ends of roasts. The famed historic Durgin-Parks restaurant in Boston solved their end roast problem years ago with a "till it's sold out" daily special of beef and onions. I've enjoyed it many times and borrowed the idea for The Fort, where I serve the tender meat and gravy over noodles, rice, or mashed potatoes. It cooks for twelve hours, so start well ahead of time.

I imagine that in the days of Bent's Fort, Charlotte Green, who ran the kitchen at "Fort William," as Bent's Fort was called, must have made the same dish, using either onions from the fort garden or wild onions from the banks of Timpas Creek or the Arkansas River.

Serves 6

¼ cup cooking oil
¼ cup butter
6 cups coarsely chopped yellow onions
4 pounds cooked prime rib roast ends or 4½ pounds raw lean
     rib eye roast
1 cup all-purpose flour
2 cups red wine
4 cups beef broth
3 bay leaves
½ teaspoon orange oil (see Suppliers, page 303), or 2 teaspoons
     grated orange peel
2 teaspoons dried thyme

3 tablespoons Hungarian Noble Sweet paprika (see page 188)

½ teaspoon grated nutmeg

Salt

Coarse black pepper

1 teaspoon melegueta pepper or cubebs (optional)

6 cups cooked noodles, rice, or mashed potatoes, for serving

Heat the oil and butter in a tall stockpot until smoking. Add the onions and brown them, stirring constantly.

Cut the meat into 1-inch cubes.

Pour flour into a paper bag and add the meat cubes, shaking to coat. Move the onions aside in the pot and brown the meat on all sides. Add the red wine, beef broth, bay leaves, orange oil, thyme, paprika, nutmeg, salt, pepper, and melegueta pepper to taste. Cover and leave on low heat overnight, at least 12 hours. The meat will be so tender that it will turn into shreds if stirred.

Serve over the noodles, rice, or mashed potatoes.

Blacksmithing at a
Fort Rendezvous.

From the Fields and Forests

Fort Tamale Pie

One evening a few years before building The Fort, my wife and I had a picnic at Elitch Gardens, a Denver amusement park. We needed an easy casserole for six people and had some blue cornmeal from New Mexico on hand. Layering blue cornmeal mush with red chile–cooked hamburger, ripe olives, cheese, and onions, we concocted a dish that was to become immensely popular at the restaurant. For large parties we prepared tamale pies in a Dutch oven or large *cazuela*, a Mexican casserole dish.

Serves 6

Vegetable oil to wipe the skillet
1 pound coarsely ground beef or buffalo chuck (put through the chile plate of the grinder twice, to give it a nice meaty texture)
1¼ large yellow onions, finely diced
2 cloves garlic, minced
1½ teaspoons Mexican leaf oregano
½ teaspoon ground fennel
1 teaspoon salt (less if your chicken broth is salty)
2 cups pine nuts or coarsely chopped walnuts
⅓ cup Red Chile Puree (page 83)
2 quarts chicken broth
2 cups blue cornmeal
½ cup cold water
1 cup medium whole pitted ripe olives
8 ounces sharp cheddar cheese, grated (2 cups)
½ cup each red and green pepper strips, cut attractively, for garnish (optional)
Avocado, cut into attractive slices for garnish (optional)
¼ cup toasted pine nuts or whole walnut halves for garnish (optional)
Several sprigs parsley or cilantro for garnish

Wipe a large skillet with oil and brown the meat in small batches over high heat, removing to a bowl as each batch is cooked. Cooking too much meat at once will steam it rather than brown it.

In the same pan, brown the onions, garlic, oregano, fennel, ¼ teaspoon salt, and nuts. Add to the meat. Add the Red Chile Puree and mix well.

Bring the chicken broth to a boil in a large stockpot. (The cornmeal will bubble and splash if the pot isn't deep enough.) While the broth is heating, combine the blue cornmeal and cold water, and whisk well. This will keep it from clumping when it's added to the hot broth. When the broth reaches a boil, stir in the cornmeal mixture. If you are using a salty chicken base, don't add more salt. Otherwise, add the remaining ¾ teaspoon. Lower the heat and simmer, stirring often, for 20 to 30 minutes, until the cornmeal mush is smooth and very thick. (A spoon should almost be able to stand upright in it.) Be sure to scrape the bottom as you stir to prevent scorching.

Preheat the oven to 375°F. Spray Pam or another nonstick baking spray into a 4-quart *cazuela* or other casserole that can go to the table. Pour half the mush into the dish, then alternately layer the meat mixture and the olives. When both are used up, top with half of the grated cheese and then the remaining cornmeal mush. Bake approximately 1½ hours. Do not underbake, or the mush will not cook through. (It'll still taste great, but it won't look very good.)

Remove from the oven and top with the remaining cheese. You may garnish the pie with wheel designs made of strips of red and green pepper, avocado slices, and toasted pine nuts or walnuts. These will sink into the cheese as the cheese melts. Return to the oven for 15 minutes more, allowing the cheese to brown a bit. Sprinkle with parsley or cilantro.

Toasting Nuts

Many of the recipes I use call for toasted nuts. Nuts lend nice texture and flavor to dishes, and toasting them brings out the flavor of their oils.

To toast nuts, spread them on a baking sheet and place it in a preheated 400°F oven for 4 to 6 minutes, turning the nuts about halfway through. Watch them carefully because nuts burn easily.

Because pine nuts and slivered almonds are very small, stir them every minute or so as they cook, until they're golden brown.

When cooking with hazelnuts, always remove the dark skins before adding the nuts to the dish. The conventional method for doing this is to rub them in cloth towels after allowing them to cool, but I find it more effective to place them in an electric mixer with a whisk attachment. Whisk them at low speed for 10 minutes, then rinse and dry the nuts.

Toothless Charlie's Ground Steak

My mother didn't enjoy cooking but encouraged my sister Mary and me to experiment, and always volunteered to do the dishes after our culinary explorations. (Pretty nice!) Early on, I discovered that a dash of vanilla is excellent with chopped meat. Mary taught me that kneading cracked ice into ground beef immediately before cooking helps hamburgers retain moisture and makes them extra delicious. And it was from the mother of an Italian girlfriend that I learned that tenderloin makes absolutely the best chopped steak. It's expensive but delicious. Some people think that chopping up tenderloin is a travesty—but they usually don't add vanilla and ice, either.

We served this dish in The Fort's early years and finally named it after friend Charlie Randall, Chief Big Cloud. Charlie's teeth weren't in great shape, and he found this ground steak easy to eat.

Serves 6

6 8-ounce beef or buffalo tenderloins, chopped into ¼-inch pieces
½ cup finely minced white onion or Bermuda onion
2 tablespoons Worcestershire sauce
2 teaspoons seasoned salt
1 teaspoon vanilla extract
1½ cups finely crushed ice
Salt
Freshly ground black pepper
Toasted walnut halves for topping (optional)
1 large bunch whole parsley leaves for serving

Heat a skillet or charcoal grill to high heat. Combine all the ingredients except the walnuts and parsley leaves in a large bowl. Divide the mixture into 6 equal portions and form patties approximately 1 inch thick. Be careful not to compress the meat too much. I prefer these medium-rare, with a well-done outer crust. You can ensure this by waiting until your grill or skillet is really hot before the meat goes on. Season with salt and pepper while grilling, and try to turn only once. If Uncle Charlie is indeed toothless, then don't add nuts. But I enjoy these best topped with toasted walnut halves, or "eagles," and placed on a bed of parsley.

NOTE: If using buffalo, be sure to watch it carefully on the grill. The meat's leanness makes it very easy to overcook, and overcooking buffalo *is* a travesty.

Buffalo Drive Buffalo Burgers

At 4 A.M. on a winter morning, with the outside temperature at −18°F, my wife and I gathered at buffalo rancher Brian Ward's for a two-day buffalo drive. The San Luis Valley in south central Colorado was stunningly beautiful with snow everywhere and the distant mountains holding back the approaching dawn. By 6 A.M. we were moving five hundred cows in a drive that would end the next day thirty-four miles away at Zapata Ranch.

Yes, Virginia, there still are real cowboys who can push a herd. My job was to build a fire midway along the route the first day and feed the dozen men and two women riders. By the time the herd arrived at about 2 P.M., my charcoal was just right and the burgers were on, with special potatoes on the side (see Sam's Buffalo Drive Fry Pan, page 180). The cowboys and girls ate in the saddle and then were off again. Here's how we do burgers for hungry cowboys and mountain men.

Per person:
6 ounces ground buffalo with 12 percent fat (see Notes)
Salt
Freshly ground black pepper
1 large bun (sourdough onion is my favorite; see Notes)
Sam's Secret Sauce (recipe below)
1 green chile, peeled and stemmed
1 very thin slice sweet onion (preferably Vidalia, Walla Walla,
    Maui, or Texas Sweet)

Hand-form the burgers into 6-ounce patties. A tuna can with the top and bottom cut out makes a good form. Grill the patties to medium-rare or medium. Sprinkle with salt and pepper while they're cooking. *Do not* pat or squash the burgers down while they're cooking. That squeezes important juice from them, turning them dry and mean!

Place the buns facedown on the grill to toast lightly. Dress them with Sam's Secret Sauce. Place a burger on each bun and garnish with green chile and sweet onion.

From the Fields and Forests

Sam's Secret Sauce
Makes enough for 6 burgers

1 **cup mayonnaise**
¾ **cup Heinz Chili Sauce**

Combine the ingredients and mix well.

Sam's Secret Sauce keeps well and is also great on a grilled turkey sandwich with green chile pod and Swiss cheese.

NOTES: Buffalo meat is less than 2 percent fat, and a good burger needs at least 12 percent. So, if you are using buffalo instead of beef, ask your butcher to add either buffalo, beef, or pork fat to the grind and to put it through the chili plate of the grinder twice.

I like sourdough buns with minced onion baked on top. The dough for sourdough bread is available frozen at groceries. Roll sourdough into one long log, about half the diameter you want your buns, then cut it crosswise to make 1-inch-wide disks. Place these on a greased or parchment-lined baking sheet and allow to rise following the directions on the package. Meanwhile, whisk together ½ cup milk and 1 egg. Just before baking, brush the buns with this mixture. While they're still wet, sprinkle bits of finely minced onion on each bun and bake according to the package instructions. Keep an eye on them because they'll bake much faster than a single loaf of bread.

Elk Medallions with Cranberry Cream Sauce

Serves 4

2 teaspoons fine sea salt
½ teaspoon lemon crystals (citric acid or sour salt)
1 tablespoon medium-ground black pepper
12 2-ounce elk medallions (good substitutes are venison and beef tenderloin)
1 to 2 tablespoons butter
½ cup cranberry chutney (see Note)
⅓ cup Cointreau
⅓ cup chicken broth (canned is fine)
¾ cup heavy cream
Fort Rice Pilaf (page 169)

Heat a cast-iron skillet on the stove over medium-high heat. Combine the sea salt, lemon crystals, and pepper, and rub each steak on both sides with the mixture.

Melt the butter in the skillet and add 4 to 6 medallions without crowding them. Sear them on both sides to medium-rare and set aside while the next batch is cooking. When all the medallions have been cooked and set aside, add the chutney, Cointreau, and broth to the pan, scraping the skillet to deglaze and incorporate the drippings on the pan bottom to the sauce. Simmer for about 3 minutes to reduce slightly. Add the cream and simmer another 5 minutes to create a medium-thick sauce that will cling to the meat.

Return all the medallions and their accumulated juices to the skillet and rewarm briefly. Serve with rice.

NOTE: If cranberry chutney isn't available, use another chutney of your choice. You may also use ½ cup cranberry relish combined with 1 tablespoon grated fresh ginger, 1 chopped serrano chile, and 2 tablespoons finely chopped green onion.

From the Fields and Forests

Golden Elk Medallions with Purple Potatoes

Mark Jakobsen, our Hawaii-raised chef, created this spectacular dish using elk medallions, called *cervina* in New Zealand where much of it is raised. The recipe was featured in a national chef's magazine and is one of our prettiest dishes in its golden presentation.

It takes two days to prepare, so start well ahead of time. The demiglacé stores very well, however, and can be made ahead of time. A time-saving alternative to making your own is using a high-quality commercial beef demiglacé.

Demiglacé of Elk Bones (or substitute 1 quart commercial demiglacé):
8 pounds elk bones
4 tomatoes, quartered
1 onion
2 carrots, unpeeled and cut into pieces
1 celery stalk, cut into pieces
6 quarts water
2 bay leaves
1 tablespoon cracked black pepper
1 tablespoon thyme
Salt

Marinade:
½ cup olive oil
¼ cup red wine
3 cloves, minced
1 sprig fresh rosemary
½ teaspoon dried thyme
2 tablespoons finely diced purple onion
2 tablespoons finely diced red bell pepper

3 2-ounce square-cut elk tenderloin medallions per person

Potatoes, per person:
½ Colorado yellow or Yukon Gold potato
½ Peruvian purple potato
4 tablespoons butter
¼ cup heavy cream
Salt

White pepper
¼ teaspoon ground nutmeg
1 teaspoon grated Parmigiano-Reggiano cheese
¼ sheet gold leaf (optional)
½ carrot, peeled, sliced, and steamed (optional)
2 asparagus stalks, steamed and cut in half (optional)

Pastry, per person:
6 6-inch-square sheets filo dough
2 tablespoons butter, clarified
1½ teaspoons Panko bread crumbs (Japanese breading, to absorb extra liquid)

At least 1 day before serving, make the demiglacé.

Preheat the oven to 350°F.

Roast the bones in a shallow roasting pan for 1 hour, then add the tomatoes. Roast 45 minutes more.

While the bones are roasting, make a *mirepoix* (a mixture to enhance flavor) of the onion cut in half and caramelized in a large skillet over medium heat and the carrots and celery.

Place all ingredients for the demiglacé into a stockpot and simmer overnight. The next day, discard the bones. Strain the broth through a conical sieve, then press again through dampened cheesecloth. Return to the stockpot and reduce the broth to 1 quart by simmering and whisking into a demiglacé.

In a nonreactive container, combine all the marinade ingredients. Add the elk medallions and allow to marinate for 6 hours.

At least 3 hours before serving time, preheat the broiler or heat the grill to high, and cook the medallions (preferably over mesquite) until they are rare, turning when half done.

Place on paper towels to absorb extra liquid and cool to room temperature.

Peel and quarter the potatoes, and place the different potatoes in 2 separate pots. Cover with cold water, bring to a simmer, and cook until a knife can be easily inserted, about 20 to 30 minutes. When the potatoes are done, drain the water and return the potatoes to the pots placed over very low heat to evaporate the last of the water. This takes just 1 to 2 minutes and gives you fluffier potatoes.

While the potatoes are boiling, preheat the oven to 350°F and make the elk medallion packets.

Brush each sheet of filo dough with the butter. Use 2 sheets, one on top of the other at a 45-degree angle, to make the packets. Sprinkle the Panko crumbs in the middle of each pair of sheets, then place an elk medallion in the middle of each packet. Fold the sides of the filo dough upward, crimping them together securely to make a purselike bag and pinching gently to seal.

When you're ready to mash the potatoes, combine the butter, cream, salt, white pepper, nutmeg, and cheese, and heat in the microwave (don't boil it). Add to the potatoes and mash with a potato ricer. *Don't use a food processor!* It breaks down the cells, and you will end up with a gluelike substance that has very little resemblance to mashed potatoes.

Bake the elk medallion packets on a parchment-lined baking sheet for 12 to 15 minutes. When the dough is golden brown, they are done.

While the medallions are baking, steam the carrots and asparagus.

To serve, place a portion of each kind of potato side by side at the top edge of the plate, pour 3 tablespoons of demiglacé in 3 spots at the center of the plate, and place 1 elk medallion packet on each.

Just before serving, use scissors to cut the gold leaf into fine confetti over waxed paper and tilt the paper to sprinkle the gold leaf over the packets. Serve with steamed carrots and asparagus. The various colors of carrot orange, green, yellow, purple, and gold make for a superb eye and palate pleaser.

Elk Sauerbraten

Using a basic sauerbraten recipe from my friend Bob Larson in Germany, we put elk roast in a large crock, using red wine and red wine vinegar, juniper berries, bay leaves, onions, and the like. We marinated it for four days, then roasted it and made a sauce from some of the marinade mixed with gingersnaps in the traditional manner. At The Fort we actually had guests who didn't know each other sharing samples of it because of its extraordinary good taste.

Serves 6

3 pounds elk round steak (good substitutes are venison or beef round steaks), preferably 1 piece or large pieces
1 tablespoon salt
½ teaspoon pepper
2 onions, sliced
1 carrot, sliced
1 stalk celery, chopped
1 teaspoon juniper berries
4 cloves
4 black peppercorns
2 cups (about a half bottle) red wine
2 cups red wine vinegar
2 bay leaves
6 tablespoons butter
1 tablespoon kidney fat or cooking oil
5 tablespoons flour
1 tablespoon sugar
8 to 10 gingersnaps, crushed
Dumplings for serving

Wipe the steak with a damp cloth and season with salt and pepper. Place the steak in an earthen, glass, or other nonreactive bowl along with the onions, carrot, celery, juniper berries, cloves, peppercorns, wine, vinegar, bay leaves, and enough water to cover the meat. Cover and refrigerate for 4 days.

On the fifth day, remove the bowl from the refrigerator and drain the meat, reserving the liquid. Heat 1 tablespoon butter and 1 tablespoon kidney fat in a large nonreactive stockpot and sear the elk on

From the Fields and Forests

both sides. Add the marinade liquid and bring to a boil, then lower the heat and let simmer about 3 hours.

Melt the remaining butter in a skillet. Stir in the flour until smooth. Blend in the sugar and let brown to a nice dark color. Add this mixture to the simmering meat mixture. Cover and continue cooking until the meat is tender, about 1 hour longer.

Remove the meat to a warm serving platter. Stir the crushed gingersnaps into the pot juices and cook until thickened. Pour the gravy over the meat and serve with dumplings and a fine full-bodied red wine.

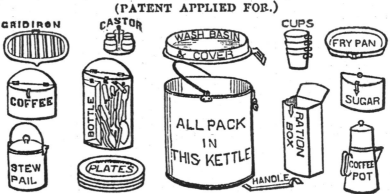

General Armijo's Grilled Double Lamb Chop

General Manuel Armijo was the last governor of New Mexico under Mexican rule. It was no coincidence that he was the last Mexican governor. Many mean things were said about him by those who felt he had sold out New Mexico to the Americans. The truth was that Mexico didn't have any money to fight a war against General Stephen W. Kearny's army, so Armijo took a big bribe and skedaddled. Detractors said that earlier in his career he'd been a sheep thief. He stole people's sheep, then sold them back to the original owners. Our lamb chop is named in this scoundrel's memory.

Serves 6

    3   teaspoons fine sea salt
    ¾   teaspoon lemon crystals (citric acid or sour salt)
    4½   tablespoons medium-ground black pepper
    6   1-pound double rib or loin chops, trimmed of fat
    Canola or vegetable oil
    Mango Chutney (see Suppliers, page 303), Peanut Red Chilli
        Sauce (page 82), Uchucuta Sauce (page 85), or Red Chile
        Sauce (page 84)

If you can't find a butcher to cut double chops, buy the thickest rib or loin chops you can find (see Notes).

Preheat the oven to broil or heat a grill to high. Combine the sea salt, lemon crystals, and pepper, and rub each chop with the mixture, then brush with oil. Place the chops about 6 inches from the heat source. The grilling time will depend on the thickness of the chops. For a chop that's a nice juicy, pink, medium-rare on the inside and wonderfully charred on the outside, about 7 minutes per side will do. Before turning, swab the tops with oil.

This is good served with many different sauces—Mango Chutney, Peanut Red Chilli Sauce, or Uchucuta Sauce. At The Fort we serve it with Red Chile Sauce on the side.

Notes: While you can find a lot of New Zealand lamb, it's usually too young to have much taste. I prefer a *hoggit,* or yearling lamb, because the meat is much more flavorful.

From the Fields and Forests

If you are preparing this dish for a large number of people, butterflied leg of lamb works very nicely and is a bit less expensive. Because the meat is not of uniform thickness, there will be medium-rare to well done, to satisfy the various palates of your guests.

If you can find a good butcher, have him cut the lamb chops to order. Starting with a whole lamb, he should use the bandsaw to cut away the front end and back legs, leaving just the rib cage and the rear loin. Then he should cut the lamb crosswise with the saw guide at 2 inches. Ask him to trim off the flippy ends of the ribs, sometimes called wings. This will leave you with M-shaped chops, with ribs on either side of the spine. Each should weigh at least a pound.

Peanut Red Chilli Sauce

For this spicy sauce my favorite ingredient is Linghams Sweet Red Chilli Sauce, available at many Vietnamese, Thai, and other Asian groceries. Other sweet chilli sauces may work well, too, but there is no American equivalent. I also use freshly ground peanut butter, found in natural food stores, because it contains no added sugar. The chilli sauce is sweet enough on its own.

Makes about 2 cups (serves 6)

8   **ounces sweet red chilli sauce**
8   **ounces chunky peanut butter**
1   **tablespoon soy sauce**

Combine the chilli sauce with the peanut butter and soy sauce. Serve with General Armijo's Grilled Double Lamb Chop (page 81) and be carried into ecstasy. If you make your own jerky, this is wonderful to swab on the meat before drying.

Red Chile Puree

Way back in 1949 when I owned a toy store in Santa Fe called La Boutique Fantasque, artist Will Shuster painted a jack-in-the-box sign for the top of a tall pine pole that had been cut and drawknife-peeled by Taos wood-carver and furniture maker Elidio Gonzales. Elidio, a small, thin man with soulful eyes, looked as I imagined Don Quixote might look. My wife and I became great admirers of his craftsmanship, and as time passed, his Spanish Colonial furniture was sought by the likes of author Leon Uris and actor John Wayne. Many years later he carved The Fort's doors and chairs.

One Thanksgiving, Elidio invited us to his home. Atop his big carved table were laid a roast turkey, salad, hot flour tortillas, and mashed potatoes topped, instead of with gravy, with red chile puree! What a wonderful discovery that turned out to be. In addition to topping mashed potatoes with it, we use this puree in Fort Tamale Pie (page 70), New Mexico Village-Style Chile con Carne (page 120), and many other dishes. It's also the base of the versatile, smooth, and spicy Red Chile Sauce (page 84), which we love with Santa Fe Pork Chops (page 122), steaks, enchiladas, and just about anything else fit to eat!

Makes about 1½ cups

- 12 **dried New Mexican red chiles, lightly oven-toasted, stems broken off, and seeds shaken out, or ½ cup pure New Mexican red chile powder (medium to mild; Medium Dixon is best)**
- 1 **clove garlic**
- ½ **teaspoon salt**
- ½ **teaspoon dry Mexican leaf oregano**
- ½ **cup hot water**

Place all the ingredients in a blender and zap into a smooth puree. Be sure to blend long enough to completely puree the garlic. The mixture should be loose and pourable. If necessary, add a bit more water.

From the Fields and Forests

Red Chile Sauce

Serve this on the side with chicken, guinea hen, pork, beef or buffalo steaks—you name it!

Serves 8

    3 ounces canola or other vegetable oil
    4 tablespoons flour
    1 cup Red Chile Puree (page 83)
   ½ teaspoon salt (unless broth is salted)
    1 cup chicken broth (undiluted canned is fine)

Heat the oil in a sauté pan. Stir in the flour and cook to a golden brown. Add the red chile puree and salt, and cook another 30 seconds, stirring constantly. Add the broth little by little, whisking it smooth. Add enough broth to make a medium-thin sauce.

Uchucuta Sauce

On a trip to Peru to study distant native American foods, I discovered that the dishes served to tourists hide the country's chile culture. After searching hotel and restaurant menus unsuccessfully for them, I finally discovered a 5-inch green chile called *rocoto* in the markets. Hot chiles are eaten everywhere in Peru, such as in this tasty sauce, but foreign visitors may come and go without ever encountering home-cooked chile. Pour this over a cold peeled boiled potato or over hard-cooked egg halves, serve with broiled fish, shrimp, pork chops, or lamb medallions, and pronounce it "oo-choo-COO-ta."

Makes 1½ cups

    8 ounces (1 cup) fresh ricotta or cottage cheese
    1 or 2 serrano chiles, finely minced (use more for a hotter
      sauce)
    ¼ cup roasted peanuts, preferably dry-roasted
    ¼ cup parsley leaves
    ¼ cup green onion pieces
    ⅛ cup milk or half and half
    1½ teaspoons olive oil
    ¼ teaspoon salt
    1½ teaspoons cilantro leaves

Put all the ingredients into a blender or processor and puree into a sauce. This tastes best when allowed to mellow for 24 hours in the refrigerator. It may discolor slightly, but that's okay. Feel free to use more chiles or cilantro; the peanuts shouldn't dominate. When ready to serve, adjust the taste and thickness with salt and milk.

From the Fields and Forests

85

Lamb Loin with Salsa Verde in Tissue Bread

Each year we give a recipe with our Christmas cards. In 1994, after a trip to Turkey, I found myself craving lamb and put together this combination. The textures of crisp filo with the lamb and salsa make for an extraordinary eating experience. It's easy and may be prepared several hours before dinner, then finished in the oven in less than fifteen minutes.

While in Turkey I learned to eat meat from only the left leg of a lamb. Lambs, they say, always rise on their right legs, making the right leg meat tougher! I suspect that the difference is negligible, but it's fun to tease your butcher by demanding to know the exact origin of your lamb leg.

Makes 8 pastries (serves 4)

Salsa verde:
- 1 cup parsley leaves (no stems)
- 1 cup cilantro leaves
- 3 serrano chiles
- 2 tablespoons olive oil
- Juice of 1 large lime
- ½ teaspoon salt

- 1¾ pounds lamb tenderloin or sirloin, cut into ¾-inch cubes (no smaller or the lamb will overcook)
- 1 16-ounce package frozen filo dough, thawed
- Approximately ½ pound (2 sticks) butter, melted
- Green salad (optional)
- Fort Rice Pilaf (page 169; optional)

Make the salsa verde by mixing all the ingredients in a blender or food processor. The sauce should taste green and herby; add more cilantro if you wish. (Many people feel that cilantro is best in small amounts. If you are one of these, feel free to use less than a cup.) Marinate the meat in the sauce for 2 hours or more.

The lamb packets may be prepared ahead of time. If baking immediately, preheat the oven to 350°F.

Divide the meat into 8 portions. Use 1 full filo sheet for each portion. Brush half of the sheet lengthwise with melted butter, then fold

over the unbuttered side and brush that with butter. Keep the other sheets covered with a damp cloth to keep them moist and pliable. If a sheet does tear, simply patch it together.

For each roll, place a portion of the meat crosswise about three-fourths of the way down the sheet, leaving several inches of filo on both sides. Fold the bottom of the dough over the meat, then fold over the sides. Roll up the dough tightly, place seam side down on a baking sheet lined with parchment paper, and brush with butter. They will look like Thai egg rolls or burritos. At this point they may be covered and refrigerated for baking later.

Brush tops with butter again just before baking. Bake about 15 minutes, until golden brown. If they haven't browned in this time, turn the oven temperature to 400°F to brown them quickly. Keep an eye on them! The lamb will be deliciously medium-rare. Serve with salad and Fort Rice Pilaf.

Buffalo Liver with Cassis and Huckleberries

After a successful hunt, mountain men and Native Americans always went for the delicious and nourishing buffalo liver first. They were likely to eat it raw, of course, as did Lakota Indian Charlie Randall, who lived with us in 1963 and loved watching "white eyes" nearly faint when he slipped a bit of buffalo liver into his mouth.

Unfortunately, most people have been turned off to liver by the opposite experience—overcooking. Ever since I learned to eat liver medium-rare, I have loved it, as I hope you will when you taste this adaptation of a calves' liver dish I first enjoyed in France.

The wild huckleberry preserves taste much like blueberries and add a uniquely American flavor. When preparing this dish for our annual Awful Offal dinner, we use preserves from the north end of Flathead Lake in Montana, where the bear population enjoys the berries as much as we do. (Carry a 10 percent pepper mace with you when picking!)

Serves 6

2 to 2½ pounds buffalo or calves' liver, cut into ½-inch-thick slices

2 cups milk

3 tablespoons all-purpose flour, plus enough for dusting

4 to 5 tablespoons canola oil

3 to 4 tablespoons butter

1 cup chicken broth

½ cup cream

¼ cup crème de cassis (or black currant syrup for a nonalcoholic substitute)

2 tablespoons huckleberry preserves (see Suppliers, page 303) or mixed berry or blueberry preserves

Salt

Freshly ground white pepper

6 sprigs parsley for garnish

Soak the liver in milk for 2 hours. Dry the liver, then dust with flour.

In a sauté pan, heat 2 tablespoons of canola oil and 1½ table-spoons butter over medium heat. When hot, place half of the liver in the pan and cook quickly to medium-rare, about 2 to 3 minutes on each side. (Remember that the slices will cook faster if they are less than ½ inch thick.) Remove and set aside, covered, in a warm place. Use another 2 tablespoons oil and the remaining butter to sauté the remaining liver and set aside with the first half.

Add 2 tablespoons flour to the pan; if no fat is left in the pan, add another tablespoon of oil or butter. Cook and stir until slightly browned, then whisk in the chicken broth and cream, scraping up all the browned bits from the pan to incorporate them into the sauce. Add the crème de cassis, huckleberry preserves, salt, and pepper. Whisk until smooth and slightly thickened. Serve over the liver and garnish with parsley.

Buffalo Liver with Bacon and Onions

Serves 6

6 slices bacon, preferably thickly cut

6 tablespoons canola oil or a combination of canola oil and butter (or substitute bacon drippings for 3 tablespoons of oil)

2 large sweet onions, peeled and sliced into ⅜-inch rings

2½ pounds buffalo or calves' liver, cut into ½-inch-thick slices

Cut the bacon slices in half and gently fry until crisp. Remove from the pan and blot but retain the bacon drippings if you want to cook the onions in it; it gives them a marvelous flavor. If you prefer to use canola oil, then drain off all the bacon fat and wipe the pan before heating the oil. Since the liver will cook more quickly than the onions, cook them in separate pans.

Heat the bacon drippings or 3 tablespoons of oil until very hot and smoke begins to rise. Add the onion slices and sear them. A bit of the burned onion flavor is excellent, so don't worry if a little bit of the onion burns black.

When the onions are about half-cooked, heat the remaining 3 tablespoons of oil in a second pan and sauté half of the liver about 2 to 3 minutes on each side, until medium-rare. Watch carefully: The liver will cook faster if it is sliced thinner than ½ inch. Remove and set aside, covered, in a warm place. Sauté the remaining liver. Place all the liver on a serving platter and top with the onions and then the strips of bacon.

Thanksgiving Buffalo Hump Roast

While researching for *Eating Up the Santa Fe Trail*, I read so many accounts of Native Americans and mountain men feasting on buffalo hump that I just had to taste it myself. One day I called one of my bison suppliers, Bob Dineen of Rocky Mountain Natural Meats.

"What about the hump?" I asked. "Is it any good eating?"

"Don't know," he replied. "But I'll try to cut you one."

A week later I went to his shop to see the hump. The buffalo is unique among animals in that it sports on top of its upper spine a row of five tall bones, like dorsal fin bones. They're sometimes called "feather bones," and Native American artists used the porous ends of the bones as paintbrushes. Each of the bones is 2 inches wide and ¾ inch thick at the base, and stretches upward 14 to 18 inches. The bones and five muscle groups around them form the hump, which weighs about 90 pounds in a young, dressed-out 600-pound animal.

Two of the muscle groups hold up the buffalo's big head and are very tough. Two, back along the sides, are good meat, a little more tender than top round. Then, in the center, there's a very tender portion you can cut with a fork.

The hump roast we serve consists of the tender center portion, with the bones arcing spectacularly skyward. It makes a splendid presentation and is best eaten on Thanksgiving or other special occasions when lots of time is set aside for gnawing on the long, meaty, savory roasted hump bones!

To obtain a buffalo hump, see Suppliers (page 303), and follow the recipe for World's Best Beef or Buffalo Prime Rib Roast (page 50).

Brains in Black Butter

Lambs' brains are simply delicious when crisp on the outside and topped with melted brown butter. I first tasted this dish years ago at a French restaurant near Estes Park, Colorado. It is now a standard at our annual Awful Offal dinner.

Serves 4

1 lamb's brain
Milk for soaking
8 tablespoons (1 stick) butter
3 tablespoons canola or peanut oil
1 serrano chile, seeded and finely minced (remove ribs and seeds before mincing for a milder dish)
½ cup flour
4 sprigs fresh cilantro

Slice the brain horizontally into ½-inch-thick slabs, then cut each slab into 4 pieces. Soak them in milk for 3 hours; drain and pat dry.

Heat the butter and oil in a skillet until not quite smoking. Dust the brain pieces with flour and quickly sauté. When they turn golden brown, place them on dinner plates. Turn the heat to high and let the butter solids turn a dark brown. Quickly sauté the chile pepper in the browning butter, then pour over the brains and garnish each plate with a cilantro sprig.

THE FORT COOKBOOK

Broiled Lamb Kidneys à la Tortilla

Many years ago there was an Afghan restaurant in Denver called the Khyber Pass; sadly, it is no longer in existence. My favorite dish consisted of a round of flatbread much like a flour tortilla, rolled around chile-sprinkled, broiled lamb kidneys. I have made it for friends and like the minimum of effort it requires, which allows the cook to enjoy the party.

Serves 6

18 lamb kidneys
2 cups milk
½ cup olive or salad oil
Salt
12 flour tortillas
1 tablespoon ground hot chile pepper

Cut the white portion away from the lamb kidneys and discard. Slice the kidneys in half and soak in the milk for 2 hours.

Preheat the broiler and place the rack 8 inches from the heat. Remove the kidneys from the milk and brush with oil. Broil for 8 minutes, sprinkling with a bit of salt when just about done. The kidneys should still be medium-rare. Avoid overcooking! Remove from the oven and cut each half kidney into 3 pieces.

While the kidneys are broiling, wrap the tortillas in aluminum foil and heat them on the bottom rack of the oven.

Place 9 kidney pieces in each tortilla and dust with the chile pepper. Roll it up and eat!

Tortillas

In Spain a tortilla is a potato omelet. In New Mexico and Mexico they are similar to what we're used to in the United States, and there are two kinds. The first is a wheat flour cake between 6 and 12 inches wide and up to ½ inch thick. It's sometimes leavened with yeast but more often with baking powder. These are baked on a griddle, skillet, or *comal,* a sheet of steel.

Corn tortillas are also baked in a skillet or on a *comal,* but they are smaller cakes of hominy cornmeal, salt, and water. The cornmeal comes from kernel corn cooked in slaked lime (calcium hydroxide), which helps remove the tough outer skin.

An alternative to premade flour tortillas is a simple home-cooked bread dough tortilla. Simply make dough according to your favorite white bread recipe. Then roll an apple-sized ball of dough into a thin, flat 8-inch round. Heat a 10-inch or larger skillet over medium heat, drop in ½ teaspoon salt to keep the dough from sticking, and panfry the tortillas. Turn when browned lightly and still flexible.

Skewered Broiled Lamb Sweetbreads

A few years ago we were invited to a potluck with a twist—each couple brought some form of offal: animal organs. I had prepared buffalo tongue and buffalo testicles, but the hit of the evening was the plate of bamboo-skewered broiled lamb sweetbreads. They were simply pecan-size pieces dusted with sea salt and a mixture of red and black pepper—crisp on the outside and tenderly delicious on the inside.

Having learned my lesson, I brought these to the next potluck I attended. Almost everyone asked me for the recipe!

Serves 6

  12 **bamboo or metal skewers**
1½ **pounds lamb sweetbreads**
    Milk for soaking
   2 **tablespoons butter, melted**
    Sea salt, finely ground
    Mixed cayenne and finely ground black pepper
   6 **cups cooked white rice, for serving**

If you are using wooden skewers, soak them in water to keep them from burning on the grill.

Soak the sweetbreads in milk for 3 hours. Remove them and heat the milk in the microwave to boiling. Remove the milk from the microwave and add the sweetbreads to gently poach them, about 5 minutes. Remove the membranes, dry the pieces, and skewer them. Brush with butter and dust with salt and pepper.

Place them on a hot charcoal grill or under a broiler, 3 to 4 inches from the flame so that they brown quickly without overcooking inside. When browned on one side, turn the skewers to cook the other side. Serve these over a bed of rice, and feast.

From the Fields and Forests

Moose Nose

Moose are still one of the most magnificent large animals in the West. The surprise of coming across one drinking from the edge of a mirror-smooth lake at dawn can be a great treat. We once had a mother moose and her half-grown calf join a herd of riders in the Teton wilderness. They stayed with the group for several days and hung their heads low, trying to blend in with the horses!

Our 1965 appetizer menu offered "Cold Boiled Moose Nose, with piquant sauce . . . $2.50." One night a Denver man brought a guest from New York, who insisted that it couldn't *really* be moose nose. His host insisted. The easterner offered a $100 bet that it wasn't real. "Bring out the moose nose!" they demanded. So I went to the walk-in and lifted out a platter with the nose. The New Yorker paid for his disbelief.

I had read about "mouffle," as moose nose is called in the Northwest Territory, so I asked my game purveyor, Bill Brogan of Montana's Cinnabar Game Farm, to get me a couple of noses. In due time they arrived, swathed in plastic. They were dark, hairy, over two feet in length, and surprisingly light.

I built a steady fire in The Fort's courtyard and impaled a nose on a long metal rod. Then I toasted it like a giant marshmallow over the open fire. The smell of the burning hair wasn't too pleasant, and a few arriving dinner guests looked unhappy. When all was singed off, I

soaked it in salt water overnight and used a wire brush to loosen and remove any residue.

The next day I discovered that the nose's sinus cavities also contained hair, so I cut them open and applied a gas torch, more salt water, and a wire brush. It was now ready to cook. Into a pot of water it went with a splash of white vinegar, a chopped onion, and several bay leaves, plus some black peppercorns and a little salt. I cooked it for five hours at a slow simmer, then moved it to a tray.

A moose nose is constructed of long-fibered meat and a lot of cartilage, which was softened by the boiling and pleasantly crunchy when cool. On the tray it makes its own aspic. Moose nose tends to be bland, tasting like pickled pigs' feet. We served it sliced into thin slabs with some nose aspic and a piquant sweet chile sauce.

Serves 25 trusting friends

1 **moose nose**
2 **cups white vinegar**
1 **onion, chopped**
Several bay leaves
2 **tablespoons black peppercorns**
2 **tablespoons salt**
1 **cup sweet red chile sauce such as Buffalo Eggs Sauce (page 25) or any commercial brand**

Prepare as explained above.

From the Fields and Forests

Governor Bent's
150th Inauguration Dinner Menu

Buffalo Tongue en Gelée
Roast Quail on Toast with Foie Gras
Robert Mondavi Woodbridge Cabernet Sauvignon
Robert Mondavi Woodbridge Sauvignon Blanc

Fort Dinner Salad

Roast Bison with Grilled Green Chile and Corn Pudding
Geyser Peak 1994 Cabernet Sauvignon

President Andrew Jackson's Trifle
Gruet Sparkling Wine Opened by Tomahawk
Coffee or Tea

From the Yard: Poultry and Pork

———◆———

EVERY FUR TRADE FORT IN THE 1830S KEPT ONE YARD FOR TURKEYS AND chickens and another for goats and pigs that were brought west with the wagon trains. This guaranteed a steady supply of fresh meat and eggs, and provided an alternative to buffalo and other game. At Bent's Fort, hunters brought in many game birds, too: duck, plover, teal, goose, and crane. The fort even kept several pet peacocks, but it's doubtful that they were eaten.

Throughout New Mexico, fowl was prevalent in the 1800s. They were inexpensive, quick to reproduce, and a source of egg money; chickens were raised by almost everyone. Even today in Santa Fe, chickens are raised within the city limits.

The long history of poultry and pork in the West is evident during our annual fall rendezvous, when The Fort becomes a bustling 1840s center of trade, games, and eating.

Fall Rendezvous

One day every October, The Fort's portals are thrown open at high noon to the tolling of the bells in the watchtower, and The Fort Rendezvous and Fandango begins. The courtyard is transformed into a market where a passel of traders come from near and far to sell their period ware. Tinsmiths and blacksmiths and silversmiths gather; gun and knife makers display beautiful handmade products. An expert on trade beads sets out her collection, with examples in every shape, size, and color. Shirts, coats, pants, trade beads, silver jewelry, sculptures, furs, blankets, and even hats are sold, all conforming to the 1850 cutoff date for authenticity.

Thousands of people come throughout the day to see the "doin's," and over a hundred mountain men, women, and children wear authentic 1840s garb, many in buckskins sewn by hand. Prizes are given for best costumes, and the mountain men engage in competitions for knife and tomahawk throwing, black powder long-gun shooting, and fire starting with flint and steel. The best time that has been achieved for burning through a string stretched horizontally eight inches above ground, with a fire started with flint and steel, is seven seconds!

Carding and spinning, gun making, storytelling, and atlatl-throwing demonstrations are just a few delights of the day. Our own phrenologist, Dr. C. C. Cochran III, is in residence to "read" the character bumps on heads of paying clients. Believed to be an accurate science in the 1840s, phrenology is enjoying a renaissance at The Fort.

Through the afternoon a military brass band with nineteenth-century instruments plays lively songs, and reenactors periodically fire our six-pounder and mountain howitzer black powder cannons.

Food at the rendezvous consists of Sioux washtunkala jerky stew; Mountain Man Boudies (page 20), Lakota Indian Fry Bread (page 217), Posole with Pork (page 123), and New Mexico Village-Style Chili con Carne (page 120). Steaming loaves of Indian Horno Bread (page 212) come out of the adobe horno beehive oven in the courtyard every forty-five minutes.

At six o'clock the "skinners," as buckskinners are called, gather in

From the Yard

the St. Vrain Dining Room for a buffler dinner. At the first rendezvous we passed a platter of raw buffalo liver as Native Americans and mountain men had enjoyed it in the nineteenth century after a hunt. None of the first table of skinners would taste it. Then it reached Carrie. Slight and blond and wearing an early Victorian dress, she popped a piece in her mouth and swallowed it right down.

"Sorts the men from the boys!" she said. The sheepish men all followed suit, and raw buffalo liver before dinner became a tradition.

Bowl of the Wife of Kit Carson

In the spring of 1961, two years before opening The Fort, my family and I found ourselves stopped during a road trip to Mexico in Durango, some six hundred miles south of the border, driving a tiny English Morris Mini-Cooper S. Today a city of several hundred thousand, Durango was then less than half that size. We were told that the best place to eat was the drugstore. Following that lead the next morning, we watched a stream of young children coming in from the fields to fill family lunch buckets with a special soup. It smelled so good that we tried it.

The bowls we were served held a heady, spicy broth of chicken, with nice bites of white meat, nutty garbanzo beans, rice, a touch of oregano, avocado chunks, and pieces of white cheese. The secret of its great taste, though, was the chipotle chile, smoked jalapeño, that gave the soup a distinctive bite and delicious smoky flavor.

Caldo Tlalpeño was its proper name, we learned, and when The Fort opened, it went on the menu. Nobody could pronounce it (or knew what it meant), so it didn't sell until one day Leona Wood, the septuagenarian who ran our gift shop trade room on weekends, exclaimed, "I remember my grandmother serving us this dish!" Miss Wood happened to be the last granddaughter of frontiersman Kit Carson. And so "The Bowl of the Wife of Kit Carson" was christened. For thirty-four years it has been a signature dish of The Fort.

Serves 4

2 whole boneless, skinless chicken breasts (approximately 2 pounds)

1 quart chicken broth (canned is fine)

Pinch of dried Mexican leaf oregano

1 cup cooked rice

1 cup cooked garbanzo beans, preferably from dried (if using canned, be sure to drain well)

1 ripe avocado, peeled, pitted, and chopped

1 chipotle chile, packed in adobo, minced

4 to 6 ounces Monterey jack or Havarti cheese, cubed (1 cup)

4 sprigs cilantro (optional)

Place the chicken breasts in a pot with the broth. Bring to a boil, then turn off the heat, cover, and poach for 12 minutes gently. Remove from the pot and cut into strips 1½ inches long. Return the chicken strips to the broth and add the oregano, rice, garbanzo beans, avocado, and chipotle.

Divide the cheese among 4 deep soup bowls.

Quickly heat the soup again to a quick boil, then ladle it into the bowls. Garnish with a cilantro sprig.

This dish may be made a day ahead, but don't add the avocado until reheating the soup for serving. The chipotle flavor will intensify overnight and the dish may seem hotter. For a more intense flavor, add some of the adobo from the peppers.

Country Captain Chicken

One of my favorite dishes in the first year at The Fort was Country Captain Chicken, an American version of an East Indian curried chicken. The tale holds that the recipe was brought back to South Carolina, where rice is a significant crop, in the 1700s by an American skipper who had sailed to India. In its current form it is a mild curried chicken and rice.

This recipe is adapted from *American Heritage Cookbook* and is the one we used at The Fort. Don't let all the ingredients scare you away—putting them together is quick and simple.

Serves 4

3 pounds skinless chicken parts, bone-in
¼ cup flour
1 teaspoon salt
¼ teaspoon pepper
4 to 5 tablespoons butter
⅓ cup finely chopped onion
⅓ cup finely chopped green bell pepper
1 clove garlic, crushed
1½ teaspoons curry powder
2 or 3 curry bush leaves (optional; see page 105)
½ teaspoon dried thyme
1 pound canned stewed tomatoes
3 tablespoons dried currants
4 cups cooked white rice
Blanched sliced almonds, toasted, for accompaniment
Chutney for accompaniment

Coat the chicken in a mixture of the flour, salt, and pepper.

Heat 4 tablespoons of the butter in a large skillet. Add the chicken and brown well on both sides. If all the fat is absorbed before the chicken browns, add the remaining tablespoon of butter. Remove the chicken and set aside.

Add the onion, green pepper, garlic, curry powder, curry bush leaves, and thyme to the skillet and cook for a few minutes over low

heat, stirring in all the brown particles. Add the tomatoes and chicken, cover, and simmer for 20 to 30 minutes, until tender.

Just before serving, stir in the currants. Serve over the white rice, with the almonds and chutney on the side.

Curry Bush

If you're feeling really adventuresome, call your local botanical garden or horticulture center and ask if you might have a few leaves from a wonderful plant called the karapincha, or curry bush. This plant produces a small leaf similar to a boxwood leaf, and it tastes marvelous when heated in oil. While it doesn't go into all curry dishes, in Sri Lanka the butcher often encloses a few sprigs with a meat purchase, just as American butchers often add parsley.

Santa Fe Chicken Breast

Northern New Mexico was for two hundred years considered the "boonies" of the Spanish empire. Every two years a wagon train arrived from Mexico carrying goods such as fabric, iron, religious objects, sacramental wine, and condado almonds from Spain. And chocolate, too! But most dishes were influenced more by the local Pueblo Indian diet. Chile, corn, beans, and squash were the staples; meat was a luxury. But the chile, originally from central Mexico, reached its highest flavor when cultivated in New Mexico.

The Chile Shop on Water Street in Santa Fe sells a most excellent pure red chile powder called Dixon, which is recommended for recipes throughout this book. It has the wonderful pungent pepper flavor while offering a modest bite on the tongue.

Serves 4

2 cups chicken broth (homemade or from bouillon cubes)
4 6- to 8-ounce skinless, boneless split chicken breasts
2 cups Red Chile Sauce (page 84)
8 ¼-inch-thick slices Muenster cheese
Ripe olives
Shredded lettuce
Radishes, cut in half
Red and green bell pepper pieces (optional)

In a saucepan, heat the chicken broth with the breasts until boiling, cover, and turn off the heat. Let them poach for 12 minutes, then drain.

Preheat the oven to 450°F.

Pour ¼ cup Red Chile Sauce on an ovenproof oval plate. Lay the chicken breasts on it. Pour more sauce over the chicken breasts, then lay the slices of cheese on top. Place in the oven for 3 minutes, or until the cheese is bubbling and browning. Garnish with the olives, lettuce, and radishes. For a special look, make a star or circle pattern of green and red pepper pieces on the cheese before it melts so that it can be seen after the cheese has melted.

VARIATION: Nothing tastes better with this Red Chile Sauce than an egg. In traditional Santa Fe style, fry an egg sunny-side up separately, and just as you serve the chicken dish, slip the egg onto the cheese.

THE FORT COOKBOOK

106

The combination of tastes—chicken, toasted cheese, red chile, and fried egg—is wonnderrrfulll.

Variation

Tamarind-Chile Chicken

In Costa Rica we once went to a local rodeo, where we sat in rickety bleachers to watch the steer throwing—novice cowboys wrestling young steers to the ground, with considerable effort and only partial success. Hanging down beside us were the branches of a big tamarind tree. They bore long, brown pods that looked as if they were made of paper. A friend showed us how to break them open and remove what resembled a prune. We sucked the fruit's meat from a large pit, and it was delicious, with a sweet-sour dried-fruit-like taste.

Tamarind is used worldwide for its exquisite flavor: in sauces such as Worcestershire, A.1, Tabasco's Caribbean sauce, and Crosse & Blackwell's superb steak sauce. Big glass jars of *tamarindo refresco* with ice are hawked on the streets of Mexico. In Italy, snow cones with tamarind syrup delight adults and children alike. We tried tamarind with cream, red chile, and honey. What a sauce! We liked it so well that we used it to dress corn on the cob in addition to this tasty chicken.

Serves 6

Tamarind-Chile Sauce:
2 cups heavy cream
¼ cup Red Chile Sauce (page 84)
1 teaspoon tamarind concentrate
2 teaspoons honey

6 6- to 8-ounce skinless, boneless split chicken breasts, poached

Simmer the heavy cream in a saucepan over medium-high heat for about 5 minutes to reduce. Add the Red Chile Sauce, tamarind, and honey. Return the poached breasts to the sauce for a few minutes to rewarm before serving.

From the Yard

Cha-Cha Chicken

Our first manager, Luis Bonachea, brought us this great recipe from Cuba. Combining sweet and tart fruits with meat is typical of Caribbean cooking, and in this dish the fruit sugars in the marinade caramelize on the chicken with a superb "agri-dulce" sweet-and-sour taste. Drummettes prepared ahead of time make a great party appetizer.

Serves 4

Marinade:
2 cups orange juice without pulp
¼ cup soy sauce
5 tablespoons honey
4 tablespoons fresh lime juice
3 tablespoons butter, melted
2 tablespoons chopped fresh parsley
2 tablespoons chopped cilantro
2 tablespoons dry mustard
2 tablespoons finely minced fresh peeled ginger
½ teaspoon cayenne plus some for sprinkling
2 cloves garlic, minced

4 chicken halves or 2 Cornish hens cut in half, or bone-in split chicken breasts, thighs, and drumsticks
Several orange and lime slices
Dash of salt
Cayenne
Fresh mint sprigs for garnish
4 cups cooked saffron rice (optional)
3 tablespoons toasted pine nuts for garnish (optional)
Zest of 1 orange, grated, for garnish (optional)

To make the marinade, mix all the marinade ingredients in a food processor.

Place the chicken in a plastic or glass bowl and cover it with the marinade and the orange and lime slices. The chicken needs only a few hours to marinate, but longer is better and overnight is dandy.

When you're ready to cook the chicken, preheat the oven to 325°F.

Remove the chicken from the marinade and place it on a baking pan completely lined with aluminum foil that has been coated with oil. (Use extra-wide foil; overlapping 2 pieces will leave a sugary mess beneath them. Parchment paper also works, but be sure to cut it large enough to extend all the way up the sides of the pan to prevent the syrup from leaking beneath it.) Sprinkle with salt and cayenne, and bake for 35 minutes, then raise the heat to broil and cook another 10 minutes, until the skin is nice and crispy.

Garnish with the mint sprigs. As an entree, serve over a bed of saffron rice with toasted pine nuts and orange zest.

NOTE: If your baking pan does get coated with syrup so that the foil sticks, run hot water over the pan. This will melt the sugar and allow you to peel off the foil.

Chicken Adobe

This has been one of our most popular dishes for many years.

Serves 4

    4 8- to 10-ounce boneless, skinless chicken breasts, unsplit
    6 ounces ham, sliced into 4 equal pieces
    6 ounces Monterey jack cheese, cut into 4 sticks approximately
        1½ inches by ½ inch
      Canola or peanut oil to fill a skillet ½ inch deep
1½ cups finely ground tortilla chips
 ½ cup bread crumbs
 ¾ cup flour
  1 to 1½ cups milk

Lightly pound the chicken breasts to flatten. If one is particularly thick, you may want to butterfly it. Wrap each slice of ham around a slice of cheese. Place one slice on each chicken breast, folding the short ends of the chicken onto the slice and then folding the larger sides on top. Place seam side down in a pan so that the smooth, pretty side is showing, and freeze.

Heat the oil over high heat and preheat the oven to 350°F.

Mix the ground tortilla chips thoroughly with the bread crumbs. This should make enough breading, but if you are using very large chicken breasts, you may need more. Dip the frozen chicken breasts first in the flour and then in the milk. Pat on the tortilla/bread crumb mixture firmly.

Fry the chicken breasts one at a time on all sides until brown. Place on a baking sheet and finish in the oven for approximately 20 to 25 minutes. This technique allows the chicken to cook evenly and thoroughly with minimal frying.

Chicken Colorado Style

This quick and scrumptious dish is a western variation on a recipe for Chicken Virginia Style from *The Improved Housewife,* an early nineteenth-century cookbook by Mrs. Webster. We've kept her original batter recipe. The eggs form a wonderful custard that blends deliciously with the pine nuts and chiles.

Serves 7 or 8

1   to 2 tablespoons vegetable oil
1   4-pound roasting chicken, cut into pieces, skin and excess fat removed
3   eggs
2   tablespoons melted butter
2   tablespoons flour
1   pint half-and-half
⅓   cup concentrated chicken broth
3   to 4 ounces chopped mild green chiles (for more bite, include a few chopped hot fresh chiles)
2   ounces bottled pimento-stuffed green olives
2   scallions
2   tablespoons toasted pine nuts
Dash of paprika

Preheat the oven to 350°F. Butter a 6- to 8-quart casserole.

Heat the oil in a skillet and brown the chicken on all sides; place in the buttered casserole.

Combine the eggs, butter, flour, half-and-half, and chicken broth in a blender and pour over the chicken. Sprinkle with the green chiles and whole olives, which will disappear into the batter. Slice the scallions lengthwise into thin strips and lay them across the top. Bake for 45 minutes. Just before serving, sprinkle with the pine nuts and paprika for color.

From the Yard

Sam's Own Cilantro/Serrano Chile Chicken Breast

Only a few guests have ever tasted this dish at The Fort, but every cook there knows how to make it. The reason? Although it's not a regular menu item, it's my favorite way to cook chicken, so I often ask for it. It's fast, it's simple, and if you like the combination of cilantro and serrano chile, you'll find it delicious. Sharply pepper hot, the chiles offset the mildness of the chicken.

Serves 4

2 tablespoons olive oil
4 6- to 8-ounce skinless, boneless split chicken breasts
2 serrano chiles, finely minced (remove the ribs and seeds before mincing for a milder dish)
2 tablespoons whole cilantro leaves
2 green onions, finely sliced diagonally
Pinch of salt
¼ cup finely diced red bell pepper
Cilantro sprigs for garnish

Heat the olive oil, and when it is quite hot, quickly brown the chicken. Remove from the pan and set aside. Lower the heat and sauté the rest of the ingredients in the pan until the onions and chiles are slightly browned.

Return the chicken to the pan and turn it in the chiles and onions. Serve, garnished with sprigs of cilantro.

Chicken Almendra

Almonds and chicken are often found together in Mexico, where I first came across this easy-to-make dish that we serve to luncheon parties. It's simply delicious, with the taste of toasted almonds in a candied, crispy almond base.

Serves 4

4 6- to 8-ounce skinless, boneless split chicken breasts
1 tablespoon canola oil
1 tablespoon butter
1 cup sliced almonds
½ cup sugar
6 tablespoons Di Saronno Amaretto or other almond liqueur

Preheat the oven to broil.

Sauté the chicken breasts in the oil and butter until cooked through. Set aside.

In a small bowl, mix together the almonds, sugar, and Di Saronno Amaretto.

Cover a baking sheet with aluminum foil that has been either buttered or sprayed with a nonstick spray. Spread the almond sauce evenly on the foil. Broil, watching carefully, until the sugar has caramelized, then remove from the oven. When it has cooled slightly, return the caramelized sauce to the bowl and crush.

Place the sautéed chicken breasts on a baking sheet lined with foil and top with the almond mixture. Broil for 2 to 3 minutes, until the topping melts. Watch it carefully. Any leftover almond mixture is great over ice cream—or as a cook's treat!

From the Yard

Wedding Salad

One April evening in 1969 a beautiful petite blond guest asked me to autograph a cookbook. With pen in hand and roving eye, I asked her name so that I could write it in the book.

"Carrie," she said.

"Miss or Mrs.?" I inquired.

"Miss!" she answered. My day brightened. I gave her and her date (whom I don't remember) a tour of the restaurant and determined to learn more about her.

Just over two years later, on May 2, 1971, Carrie and I were married at dawn on the huge red rock overlooking The Fort. That evening we invited about eighty friends to a wedding party buffet. We served large steamboat roasts of buffalo, Indian Horno Bread (page 212), and what we later christened "Wedding Salad."

Serves 12

3 pounds boneless, skinless chicken breasts
2 cups chicken broth (canned works fine)
4 8-ounce russet potatoes
¼ cup plus 2 tablespoons sugar
¼ cup plus 2 tablespoons cider vinegar
1 cup frozen green peas
4 8-ounce jars pickled artichoke hearts in oil and vinegar
1 can pitted whole ripe olives, drained (sliced will work also, but whole olives look nice and have more flavor impact)
2 cups sour cream (light sour cream if you prefer)
Salt
Cayenne
Bibb lettuce, rinsed well, to line the bowl
1 cup coarsely chopped English walnuts, toasted
6 red radish crowns
3 hard-cooked eggs, halved or quartered
Paprika for garnish

Poach the chicken breasts by placing them in a saucepan with the broth. Bring to a simmer, then turn off the heat and cover for about 12 minutes. It's important not to overcook them because they'll turn

rubbery, but be sure there's no pink left in the middle. Remove and cut into ¾-inch cubes.

Peel the potatoes, cut them into ¾-inch cubes, and boil in enough water to cover for about 12 minutes, or until a knife can be easily inserted in them. (Try one; your teeth are the best indicator.) Do not overcook or they will fall apart. Carefully remove from the water and drain.

Dissolve the sugar in the vinegar in a large bowl and gently toss with the potatoes when they're just cool enough to touch. Mix in the chicken and refrigerate.

Blanch the peas by pouring them into boiling water for 1 to 2 minutes, or microwave them with a few tablespoons of water for about 1 minute, then drain.

Cut the artichoke hearts into quarters and stir them along with their liquid into the potatoes. Fold in the olives and add the sour cream a little at a time. (The amount of liquid from the artichokes will determine how much you'll need. Light sour cream tends to be runnier than regular.) Add the salt and cayenne to taste.

Line a large salad bowl with the lettuce. Add the potatoes, top with the peas and toasted walnuts, and garnish with the radish flowers, egg halves or quarters, and paprika.

Turkey with Piñon Stuffing

For over a third of a century The Fort has served tom turkey with pine nut stuffing to the delight of Thanksgiving Day guests. For years the turkeys were cooked in a smoke oven, but since twenty-five or more big birds are now needed, we oven-roast them.

Serves 8

Stuffing (see Note):
½ pound chestnuts, either fresh roasted, peeled, and chopped, or dry-roasted from a jar (available at specialty groceries)
8 tablespoons (1 stick) butter
1 clove garlic, crushed
2 cups stale bread cubes
⅔ cup chicken broth
2 tablespoons dry sherry
½ cup heavy cream
½ cup chopped hot green chiles, canned or fresh, roasted (see page 140)
2 shallots, minced
2 stalks celery, diced
½ cup chopped parsley leaves
¼ cup whole cilantro leaves
1 tablespoon freshly ground black pepper
1 teaspoon chopped fresh rosemary
1 teaspoon salt
2 pinches fresh thyme leaf or 1 pinch dry
½ cup toasted pine nuts

1 15- to 20-pound turkey
½ pound (2 sticks) unsalted butter
Salt
Freshly ground black pepper
1 cup dry white wine
3 tablespoons fresh or 1 tablespoon dry rosemary

To roast the chestnuts, cut an X on the flat side of each nut. Place the nuts in a dry cast-iron skillet and toast over medium-high heat, shaking the pan often, until the shells start browning and the edges of

the X begin to pull away from the nut. Parts of them will be quite dark, and they will smell wonderful! Chestnuts peel more easily when they're warm. Use a sharp paring knife to peel back both the outer shell and the inner membrane. The inner membrane can be quite stubborn, but the result justifies the effort.

For the stuffing, melt the butter in a sauté pan and cook the garlic until golden. Add the bread cubes and stir constantly until golden. Remove the mixture and set aside. In the same pan, combine the remaining ingredients except the chestnuts and pine nuts. Simmer for 2 minutes to release the flavors, then add the bread cube mixture, chestnuts, and pine nuts. Mix well, cover, and bring to room temperature before using to stuff the bird.

Preheat the oven to 325°F.

To prepare the turkey, melt the butter and stir in the salt and pepper. Rub the turkey with the butter mixture inside and out. Use the remaining butter to make the basting sauce. Combine the butter with the wine and one-third of the rosemary in a small saucepan. Boil for 2 minutes on high heat, then remove from the heat and use to baste the turkey every 15 minutes.

Fill both cavities of the bird with the stuffing. Sew up with a trussing cord and bind the wings and drumsticks tight alongside the bird's body. Cover the wings and drumsticks with aluminum foil for the first hour to prevent overcooking.

Sprinkle the remaining rosemary over the bird.

Place the turkey on a rack in a shallow roasting pan. Do not add water. Cover the turkey with a loose tent of aluminum foil and roast for 15 minutes per pound plus 1 hour for the stuffing.

Remove the foil 30 minutes before roasting is done. Test for doneness with a reliable meat thermometer; this is the only way to be sure it is done. The final temperature for safety and doneness is 180°F in the thigh and at least 165°F in the breast and stuffing. The juices should run clear, not pink. Test the temperature early and often. An overcooked turkey is dry, tough, and pasty in texture.

HICKORY-SMOKED TURKEY: You can also use a covered barbecue or smoke roaster to cook the turkey and use damp hickory chips on the fire for a smoke flavor. Don't overdo the amount or length of smoke—15 minutes of smoke is enough. Roast the bird in a pan at 375°F until a meat thermometer measures 180°F in the thigh and at least 165°F in the breast and stuffing, 4 to 6 hours,

depending on size. A pan of water in the cooker under the bird helps to keep it moist.

NOTE: You may make the stuffing a day ahead of time and refrigerate it overnight, but warm it before you stuff the bird. Bringing the stuffing to room temperature before filling the bird is necessary to allow the stuffing to cook all the way through. Be sure to remove all stuffing from the carcass after dining and store in a separate bowl.

Pine Nuts

Pine nuts in New Mexico and Colorado are called *piñones* (peen-YO-nays). These were gathered by Native Americans in winter. After the first snowfall, the tracks of ground squirrels were followed to the burrows, where several gallons of nuts could be dug up. Some were always left for the squirrels' winter rations. Indians roasted the pine nuts and then ate them by cracking the shells between the teeth and skillfully extracting the meat with the tongue. Today, Santa Fe's movie theater floors, when the show is over, are a carpet of empty pine nut shells.

Santa Fe Pork Adobada

From the 1607 settlement of Santa Fe onward, the wealthy landowners generally raised beef while the small farmers and townspeople consumed mostly sheep, chickens, and pigs.

The tradition of eating pork lives on in New Mexico in many wonderful dishes. The Christmas holiday season is pork posole time. But all year round, pork-filled tamales, roast pork, barbecued ribs, deep-fried pork pieces called *carnitas,* and all parts of the pig are enjoyed. Pork *adobada* (in a chile marinade) is one of the most popular dishes in all of New Mexico. We served it in the early days of The Fort.

Serves 4

Marinade:
½ cup medium red chile caribe (coarsely ground chile; see Notes)
1 cup chicken broth
½ teaspoon Mexican leaf oregano
2 cloves garlic, minced
½ teaspoon salt

6 7-ounce lean pork rib chops, thickly cut (see Notes)
4 cups cooked white rice or mashed potatoes

Combine the marinade ingredients in a nonreactive bowl and dredge the pork chops in it. Refrigerate for at least 4 hours. They're best when marinated at least 8 hours and are delicious when marinated for up to 2 days, as long as they're refrigerated.

Preheat the oven to 350°F.

Transfer the chops and marinade to a foil-lined pan and bake, covered with a sheet of foil, for 45 minutes. Remove the foil during the final 10 minutes of baking. Check to make sure that the chile doesn't burn. If it threatens to, cover with foil for the last few minutes of baking. Serve over white rice or with mashed potatoes.

NOTES: For my particular taste, I like the Dixon ground pure New Mexico red chile (medium-hot) mixed half and half with Hatch mild red chile powder. If only mild red chile is used, this sauce is not very pepper-hot, but it still has a nice, delicious paprika-ish piquancy.

This is also wonderful using country-style pork ribs cut from the front end of the loin. Country-style ribs need more cooking time, at least 1½ hours, to become fork-tender.

From the Yard

New Mexico Village-Style Chili con Carne

When I first lived in Santa Fe, I learned from restaurateur Luis Salazar how to make real New Mexican chili con carne. Mr. Salazar had grown up in Santa Fe and came from a long line of Santa Feans. At his Original Mexican Cafe on College Street, everything was made from scratch. He boiled blue kernel corn in huge kettles with slaked lime to make posole and the masa for corn tortillas. He dried ripe red Española Valley chiles and then stemmed, cleaned, and cooked them to make red chili con carne—chile with meat.

His chili con carne recipe reflects the cuisine of the little villages north of Santa Fe, which is very different from those of southern New Mexico, Texas, and Arizona. It contains no beans, no tomato, no onion, no cumin, and only a slight touch of garlic and Mexican leaf oregano. Twice-cooking the pork results in browning and caramelization for depth of flavor.

This dish is easy to digest because it contains no tomatoes, whose acids contribute largely to indigestion. Once you taste it, you may never go back to tomato and kidney bean–based recipes.

Serves 10

4   pounds bone-in pork shoulder (also known as pork butt), fat cut away and chopped into fist-size pieces
3   quarts water or enough to cover the meat in a pot
2   tablespoons vegetable oil or rendered pork or bacon fat
½   cup cornmeal
½   cup cold water
1   cup Red Chile Puree (page 83)
1   teaspoon dried Mexican leaf oregano
Salt

For best results start this recipe a day ahead to give the broth time to cool completely so that it can be thoroughly defatted.

Slowly boil the pork in water for 1½ hours. Remove the meat to a large bowl and place the broth in the refrigerator. When the pork is cool enough to touch, cut the meat away from the bone and chop into ¼-inch cubes. Store in the refrigerator until ready to use.

Defat the pork broth and bring to a simmer.

Heat the oil in a deep skillet until smoking. Dry the pork cubes with a paper towel and sear in the oil until thoroughly browned. Add the browned meat to the broth. Add a bit of broth to the skillet to deglaze.

Stir together the cornmeal and water. Add the mixture to the broth in the skillet, stirring well to thicken.

Remove about ½ cup broth from the stockpot and set aside in case the chili needs thinning after it has simmered. Pour the broth and cornmeal mixture into the pot and add the Red Chile Puree. Adjust the flavor with oregano and salt. Simmer for 25 minutes, then serve.

NOTE: The longer you simmer this, the more tender the pork will be and the thicker the chili. Adding more cornmeal will thicken it, too.

Santa Fe Pork Chops

Hardly anything in the world is better tasting than a morsel of broiled pork, all browned and caramelized from the heat and yet moist, white, and succulent in the middle. Add to this a dip into a small cup of Red Chile Sauce, and ecstasy prevails.

Ask your butcher to cut thick rib or loin chops, not less than 1 inch and preferably 1½ inches thick. They'll be between 8 and 9 ounces. If your guests are modest eaters, allow for one chop per person. At The Fort we serve two chops per person. Really too much, but people like to take 'em home for breakfast.

Serves 4

    8 8-ounce lean rib or loin pork chops
    Olive oil for rubbing the pork chops
    1 cup Red Chile Sauce (page 84)

Before cooking the pork, rub with a little bit of olive oil to keep the chops from sticking to the pan. Broil or grill the chops about 4 inches from the heat source, but juicier chops often result from "pan-grilling" them over high heat in a dry cast-iron skillet, preferably with a ridged bottom, for 5 to 8 minutes per side, depending on thickness.

Heat the Red Chile Sauce and serve in a gravy boat or in individual ramekins to dip the meat.

Posole with Pork

Visit any grocery store in Santa Fe at Christmas, and you'll see lots of people buying pork for making posole. While *posole* is the name of the dish itself, it is, literally, hominy corn—kernels whose hard shells have been removed by boiling in slaked lime. The remaining meaty center is sold fresh or dried throughout the Southwest. Ground to a paste, it's used for making corn tortillas or tamales. When left in kernel form, it is boiled, and the kernels pop rather like popcorn.

Definitely a cold weather dish, posole with pork has that slight mustiness that comes from the tiny bit of residual lime in the corn. This recipe is a traditional one served at The Fort Rendezvous and Fandango and other celebrations.

Serves 12

1 tablespoon vegetable oil or bacon fat
2 onions, chopped
2 pounds pork shoulder, cut into fist-size chunks
4 quarts chicken broth
1 bay leaf
1 sprig fresh oregano
½ cup fresh red chile puree or 4 to 6 tablespoons mild or medium-ground pure New Mexican red chile (Dixon is best)
2 cups wet or dry white posole corn, soaked overnight if dry
2 teaspoons salt
1 whole skinless, boneless chicken breast, cut into bite-size pieces (optional)
1½ pounds shredded mild cheddar cheese (6 cups) for topping

In a large stockpot, heat the oil and fry the onions about 2 minutes, until transparent. Add the pork and cook, turning occasionally, about 4 minutes, until brown.

Deglaze the stockpot with a little of the broth, scraping the bottom to loosen all the browned bits and incorporate them into the broth. Add the remaining ingredients except the chicken and cheese, and simmer, covered, for 5 to 6 hours, stirring regularly. Keep the solids under liquid by adding hot water when necessary. The dish is ready when the pork is tender and the posole has popped. It will look like wet popcorn.

Add the chicken, if using, and simmer for another 12 minutes, until the chicken is cooked. Serve hot in bowls and top with the shredded cheese.

From the Yard

123

Charbroiled Quail Glazed with Red Chile Honey

Bees came to North America from Europe with the settlers. Honey was the settlers' main sweet because cane sugar from the Caribbean was expensive and not readily available. Native Americans recognized the honeybee as an early warning of white encroachment. Their presence indicated that settlers were within fifty miles.

Quail, in contrast, are indigenous to the North American continent. In the Old West, hunters could usually shoot birds when red meat was scarce. Quail, grouse, and prairie chicken were often eaten on the trail and at military and fur trade forts.

Serves 4

Glaze:
1 rounded tablespoon pure ground New Mexico red chile (Dixon is best)
1 cup honey

8 partially boned quail (see Note)
Canola oil

Simmer the chile in the honey for 10 minutes to combine their flavors.

Brush the quail with the oil and charbroil them over a slow part of the grill for 5 to 8 minutes per side. Brush both sides of the birds with glaze when they are nearly cooked. If you glaze them too soon, the honey will burn, and you will end up with charred quail. After placing the quail on the plate, brush them once more with glaze.

NOTE: If you use quail that aren't partially boned, allow them longer cooking time.

Teriyaki Quail

The West was built in good part by Chinese and Japanese immigrants who supplied both hands and brains to build railroads and cities, ranches and farms. Also, some of the first trappers who had been brought to our northwest coast by John Jacob Astor were Hawaiians. It is not surprising, therefore, that teriyaki came to the West early on.

At The Fort we serve well over one thousand of these quail a week. We start with partially deboned birds so that the little rib cage has been removed. The legs, thighs, and wings are still attached, and with the large breast, quail makes a delicious dish when two or three birds are served.

Serves 4

Teriyaki Marinade:
1 **cup soy sauce**
½ **cup Mirin rice wine or dry sherry**
¼ **cup sugar**
2 **tablespoons minced fresh ginger**
3 **cloves garlic, finely minced or smashed**
2 **whole star anise (found in the Asian section of most groceries or in bulk at natural food stores; optional)**
¼ **cup finely chopped orange peel**
1 **cup orange juice**
1 **cup water**

8 **2½- to 3½-ounce partially deboned quail**
4 **orange slices for garnish**

Combine all the marinade ingredients in a saucepan and bring to a boil over high heat. Lower the heat and simmer for 5 minutes. Let cool.

Place the quail in a single layer in a pan, pour the marinade over, and let the quail marinate for 2 to 4 hours. Beware of leaving the birds in for more than 8 hours because they will become unpalatably salty.

When ready to cook the quail, heat the grill to medium or preheat the broiler. Cook the quail for 3 to 4 minutes on each side. Garnish with a twisted orange slice.

From the Yard

125

Quail Salad

I often eat this at The Fort although it's not on the menu. I urge guests to order whatever they desire; our kitchen will prepare individual requests. Our policy is to be flexible and provide our guests with exactly what they want.

Serves 4

Dressing:
½ cup raspberry vinegar
¼ cup water
¼ cup olive oil
1 tablespoon sugar
1 teaspoon dillweed
¼ teaspoon cayenne pepper

4 cups mixed salad greens: romaine, dandelion greens, and so forth
1 avocado, pitted, peeled, and cut into narrow wedges or cubes
1 tablespoon small capers
1 tablespoon beni-shoga (kizami-shoga) red pickled ginger (available at Japanese groceries; optional)
¼ cup cubed jicama
1 small jar marinated artichoke hearts, cut into small pieces
8 partially boned quail (use charbroiled quail from Teriyaki Quail, page 125)
1 medium tomato, cut into wedges, for garnish
8 large radish crowns for garnish
½ cup toasted cashews for garnish
4 lemon wedges for garnish

Combine the dressing ingredients. Adjust for taste.

Toss the greens, avocado, capers, beni-shoga, jicama, and artichoke hearts with the dressing. Place on individual plates or 1 large platter and arrange the quail on top. Garnish with the tomatoes, radishes, toasted cashews, and lemon wedges.

Broiled Guinea Hen with Wild Huckleberry

Years ago in Paris I was served a roasted bird by a French friend.

"It's marvelous!" I exclaimed. "This chicken is delicious!"

"It's not chicken," she said. *"C'est un pintade."*

"Un pintade?" I asked. "What's that?"

We found the word in the dictionary and discovered *pintade* translated as guinea fowl, a bird originally from Africa. The hen was called *pintelle,* which means "painted," because of its black feathers with spatterings of white dots. In France it is easily as popular as chicken, with more than sixty million pintade consumed every year. Moreover, it is lower in cholesterol and fat than chicken and has a wonderful flavor, a cross between chicken and pheasant, without the pheasant's tendency toward dryness.

Guinea hens were commonly served in colonial America and up through the nineteenth century on American farms in the West. Gradually, fewer and fewer people raised them, and today they're virtually unknown in this country. Many older people remember them as "watch birds" on farms and ranches, recalling vividly the birds' horrible call, which they raise whenever they're disturbed (and often when they aren't).

I searched long and hard to find a purveyor, and have served both half birds and pairs of leg quarters ever since. They are both equally

From the Yard

127

good, but we find that leg quarters are much easier to eat. We marinate them in dry white wine and powdered jalapeño pepper. You cannot distinguish either the wine or the pepper in the dish, but the marinade gives the meat an especially good flavor when cooked over the charcoal grill.

Serves 4

   2 3½- to 4-pound guinea hens, split in half
   2 cups dry white wine
   2 teaspoons jalapeño powder (available in the spice aisle or
       Mexican section of most groceries)
Approximately 1 tablespoon butter
   2 tablespoons dried thyme or herbes de Provence (see Note)
Wild Montana huckleberry sauce (see Suppliers, page 303) or
       blueberry sauce for dipping

Marinate the hens in wine and jalapeño powder for 2 to 4 hours. Preheat the oven to 325°F.

Pat the birds dry and rub with butter and thyme or herbes de Provence. Place them in a baking pan, cover, and parcook for 20 minutes. If you are using a grill, begin heating it.

When the birds have parcooked, finish them on the grill or under the broiler, with the inside facing the heat source. After 5 minutes, turn the birds over to cook the skin side for another 5 to 8 minutes. If you are using a grill, rotating the birds 90 degrees halfway through will result in nice cross-hatched grid marks on the skin.

Remove from the grill or broiler and use a boning knife to separate the breast meat, cutting away the rib cage and eliminating the backbone, so that each plate holds only breast meat, thigh, wing, and drumstick. This makes it much easier for your guests, who would look most undignified struggling with an entire half of a bird.

Serve with the wild Montana huckleberry or blueberry sauce on the side, for dipping.

NOTE: Herbes de Provence is a combination of many herbs, traditionally including rosemary, thyme, basil, dillweed, cracked fennel, savory, marjoram, tarragon, lavender, chervil, and Greek oregano. It's available from specialty markets and catalogs.

Chicken Livers Volkswagen

One early summer evening years ago on a trip around the Southwest, my family and I stopped for dinner in our Volkswagen camper bus near Zuni Pueblo in New Mexico. Looking in the refrigerator, I found only a box of frozen chicken livers and a bottle of artichoke bottoms. But a little butter, broth, and a heavy dash of tequila transformed the modest ingredients into a memorable dinner. Shortly after we opened The Fort, Chicken Livers Volkswagen became a standard on the menu. My recipe has been published once before, in the VW owners' magazine!

Serves 4

12 ounces chicken livers
1½ tablespoons butter
1½ teaspoons flour
¾ cup chicken broth
3 ounces tequila
¾ cup quartered artichoke bottoms (marinated or packed in water)
Salt
Freshly ground black pepper
Toasted white bread, 1 or 2 pieces per person (optional)
4 cups cooked white rice or your favorite noodles (optional)
Parsley for garnish

Wash and separate the livers.

Heat the butter on medium-high and gently sauté the livers to medium-rare. Move them to the side of the pan and add the flour, whisking it together with the butter to form a roux that will thicken as it cooks. When it becomes slightly browned, add the chicken broth and tequila. Mix the livers into the sauce, scraping the pan to deglaze and whisking the sauce to ensure smoothness. Stir in the artichoke bottoms and add salt and pepper.

To serve, place toast on each plate and pour the livers and sauce over, or serve over white rice or your favorite noodles. Garnish with parsley.

Martha Washington's
Chicken Breast with Grains of Paradise

The spice market in Fez, Morocco, boggles the mind. Booth upon booth offer so many rare and nearly extinct tastes that a trip to the market should be on the curriculum of every chef's school. On a recent trip with a culinary group, I found such rarities as "long pepper," which is not a chile pepper but was the pepper originally sought by Columbus. It was rare and expensive in medieval Europe because it had to be brought from India and was quite fragile, often developing mold en route. Other chiles replaced it when Columbus brought back capsicum (chile) seeds on his second voyage.

The spice market also sold small iridescent green/blue beetles called *mouches espagnoles,* or Spanish flies. These were the corrosive aphrodisiacs used by the Marquis de Sade to spike the court ladies' chocolate bonbons. It got him a prison sentence. It's one of some thirty to forty ingredients, in tiny amounts, in *ras el hanout,* the Moroccan equivalent of curry powder.

Another of the rare spices I found was melegueta pepper, known in the fifteenth, sixteenth, and seventeenth centuries as "Graines of Paradise." The reddish brown grain has a kind of menthol bite to it and is smaller than a black peppercorn, with a tiny white flag at its top. It seems unlikely that such obscure peppers would have been used in early America, but while reading the recently published book on Martha Washington's Custis family cookbook, I came across a chicken dish using "Graines of Paradise" and verjuice, the juice of wine grapes. It sounded like a dandy combination, and I did some experimenting. My version of the dish was on the menu in the spring of 1996.

Serves 6

6 6- to 8-ounce boneless, skinless split chicken breasts
2 cups chicken broth
2 tablespoons canola or other vegetable oil
2 shallots, finely minced
¼ cup verjuice (available in gourmet groceries or see Suppliers, page 303)
¼ cup sugar

1 tablespoon arrowroot dissolved in 2 tablespoons water
2 tablespoons butter
1 teaspoon ground melegueta pepper
1 teaspoon ground black pepper
Salt
Mint or cilantro sprigs for garnish
Red pepper slices for garnish

Poach the chicken breasts in a saucepan by covering with chicken broth. Bring to a boil, then remove from heat, cover, and set aside for 12 minutes; the breasts will poach perfectly. Pour out the broth, reserving about ½ cup and discarding the rest.

In a deep skillet, heat the oil until quite hot, then sauté the shallots until clear. Add the verjuice, sugar, reserved broth, and arrowroot to thicken. Simmer about 5 minutes to reduce to a pleasant, zingy sweet-and-sour sauce with a nice oniony base.

While the sauce simmers for a few more minutes, rub the warm chicken breasts with butter on both sides, then sprinkle top and bottom with melegueta and black peppers. Taste the sauce and adjust the flavors, adding a dash of salt. To serve, spoon sauce onto each dinner plate, place the chicken on top, and cover with more sauce. Add a few sprigs of mint or cilantro and red pepper slices for color as garnish.

Quail en Quinoa

I first tasted quinoa and quail together in Peru, and it's a dandy combination. The grain, with its texture resembling tapioca, absorbs the savory flavor of the quail. This is one of our most popular party dishes. It's easy to make and modest in price. Guests will rave. (For more on quinoa, see page 228.)

Serves 10

          6 tablespoons butter
          6 tablespoons cooking oil
        10 partially boned quail
          4 cups quinoa
        10 Portuguese hot linguisa sausages
          2 large onions, chopped medium
          4 cups chopped mild green chiles
          1 cup pitted ripe olives
        2½ quarts chicken broth
          1 cup toasted English walnut halves

Preheat the oven to 325°F.

Heat the butter and oil in a skillet over high heat and sear both sides of the quails. Remove to a cutting board and cut into quarters.

Butter a 10-quart baking dish or casserole.

In a sieve, carefully wash the quinoa in cold or lukewarm water, using your hand to stir it as water pours through to remove any of the natural soap that hasn't been removed in the milling process. Place 2 cups of the quinoa in the prepared baking dish.

Cut the linguisa sausages into bite-size pieces and arrange them on top of the quinoa. Add the quail pieces, onions, green chiles, and olives. Cover with the remaining quinoa and add the chicken broth. Seal the top with aluminum foil or a lid and bake for 1½ hours.

Garnish the casserole with toasted walnuts just before serving. This is essentially a one-dish dinner but is also a great addition to a buffet, hot or cold.

Smoked Pheasant Breast Salad

Pheasant was brought to this country from China via Great Britain and came west with the white settlers. Our fields around The Fort are full of wild pheasant, introduced by a sportsman about 1900. What a wonderful salad smoked pheasant breast makes!

Serves 4

  1 **cup sour cream**
Juice of 2 lemons
  1 **cup mayonnaise**
Dash of cayenne
  4 **cups mixed greens**
  2 **cups sliced pickled beets**
  4 **hard-cooked eggs**
  2 **6-ounce smoked pheasant breasts, warmed in chicken broth and cut into ¼-inch-thick slices to make 1½ cups**
  4 **tablespoons pine nuts for garnish**
  4 **tablespoons currants for garnish**
  8 **fresh onion rings for garnish (optional)**
16 **pickled hard-cooked quail eggs (see Note)**
12 **radish crowns**

Combine the sour cream, lemon juice, mayonnaise, and cayenne pepper. Toss this thoroughly with the mixed greens, then divide equally among 4 salad plates. In the center, overlap 6 slices of pickled beet to make a ring and place a whole hen's egg in the middle. Arrange slices of smoked pheasant breast on the beets, leaving visible the white top in the center of the hard-cooked egg. Garnish the salad with toasted pine nuts and currants. A few rings of fresh onion are a nice addition. Arrange the quail eggs around the edge of the plate with the radishes.

NOTE: If jars of quail eggs are not available, substitute 4 hard-cooked hen eggs, cut into quarters. Do not use canned quail eggs because their quality is poor.

From the Yard

133

The Fort's
Thirtieth Anniversary Dinner Menu

Hors D'oeuvres
Comanche-Style Buffalo Heart Skewers
Gwaltney Ham on Chive Biscuits
Gruet Blanc de Noir Champagne (Brut, New Mexico)

First Course
Venison Consommé
Montee de Tonnerre 1988, Chablis Premier Cru

Second Course
Charbroiled Quail Glazed with Red Chile Honey
Dominus Meritage 1986, Napa Valley

Third Course
Roast Buffalo Tenderloin Crusted with Toasted Pine Nuts and
Ancho Chiles
Cha-Cha Murpheys
Fresh Vegetable Terrine
Bee-nanas

Fourth Course
Bibb Lettuce Salad with Raspberry Vinaigrette

Dessert
President Andrew Jackson's Trifle
Coffee or Tea
Fonseca "Guimaraens" Vintage Porto, 1963

From the Garden

———◆———

A TRINITY OF INDIAN FOODS—CORN, BEANS, AND SQUASH, INCLUDING pumpkin—was grown in the garden at Bent's Fort in the 1830s. But when it comes to vegetables at The Fort, we don't limit ourselves to what was available on the plains of Colorado 150 years ago. Bringing new beans and greens to our guests is one of my favorite pursuits.

While The Fort's reputation is heavily based on red meat, with so many guests coming to eat buffalo, we often surprise them with our active interest in the vegetable world. Today, as people are becoming more open to chiles and other delicious ingredients from around the country and the world, it's fun to serve items such as shiitake mushrooms, chipotle peppers, Anasazi beans, tamarind, Colorado-grown black quinoa, melegueta pepper, damiana, toasted canola seeds, jicama, verjuice, and red chile honey.

Carrots or Beets with Red Chile Honey

In the fall we traditionally serve fresh root vegetables. Carrots are especially nice if they're not too large and pithy. This dish has a lovely sweet-and-sour quality from the vinegar and honey, plus a fruity quality with a pepper bite from the raspberry and chile. It makes carrots and beets so good to eat that even children become fans.

Nice, mild red chile honey is available in specialty stores (see Suppliers, page 303) or is easily made at home with pure New Mexico red chile powder, which has a sweet pepper-hot quality.

Another interesting note on red chile honey: It's an old Aztec remedy for mouth lesion pain. If you have bitten the inside of your cheek, take a half spoonful of the chile honey and hold it against the raw area. The combination of chile and honey doesn't heal the wound, but it does dissipate the pain.

Both carrots and beets can be cooked ahead of time, then cooked for a few minutes in the glaze to reheat.

Serves 4

2 cups raw carrots, cut in ¼-inch-thick diagonal slices, or 4 to 5 medium-sized fresh beets, stems cut to 1 inch and root ends intact (helps to keep them from bleeding)

Red Chile Honey:
½ cup honey
½ teaspoon ground pure New Mexico red chile powder (Dixon is my favorite)

Red Chile Honey Glaze:
¼ cup raspberry vinegar
¼ cup water
1 tablespoon cornstarch or arrowroot
1 tablespoon Red Chile Honey

Boil the carrots in water until just soft. If you are using beets, boil them, covered, for 30 to 40 minutes, until tender.

While the vegetables are boiling, make the Red Chile Honey. Stir together the honey and chile powder in a jar and microwave on high for 1 minute. Stir, then microwave again for 30 seconds.

Before starting the glaze, taste your vinegar to measure its tartness. If it seems quite strong, decrease the amount of vinegar and

From the Garden

137

increase the amount of water proportionately. Over medium heat, combine the vinegar, water, and cornstarch, stirring well to dissolve the cornstarch. Add the honey and continue stirring as the mixture slowly thickens. Remove from the heat and cover to keep warm.

When the carrots are done, toss them in the glaze to coat thoroughly, reheating if necessary. If you are using beets, run them under cold water, remove the root and stem ends, and slip off the skins. Drain well. Slice, dice, or cut the beets into julienne strips and toss them in the glaze to coat thoroughly, reheating if necessary. Adjust the seasoning to taste, adding more red chile honey as needed.

Fort Chile Breakfast

I thought I'd seen chiles prepared in every imaginable way. Then one morning in Santa Fe, Carrie and I went to breakfast at the home of historians Bob and Melody Utley. We entered their adobe house to the wonderful scent of roasted green chiles. When we sat down, it was to plates of whole roasted green chiles lying across toasted English muffins topped with browned butter. So simple, yet so delicious!

Serves 4

Black sesame seeds for garnish (available at groceries as sesame
   salt or gomashio but easy to make yourself; optional)
4 tablespoons butter
4 English muffins, halved
8 poblano or Anaheim green chiles, roasted and peeled (see
   page 140)

Toast the sesame seeds by heating them in a dry skillet for a few minutes.

Heat the butter in a saucepan until it begins to brown.

While the butter is heating, toast the English muffins and microwave the chiles briefly to warm them. Lay one roasted green chile over each muffin half. Pour the browned butter over the chiles and sprinkle with the sesame seeds.

NOTE: This is great made with bagels, too.

Chile

In the Middle Ages, Europeans enjoyed the pepper-hot "long pepper," brought to them from India. This was the pepper that Christopher Columbus sought. But when he arrived in the West Indies in 1492, the natives served him foods he'd never before encountered, one of which was a pod pepper, hotter than the long pepper and much more easily stored and transported. The pod pepper had actually originated on the Yucatán Peninsula. On his second voyage Columbus returned to Spain with its seeds. This chile (or capsicum, as it's also called) spread across the western world to Africa and the Orient.

Today, from the remotest Americas through Europe, across India, around the Orient, and everywhere in between, chile pods—long and short, thin or fat, red, yellow, green, brown, and purple—have traveled to tantalize man's soul.

It seems to me that much of chile's popularity worldwide stems from its ability to make otherwise unexciting cuts of meat and many kinds of starches—rice, pasta, potatoes—both flavorful and pepper-hot. One needn't be rich to enjoy it.

It's very versatile, too. The Thai spoon a bit of chicken or pork cooked in a chile-heavy curry sauce over large rice bowls. The Mexicans add chile-flavored meats to cornmeal tamales. I use it in just about everything. Eating very hot chile imparts a certain euphoria. For many (including me), it's a virtual addiction.

The word "chile" can be spelled many different ways. In one recipe in this book it's spelled "chilli" because the Lingham company in Malaysia calls it "chilli." "Chili" is perhaps the most popular spelling, but we use it only to refer to chili con carne. The spelling "chile" refers to the pod and most dishes made from it.

Roasting Green Chiles

Use fresh medium to mild poblano or Anaheim chiles.

There are several good ways to roast chiles, but this is the easiest way to ensure that they won't overcook: Prick each chile with a fork. Turn a burner on your stove to high and lay large chiles across the burner until they're a little blackened on one side, then turn over and blacken the other side. If the chiles aren't big enough to do this, impale them on the tines of a fork and hold them over the heat as you would a marshmallow. Be careful not to overburn—the pulp should still be soft under the burned skin.

If you are roasting many chiles, after pricking them place them on a baking sheet and broil them about 5 inches below the heat source. They'll roast very quickly, so watch carefully, turning once when necessary.

Place the chiles in an airtight plastic bag and cool in the freezer for 20 minutes. The chiles expand over the heat and then contract in the freezer, which makes them easier to peel. Hold each one under cold running water and gently pull off the burned skin, keeping the chile intact. Now it's ready for use.

Some people like to remove the seeds. I don't because, like the Mexicans, I believe that some seeds give life to your dish.

Shoepeg Corn with Sweet Peppers

I grew up in Pennsylvania where white sweet corn, or sugar corn, was one of the joys of summer. We called it shoepeg corn, using a name given to it in earlier centuries when leather soles and uppers were held together with little wooden pegs that looked very similar to the kernels. It is singularly delicious and makes a great summer dish when tossed with red, yellow, orange, and green peppers. At The Fort we chop up hot green chiles along with the sweet peppers to give it a little authority.

Serves 4

- 3 to 4 cups corn kernels (approximately 6 cobs; see Note)
- 1 cup diced red bell peppers
- 1 or 2 serrano peppers, diced (remove the ribs and seeds before dicing for a milder dish)
- 2 tablespoons butter
- Ground white pepper
- Salt

Heat the corn in a large saucepan with the peppers, butter, white pepper, and salt until the peppers have softened just a bit and the corn is heated through.

NOTE: Fresh corn is best, of course, and to remove it from the cob, use either a very sharp knife or a little tool made for dekerneling corn. This tool, which has a sharp metal ring with handles like ears on either side, is run down the cob neatly and quickly. Shoepeg corn is commonly available frozen in butter sauce; if you use this, you need not add extra butter. If you are using canned corn, drain it first.

Zuni Succotash with
Toasted Sunflower Seed Hearts

I make this recipe with lima, Anasazi, or Aztec beans. At The Fort each Thanksgiving Day, it is made with lima beans, as it was made by Native Americans in the northeastern United States. But Native Americans in the Southwest used Anasazi or other beans. They both used what was available to them; I suggest you do the same.

Serves 6

½ cup raw or roasted sunflower seed hearts (shelled sunflower seeds)

2 packages frozen lima beans or 1 cup Anasazi beans

2 strips bacon

2 cups fresh sweet corn cut from the cob (approximately 3 cobs; frozen or canned whole kernel corn will work, too)

1 medium onion, finely diced

1 cup canned chopped green chile

½ large red bell pepper, finely diced

½ large green bell pepper, finely diced

If you use raw sunflower seed hearts, toast them in a small dry skillet over medium heat, stirring until lightly browned, about 5 minutes.

If you are using frozen lima beans, set them aside to thaw. If you are using Anasazi beans, boil them for 2 hours until soft and mealy.

In a large skillet, fry the bacon on both sides until crisp. Remove and drain on a paper towel. Sauté the corn and onion in the bacon drippings for about 3 minutes. (If you prefer, use vegetable oil instead of the bacon fat.) Add the beans, green chile, red and green bell peppers, and sunflower seeds, and sauté for about 10 minutes, or until hot. Serve with diced bacon on top.

Dilled Zucchini

When zucchini and yellow squash are in season, we like to cook them *al dente* with dill weed and a very little bit of canola or peanut oil combined with a dash of olive oil or butter. An onion, thinly sliced, adds even more taste. Luscious!

Serves 6

1 **pound zucchini**
1 **pound yellow squash**
½ **cup canola or peanut oil**
1 **to 2 tablespoons butter or olive oil (optional)**
1 **onion, sliced (optional)**
1 **tablespoon dried dill weed**
White pepper
½ **teaspoon salt**
Squeeze of lemon (optional)

Use the smallest squashes you can find; the younger they are, the more tender they'll be and the fewer seeds they'll have. Slice them ⅜ inch thick.

Heat the oil and butter in a skillet. When quite hot, sauté the onion until it's limp. Add the squashes, stirring constantly, and sprinkle with dill. Add white pepper and salt to taste. A squeeze of fresh lemon juice gives extra zest. Do not overcook. These are better on the raw side rather than on the limp side and don't take more than a few minutes after the onion has cooked.

From the Garden

Zucchini Chips

Mexican workers at Bent's Fort cut both green and yellow squash, hanging hundreds of slices on long strings to dry. While these squash chips made great snacks, they could also be easily reconstituted for use in pies and stews.

If you find yourself with too much zucchini, try making your own zucchini chips. They're crisp and surprisingly sweet. Cut a squash into ¼-inch rounds and, using a mattress needle, string them, keeping the pieces ¼ inch from one another. Don't put too many on one string. To hang, tie the ends of each string to either side of the top rack of the oven to form a long arc. Then place an electric fan on the open oven door, leaving it to blow overnight. *Do not heat the oven.* The contained space of the oven concentrates the air from the fan, and the zucchini chips dry beautifully. When they're completely dry, store them in an airtight jar.

Shïtake Mushrooms

Colorado is a land of wonderful mushrooms. Trips into the mountains are exciting in late August and September for mushroom lovers. We find chanterelles, boletus, oyster mushrooms, and many other excellent and easy-to-identify mushrooms. Like an angler who has found a favorite fishing hole, one shares his mushrooming areas— even with his closest friends—only with great reluctance.

I once attended an annual mushroom symposium in Telluride along with a hundred or more mushroom buffs and a handful of expert mycologists. We spent the days roaming the mountains and brought home what we found. To my amazement, the experts couldn't identify with certainty nearly 40 percent of what we'd foraged. I was also surprised that a great many of my fellow mushroom aficionados were city high-rise dwellers who had come seeking knowledge on how to better raise certain "recreational" mushrooms at home.

At The Fort we serve ninety to a hundred pounds of shiitake mushrooms a week. The Mahoneys' mushroom farm, just up the road

from The Fort, is prospering and growing as the public learns about these delights. We present the mushrooms sautéed in a small iron skillet as a side dish, and many guests enjoy them atop their steaks. Not only are they delicious, but folklore indicates that they're antioxidants and offer other health benefits.

Serves 4

½ **pound shiitake mushrooms (see Note)**
¼ **cup olive oil or butter, or a combination of both**
Salt
Freshly ground black pepper

Slice the mushroom caps into bite-size pieces; they'll grow smaller as they cook, so err on the big side. Sauté the mushrooms in the oil for about 5 minutes. If using butter, it will impart a delicious flavor, while the oil will save you cholesterol and reduce the chances of burning. Add salt and pepper to taste.

We particularly like these over toast or topping a juicy buffalo steak. Use the stems to make Simple Shiitake Mushroom Soup (page 148).

NOTE: Mushrooms absorb liquid rapidly, so to clean them, simply brush off the dirt or place them in a colander and dip each in water several times. Snap off the stems (you shouldn't need a knife). If you plan to use them in another recipe, refrigerate them in a paper bag for one to two days. (Never store mushrooms in plastic—they'll turn to slime!)

Interview Breakfast

My assistant, Betsy Andrews, who helped me sift through overflowing files of The Fort's history for this book, has a memory about Christmas shiitakes from Lora Brody:

My train was eight hours late, and my stomach growled as we pulled into Union Station at close to midnight, fourteen hours after I'd boarded in Shoshone, Idaho. Nervous about my impending job interview, I hadn't been able to eat all day. A man named Sam Arnold, who I'd heard owned a restaurant called The Fort and wrote cookbooks, was in the market for an assistant.

I was to have been interviewed over dinner, but by the time Amtrak delivered me to Denver, The Fort was long closed. So the wee hours of the morning found me sitting in the Arnolds' living room, patting a huge, heavily breathing German shepherd and answering questions about why I wanted to work for Sam. I think I mentioned one too many times that Denver was close to skiing, and I went to bed feeling starved and doomed. In less than twelve hours I'd be back on the train, and no job offer had been made.

I awoke early the next morning to the aroma of fresh buttery toast. This is what heaven must smell like, I thought, and I eagerly took my place at the breakfast table. Across the kitchen, Sam toiled impressively over plates. My stomach let loose three rapid-fire gurgles, and the dog perked up his ears and tilted his head.

At last, Sam marched to the table proudly bearing the fruits of his labors: English muffin halves topped with a small pile of shiny black stuff and a large pile of shiny brown stuff. "Sautéed shiitake mushrooms and Boyajian beluga caviar!" Sam proudly announced.

Horror coursed through me. I still picked button mushrooms off pizzas. As a kid in Alaska I'd gutted salmon and bagged the slimy roe for bait. And yet here, under the critical eye of this internationally known gourmet and, more important, my potential boss, I was expected to eat fungus and fish eggs for breakfast.

My stomach seized while Carrie expounded on my good fortune. Sam must like me, she said. Sam didn't share his caviar and mushrooms with just *anyone*. It seemed that this treat had been received especially

for Christmas and was not used lavishly or wasted. I fervently wished that it had been used lavishly before my arrival. I fervently wished that I could tell them it was being wasted. I fervently wanted to ask them what kind of a friend would send mushrooms for Christmas. Instead, I tried inconspicuously to breathe through my mouth, and I paced myself.

I washed down each mouthful with a large swig of orange juice. What a dry climate Denver had, I said. Sure made you thirsty! I strove to listen attentively to Sam's discourse on the new amendment to the state constitution. I strove to acquire a taste for caviar. Sam rose to pour more coffee. Carrie rose to get more orange juice. Half my English muffin remained unmoving on my plate. Where was that German shepherd when I needed him?

I struggled along for nearly an hour, feeling valiant and very sorry for myself. But finally my plate was clean. Only a few stray black eggs and a limp slice of mushroom remained as evidence of my ordeal. I took a last gulp of orange juice and with great relief placed my napkin on the table like a flag of surrender. Sam stood to clear the table.

"We decided last night to offer you the job," he said. "When can you start?"

Two weeks later Betsy arrived early for her first day of work. The office was still in the house then, and the insistent ringing of the doorbell woke Carrie and me from a sound sleep. In spite of that, we have become great friends over the past few years, and I've delighted in introducing her to dishes she admits she'd never before imagined considering as food. Today, she likes caviar and shiitake mushrooms. And she even likes Lora Brody, having forgiven her for her taste in Christmas gifts.

Serves 2

1 **tablespoon canola oil**
1 **tablespoon butter**
½ **cup cleaned, sliced fresh shiitake mushrooms**
2 **English muffins, halved**
2 **tablespoons beluga caviar**

Heat the oil and butter in a skillet and sauté the mushrooms until soft. Meanwhile, toast the English muffins and set on serving plates. Top each half with mushrooms and spoon caviar over the top.

Simple Shiitake Mushroom Soup

Serves 4

Stems of 1 pound fresh shiitake mushrooms or 2 to 3 ounces
     dried shiitake or other wild mushrooms
1 14-ounce can (approximately 2 cups) low-fat, low-salt chicken
     broth
1 pint (2 cups) heavy cream
Dried tarragon
Dried chervil

The stems may be cleaned and placed in a pot with the chicken
broth. If you are using dried mushrooms, reconstitute them in
enough warm water to cover and don't use the stems because they'll
be too tough. Save the broth; strain out any dirt and substitute this liquid for some of the chicken broth.

Boil the mushrooms in the broth for about 10 minutes, let cool,
then puree in a blender or food processor until smooth.

Add the heavy cream, tarragon, and chervil. Simmer for 15 to 20
minutes, then pour through a chinois or conical sieve to filter out any
remaining solids. Serve with great joy and good bread.

Sgt. Ken Gilpin prepares to fire a cannon
during a wedding reception.

Pickled Beets with Hard-Cooked Eggs

When I was a little boy, every Memorial Day my family drove one hundred miles from Pittsburgh to Curwensville, my father's birthplace in north central Pennsylvania. A picnic lunch was packed to be eaten on the grounds of the cemetery. We joined the parade of families marching toward the bandstand behind a large number of World War I veterans. Ahead of them was a group of Spanish American War veterans and, in the lead, a half dozen or more men in their eighties and nineties, veterans of the Civil War.

A long, boring speech followed, and finally it was eating time. Ham, fried chicken, potato salad, pies, and cakes were all laid out on long tables and shared among families. My greatest delight was the offering of pickled beets and hardboiled eggs turned scarlet with beet juice.

Makes 2 gallons

- 20 medium-sized beets or equivalent
- Water to cover beets plus 2 cups for pickling
- 1 quart white vinegar
- 2 teaspoons salt
- 2 cups sugar
- ½ cup horseradish root cut in slices (horseradish in a jar may be used but will turn the pickling juice cloudy)
- 4 cloves
- 4 cinnamon sticks
- 2 tablespoons yellow mustard seeds
- 4 Bermuda or yellow onions, peeled and sliced ¼ inch thick
- 12 hard-cooked eggs, peeled
- 2 1-gallon widemouthed glass jars

Cut the tops of the beets to about ½ inch; leave the roots attached to minimize bleeding. Boil the beets about 20 minutes, until soft, then drain and cool under cold running water. Cut the tops and bottoms off the beets. Remove the skins using your fingers or scraping with a knife. Slice them ¼ inch thick either by hand or in a food processor. Although roasted beets are less messy and their flavor is wonderful, boiled beets retain a better, firm consistency for pickling.

Heat the vinegar with 2 cups water. Add the salt, sugar, horseradish, cloves, cinnamon sticks, and mustard seeds. Taste; if too sour, add

From the Garden

149

more sugar. Simmer the spices for 5 minutes. Pack the beet slices, onion slices, and hard-cooked eggs in repeating layers in jars, then fill the jars with the hot pickling liquid.

Refrigerate for at least several days before eating. The eggs will be jewel-like red on the outside, white and yellow on the inside. A nice serving is one egg, cut in half lengthwise, a few beets, and some onion rings.

Fort Dinner Salad

Here's The Fort's famous dinner salad, as served in nine dining rooms.

Serves 6

- 1 tablespoon raw or roasted pepitas (pumpkin seeds)
- 6 cups mixed fresh salad greens (mesclun)
- 1½ cups of your favorite salad dressing
- ½ cup finely diced jicama
- 12 slices fresh tomato or 24 cherry tomatoes, halved
- 3 teaspoons of beni-shoga (kizami-shoga) red pickled ginger (available at Japanese groceries)
- 12 pickled, hard-cooked quail eggs (sold in jars; the canned Asian ones are not very good; optional)
- ½ cup buttered toasted croutons (recipe below)

Croutons
Makes 2 cups

- 2 cups cubed Herb Bread (page 214)
- 2 teaspoons olive oil
- ¼ cup grated Parmigiano-Reggiano cheese

Preheat the oven to 350°F.

Toss the bread with the olive oil. Arrange in a single layer in a baking dish. Bake for about 8 minutes, or until golden but not dry, then toss with the cheese.

If you use raw pepitas, roast them in a dry skillet over high heat, shaking it periodically until they begin to pop.

To make the salad, toss the greens with the salad dressing and divide among chilled salad plates or shallow bowls. Add, in order, the jicama, pepitas, tomatoes, beni-shoga, and quail eggs. Sprinkle the croutons on the top.

Alligator Pear and Shrimp Salad

I grew up in Pittsburgh, Pennsylvania, in the 1920s and 30s, and no one knew much about either shrimp or avocados. The first shrimp I ever saw were in a fish shop in Pittsburgh. Quick-freezing hadn't yet been invented, and they'd been brought on ice in a fast train from the Gulf of Mexico. My father introduced me to avocados. He was an electrical engineer who designed steel-making furnaces and he traveled a lot. He loved to try new foods, and my sister Mary and I eagerly anticipated his homecomings and the culinary delights that were sure to accompany him. He first saw "alligator pears," as they were called, in 1937, I think, on the Union Pacific Railroad. He loved them and brought some home for us. We became instant fans and enjoyed my father's shrimp and avocado cocktails as a special treat.

I enjoy his Alligator Pear Sauce as an alternative to Shrimp and Avocado Sauce (page 30) and also combined with Caper Sauce (page 36) to dress salads. While this is a delicious side salad as is, it is also the perfect beginning of a delicious entree salad. Just add your favorite salad ingredients: hard-cooked eggs, olives, artichoke hearts, croutons, asparagus, tomatoes, and so forth.

Serves 4

¾ cup Alligator Pear Sauce (recipe follows)
1¼ cups Caper Sauce (page 36)
20 to 24 large shrimp, cooked and peeled
2 avocados, pitted, peeled, and sliced
3 cups mixed salad greens

Alligator Pear Sauce
Makes about 1½ cups

1 cup Heinz Chili Sauce
½ cup Heinz ketchup
1 tablespoon horseradish in vinegar
1 tablespoon small capers

Mix thoroughly and chill.

Combine the Alligator Pear Sauce and Caper Sauce.

Arrange the shrimp and sliced avocado atop salad greens on individual salad plates and dress with the sauce sparingly and attractively. Pour the remaining sauce into a small serving dish or pitcher to pass.

From the Garden

151

Bayou Salado Dressing

Just a hundred miles southwest of The Fort lies South Park, historically called the *bayou salado,* or salt marshes. In Bent's Fort's day it was considered the Eden of the American West, with its high waving buffalo grass and abundant wildlife. Two decades ago when Trader Vic's was our favorite "other" restaurant in Denver, partly because of their wonderful Green Goddess dressing, I created a variation of that dressing for The Fort. It's singularly delicious because of the anchovies. Not too much . . . just right. Needing a name for it, our dining room manager came up with Bayou Salado Dressing. It stuck, and the dressing continued to be served for many years.

Makes about 4 cups

> 3 cups mayonnaise
> ¼ cup buttermilk
> 2 tablespoons tarragon vinegar
> ¼ cup chopped chives or green onions
> ¼ cup chopped parsley leaves
> 1 large or 2 small cloves garlic, crushed
> ¼ cup fresh tarragon leaves or ⅛ cup dried
> Approximately 3 ounces canned flat anchovy fillets, rinsed and chopped (Yes, yes, you need them, and your guests will never know they're there—but they'll miss them if they're not.)

Combine all the ingredients in a blender and blend well. This dressing should be just thick enough to cling to the lettuce, but not heavy. Taste; adjust the vinegar and buttermilk.

Creamy Blue Cheese Dressing

Susan Magoffin, on the Santa Fe Trail in 1846, spoke of meeting an ugly-looking cheese near Las Vegas, New Mexico. Indeed, ripe cheeses were a regular part of the Mexican diet. Cow, goat, and sheep milk were used, but never buffalo because it's pretty tough to milk a buffalo. Doubtless in the Old West a nice moldy cheese was quite at home, but you can be sure it was a far cry from the best blue cheese made in America today, produced by Maytag Farms in Iowa. We use only Maytag in our blue cheese dressing. We crumble it but leave some large pieces so that guests know the dressing is made from real blue cheese.

Makes 2 cups

 1 **cup mayonnaise (homemade is best)**
 ½ **cup sour cream (not low-fat; it's too watery)**
 ¼ **cup milk**
 ½ **teaspoon Worcestershire sauce**
 ½ **teaspoon freshly grated white pepper**
 1 **clove garlic, crushed**
 ¼ **teaspoon salt**
1½ **teaspoons fresh thyme**
 ⅓ **cup crumbled blue cheese, with some larger pieces**

Place all the ingredients except the blue cheese in a blender or food processor and blend until smooth. Stir in the blue cheese by hand and allow to mellow for 24 hours in the refrigerator. This lasts about 3 weeks in the refrigerator.

Scandinavian Dill Salad Dressing

One of our dearest friends, now gone on ahead of us, was Astrid Gusterman. She and her husband, a talented silversmith, taught us many Swedish dishes. Astrid's delicious salad dressing is easy to make and has been a standard at The Fort for a quarter of a century.

Makes 1½ cups

  1 cup red wine vinegar
  ¼ cup water
  ¼ cup olive or canola oil
  1½ tablespoons sugar
  ½ teaspoon salt
  3 tablespoons finely chopped fresh dill weed or 1 tablespoon dried
  ½ teaspoon white pepper

Shake all the ingredients together and chill. This dressing does not emulsify at all; it will separate as you watch. You'll need to stir it again immediately before using, so it works better if you dress the greens in the kitchen rather than allowing everyone to do his own. We place the greens in a colander and pour the dressing through it, with a catch bowl below. A few tosses and the greens are nicely coated. This results in the perfect amount of dressing adhering to the greens without a messy pool of separated oil and vinegar at the bottom of the salad bowls.

Variation

Creamy Blue Dill Vinaigrette

Combine 1 cup Scandinavian Dill Salad Dressing with ½ cup Creamy Blue Cheese Dressing (page 153). Mix well. The red wine vinegar makes this blue cheese dressing pink!

Damiana Vinaigrette

Damiana is an herb that grows in northern Mexico and Arizona. It has long had a reputation as an aphrodisiac. Mexican liquor stores have stocked damiana liqueur for many years, and it is still available. Years ago it was also made and sold in California, but nowadays only the imported variety can be found in the United States. The dried herb is sold at about $7 per pound at herbal and natural food stores. The leaf has a slightly minty, bitter taste and makes a delightful tea.

It also makes a very tasty vinegar. One day I opened *Early American Times* magazine and read an article about how in colonial America, herb-flavored vinegars were made very simply at home. We tried this with the damiana and produced an excellent herb vinegar that we used in our Valentine's Day dressing. The reception was so strong that we kept it as a permanent item on the menu.

Makes 4 cups

    1   cup red wine vinegar
    2   tablespoons water
1½   teaspoons damiana
    3   cups salad oil
1½   tablespoons sugar
    ⅛   teaspoon salt
    ⅛   teaspoon white pepper

Heat the vinegar and water in a nonreactive pot to almost boiling, about 190°F. Add the damiana and mix well. Place in a sealed glass or plastic container and set aside at room temperature for 2 weeks. Pour through a strainer to remove the leaf. Add the oil, sugar, salt, and pepper. Taste and adjust to personal taste.

NOTE: Unstrained Damiana vinegar in a decorative bottle makes a wonderful gift. Include a recipe for the vinaigrette dressing.

From the Garden

Damiana Liqueur

One may make a tasty damiana liqueur by steeping a tablespoon of herb in a bottle of high-proof alcohol such as Everclear or preferably vodka. After three weeks it will have a straw yellow color. Strain out the leaf and add a finishing liquid such as glycerin to increase viscosity and then a simple syrup to taste.

Craneberry Sauce

Cranberries used to be called "craneberries," either for the cranes that nested in the bogs of the low-lying bushes or for the shape of the cranberry flower, which resembles a crane's head. Each Thanksgiving we make jarfuls of this sauce at The Fort and serve it with Turkey with Piñon Stuffing (page 116) and Zuni Succotash (page 142), and Cha-Cha Murpheys (page 174). It's also a great addition to elk and guinea hen.

Makes about 3 pints

1 quart fresh cranberries, coarsely chopped
4 cups white sugar
½ cup water
½ cup Grand Marnier liqueur
1 cup coarsely chopped pecans, toasted

Simmer the cranberries and sugar in the water over medium heat for about 20 minutes, until thickened.

When the sauce has thickened, add the Grand Marnier and pecans, and stir. Bottle and refrigerate until serving time.

Samoren Sauce

When my grandson, Oren, was ten, we worked in my kitchen at home to produce a new sauce from jalapeños. It turned out so well that we named it for its inventors and served it at The Fort as a sauce for meat. It's both sweet and sour, with a bite of mixed ginger and mustard. . . . A delight!

Makes 1 gallon or sixteen ½-pint jars

    4 pounds fresh jalapeño peppers, stems removed
    4 cloves garlic
    1 pound peeled fresh ginger
    4 pounds white sugar
    1 quart water
    2 quarts white vinegar
    2 tablespoons black mustard seeds
    2 tablespoons salt
    2 tablespoons pectin

In small batches, puree the jalapeños, garlic, and ginger in a food processor and remove to a tall stockpot. Add the remaining ingredients and bring to a boil over medium heat. Boil, stirring frequently, for about 2 hours, or until the mixture thickens and the sugar reaches the soft ball stage when dropped in cold water.

Sterilize jars by submerging them in boiling water for 6 minutes. Fill them with the sauce and seal. This makes a marvelous gift.

From the Garden

Date Raisin Chutney

Chutney was very popular on the American frontier because it was a wonderful way to preserve fruits.

Our East Indian friend Geetha Pai of Las Cruces, New Mexico, makes a wonderful chutney that we serve with guinea hen. If you can't find her bottled Indian foods, try this. It's a whole new look at chutneys and makes a wonderful gift. Just remember that since it's not sealed and put through a hot water bath, label it "refrigerate."

Makes 1 quart

1½ **cups roughly chopped pitted dates**
1½ **cups raisins (any variety)**
1½ **cups cider vinegar**
 ½ **cup dark brown sugar**
 ¼ **cup finely minced fresh ginger root**
 3 **cloves garlic, minced**
 1 **yellow or white onion, finely diced**
 1 **tablespoon black mustard seed (if not available, brown will do, or, if you must, yellow)**
 1 **to 2 serrano chiles, finely minced**
    Zest of 1 lemon, cut in small pieces

Place all the ingredients in a large stockpot and cook over medium heat, stirring frequently. After about 25 minutes, when the mixture has thickened somewhat, adjust the seasonings. Bottle and refrigerate until ready to use. This is excellent served with rice dishes, curries, and meats, especially game birds.

Father Pelayo's Green Sauce

Father Geronimo Pelayo's recipes appear throughout this book. A Spanish monk at a Mexican monastery in the late eighteenth century, Pelayo wrote a fascinating cookbook which contains many dishes that are fresh and exciting even to today's palate. This is excellent with hot roast lamb and is also a treat with cold roast beef.

Makes about 1 cup

- 1 cup parsley tops
- 3 cloves garlic, smashed and minced
- ¼ cup cider vinegar
- ¼ cup water
- 1½ tablespoons sugar
- 2 teaspoons cumin seed
- 1 slice stale, dry bread, cubed (a sturdy, country-style bread such as French, Italian, or sourdough is best)
- 2 tablespoons olive or salad oil
- 1 serrano chile, minced (or more for a hot sauce; remove the seeds and ribs before mincing for a milder sauce)

Puree all the ingredients in a blender or processor and chill until ready to use. This is best if refrigerated for a day to give the flavors a chance to blend and mellow. Serve cold.

From the Garden

Sam's Buffalo Salad

There are some special things that I particularly like in an entree salad: mixed greens, hard-cooked eggs, toasted hazelnuts or walnuts, radishes, salty pickled ginger shreds, roasted pumpkin seeds, and jicama. Tossed with a good dressing such as Bayou Salado Dressing (page 152), topped with thin, bite-size slices of cold buffalo roast meat, and sprinkled with cilantro leaves and modest amounts of finely minced serrano chile pepper, this makes a complete feast. That's a salad!

Makes 1 salad

¼ cup Creamy Blue Cheese Dressing (page 153) or Bayou Salado Dressing (page 152)

1 cup mixed fresh salad greens (mesclun)

1 hard-cooked egg, cut into quarters

¼ cup finely diced jicama

½ cup cold medium-rare buffalo rib eye roast, cut in bite-size pieces (cold beef or chicken are excellent substitutes)

2 tablespoons coarsely chopped hazelnuts or English walnuts, toasted

1 tablespoon beni-shoga (kizami-shoga) red pickled ginger (available at Japanese groceries)

1 tablespoon raw or roasted pepitas (pumpkin seeds; see Note)

1 teaspoon fresh whole cilantro leaves

½ serrano chile, finely minced (remove the ribs and seeds before mincing for a milder dish)

Juice of 1 lime

Radish roses

½ avocado, peeled, pitted, and cut into 4 slices

In a large salad bowl, toss the dressing with the salad greens, carefully coating them lightly. Arrange the other items over the greens in this order: egg quarters, jicama, buffalo pieces, nuts, beni-shoga, pumpkin seeds, cilantro, and chile. Squeeze the lime over the salad and garnish with radish roses and a fan of avocado slices.

NOTE: If you can't find canned roasted pepitas, you can easily roast them yourself in a dry skillet over medium heat, shaking the pan periodically until they begin to pop.

Jicama and Pepitas

If you walk through the markets of almost any Mexican city, you'll see vendors hawking slices of jicama (pronounced HE-ka-ma) with a squeeze of fresh sweet lime juice and a sprinkle of ground red chile. The combination is marvelous and is a good one to serve at a cocktail party. The round, tan, thick-skinned tuber from Mexico now has a regular place in North American supermarkets, but many Americans aren't yet familiar with it. With its sweet taste somewhere between a potato and a crisp apple, it's delicious in salads and as a substitute for water chestnuts in stir-fry. It's easier to peel than water chestnuts and retains its crispness, unlike water chestnuts.

Because jicama can weigh as much as 5 pounds, grocery stores will cut and sell it in halves and quarters. Once cut and wrapped in plastic, jicama lasts about a week.

Another of my favorite ingredients, which imparts a taste of the Old West, is toasted pepitas. Not only in Mexico but throughout North America, wherever pumpkins and other squash have grown, the seeds have also been popular. The Mandan Indians ground them into a meal that was used to thicken and flavor a nourishing deer or buffalo marrow soup. We buy the seeds green and pan-roast them ourselves as an important ingredient in all our salads.

Pickled Devil's Claws

In the summer of 1845, Lieutenant James Abert, a recent West Point graduate, spent some time at Bent's Fort and kept a journal documenting flora and fauna. Several entries concern a plant with large seed pods called *Myrtinia proboscidia,* or devil's claws. He wrote that when pickled, these pods resembled pickled okra and were good to eat.

In the late 1980s a retired botanist named Dexter Hess read these journals and went in search of devil's claws on the prairies south of La Junta, Colorado. Picking the seed pods at just the right time of year wasn't an easy task. Early August is a hot time in Colorado; the plant is not much over two feet tall; and more than a few rattlesnakes inhabit the plains. But Dexter and his wife gathered enough for some experiments. Pickled, the little pods were delicious, and I commissioned him to pick and pickle devil's claws for The Fort.

They should be picked in late July or early August when the pods are young and before the antennae have formed and hardened. Use a long pin to probe the pods before picking, to check for a tender tip. If hardened, the sharp hook (the devil's claw, no doubt) may cut your mouth. Eat carefully because it's nearly impossible to tell if the pods will be soft all the way through.

Pickled devil's claws have a slightly crunchy, sour pickle taste, and the seed pod and antennae are tasty as well as fun to eat. I keep a secret store of them to feed adventurous "foodies."

Makes 1 gallon

Approximately 85 devil's claw pods, picked young
1 quart fresh water
1 quart white vinegar
3 tablespoons salt
4 whole dried red chile pequin
6 fresh garlic cloves
2 tablespoons black peppercorns
6 bay leaves
2 tablespoons mustard seed
2 sprigs fresh dill

Clean the devil's claw pods and prick each with a knife to allow the pickling juices to enter.

Pour boiling water into a widemouthed gallon jar to sterilize it, then drain.

Bring the water, vinegar, and salt to a boil. Add the chile, garlic, peppercorns, bay leaves, and mustard seed. Pack the pods into the gallon jar and then add the dill. Carefully pour the boiling liquid over the pods and seal the jar.

These should sit at room temperature for 2 weeks before using. After they're opened, store in the refrigerator. We serve them as a pickle with steaks and cold meats, on salads, or as a vegetable dish on a buffet table.

The same pickling process may be used with okra.

From the Garden

The Fort's
Silver Anniversary Dinner Menu

Tossed Green Salad with Astrid's Scandinavian Dill Dressing
Pumpkin Walnut Muffins

Sirloin Steak Blackfoot Style (Your Choice of Beef or Buffalo)
Cha-Cha Murpheys
The Fort's Little Black Beans

Bee-Nanas Broiled in Their Very Own Hides
Wild Huckleberry Sundae

From the Quartermaster's Storeroom:
Beans, Rice, Potatoes, and Pasta

—•—

IN NINETEENTH-CENTURY MILITARY FORTS, THE QUARTERMASTER WAS IN charge of the stores. This included all dry and bulk food goods such as rice, pasta, grains, potatoes, pulses, and dried fruits. While Bent's Fort was not a military center, its form of organization paralleled that of the military.

In 1968 we published a small newspaper called *The Fort Cannonball*. It contained articles of interest that included historic tidbits, new dishes, and new goings-on at The Fort. According to the *Cannonball*, the quartermaster's storage room provided some good stories as well as good food.

PO' JACK DIES OF MOLASSES

Poor Jack, the Fort's pet beaver, was found dead in the storage area yesterday. Habitués of the fort will remember him in brighter days when as a kit he was found by Raul Martinez and brought here.

Employees and visitors alike were amused by his nocturnal trips to the nearby Arkansas River, where natural instinct prompted his attempts to dam the river with cut trees.

Evidence indicates that Jack was shut up in the stores area where large hogsheads of molasses were stored. His instinct was the cause of his demise, for when he commenced gnawing through one of the barrels (which looked like trees to him), out poured the sticky stuff, drowning Poor Jack. Fort personnel will remember him fondly.

—*The Fort Cannonball*, summer 1968, retelling of a story in a letter from Thomas Fitzpatrick, who was the very literate Indian agent at Bent's Fort

ROOT CELLAR HOSTS SNAKE

The cook's helper at The Fort was frightened recently when she went to the root cellar for potatoes and almost stepped on a large bull snake coiled on the first step. Throwing the door back from the underground stairwell, she commenced to run screaming back into The Fort's kitchen. When the cook went to investigate, she found that the snake had taken off for parts unknown!

The root cellar, next to the sweatbath, is made exactly like those that families in the East and Midwest had for storing their potatoes, apples, carrots, and such during the 1840s.

—*The Fort Cannonball*, summer 1968

The Fort's Little Black Beans

Our first manager, Luis Bonachea, was a delightful Cuban man with some peculiar ideas. One he'd learned from his grandfather was that when a car wouldn't run, a good kicking would fire it into life. Unfortunately, my Mini-Cooper S never responded to that approach.

One of Luis's better ideas was serving Cuban black beans, which he called the "Rolls-Royce of the bean world." His recipe was delicious, but in 1963 most Americans had never heard of black beans. Denverites unaccustomed to eating black-colored foods were skeptical, and although a few enlightened guests developed a great fondness for them, we just couldn't kick-start the Rolls-Royce of the bean world. Today, over thirty years later, it is widely recognized that beans were an important part of the Native American diet, and black beans are known as a staple of southwestern cuisine. Many fine restaurants offer black bean dishes, but rarely do they taste as good as Luis's.

Serves 8 (makes about 4 quarts)

4   cups black beans (sometimes called turtle beans)
6   quarts water
2   yellow onions, finely chopped
4   cloves garlic, crushed
3   ham hocks
4   green bell peppers, chopped
4   bay leaves
½   teaspoon powdered cloves
½   teaspoon whole black peppercorns
1   cup olive or salad oil
1   cup white vinegar
Salt

Rinse the beans thoroughly, checking for rocks or gravel. Soak them overnight in enough water to cover them by 4 inches. The next day, drain and rinse them, then place them in a stockpot and add 6 quarts of water. (Using fresh water helps the beans not be as musical—flatulence-producing—as they might be.) Add the onions, garlic, ham hocks, peppers, bay leaves, cloves, and peppercorns. Cover, bring to a boil, then simmer for 5 hours.

Check on the beans every hour or so, and if the liquid level has dropped so as to threaten to expose the beans, add more hot water.

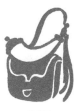

From the Quartermaster's Storeroom

(Always add hot water, never cold, to cover the beans; cold water makes them tough.) Keep the heat low and stir occasionally to prevent burning.

When the beans soften, remove the ham hocks and separate the meat from the bone. Chop the meat into bite-size pieces and add them to the beans. In the last hour of cooking, add the oil and vinegar. Add the salt just before serving.

Variation

Moros y Cristianos

This Cuban main dish, brought to us by Luis Bonachea, illustrates the pervading influence of the nine-hundred-year Moorish control of Spain. *Moros y Cristianos* means Moors and Christians; translated into culinary terms, it means black bean soup over white rice. It makes a marvelous meal-in-a-bowl that we often enjoy for Sunday night supper.

Serves 12

4 quarts of The Fort's Little Black Beans (page 157)
2⅔ cups uncooked long-grain basmati rice or long grain white rice
5⅓ cups water
Pinch of salt
½ white onion, finely diced
8 sprigs cilantro

Prepare the black beans as in the recipe, but before replacing the meat in the pot, remove the bay leaves and place ¾ of the black beans into a blender or food processor and zap them into a thick soup. Return this puree to the pot with the remaining beans and chopped ham. Cover and bring to hot soup temperature over low heat. Stir fairly often, making sure the spoon scrapes the bottom of the pot— don't scorch your *moros*!

Meanwhile, place the rice, water, and salt in a large saucepan. Cover and cook according to the directions on the package of rice. When the rice is ready, place it in large soup bowls and top with the black beans. Sprinkle on a bit of onion and a few sprigs of cilantro.

Fort Rice Pilaf

The Spanish brought rice to the New World, where it flourished. It became the main starch on the Spanish frontier because the Spaniards forced its cultivation throughout South and Central America. It was a staple at Bent's Fort because it lasted so well on the long trip west and nourished many a beaver trapper who could quickly and simply cook it out in the woods.

We present rice pilaf nightly, and it varies with the mood and season. We usually use basmati rice from Pakistan, but in recent years we have been experimenting with many new rice strains from the United States. Often we also add black quinoa for flavor, texture, and visual appeal.

At my San Francisco friend Narsai David's table, I learned to use tiny, brilliantly red barberries in my rice. They make a nice, piquantly sharp exclamation mark. They can be found in Middle East groceries and will confound the most dedicated food lover.

Leftovers make a great salad.

Serves 8

1 cup basmati rice, well washed 6 times
Water for cooking the rice and quinoa
8 strands saffron
½ cup dried currants
2 tablespoons barberries (see Notes)
1 cup quinoa (preferably black, but it's hard to find; see
   Suppliers, page 303)
½ cup toasted pine nuts
¼ cup finely diced red bell pepper
¼ cup finely diced green bell pepper
½ cup flavorful olive oil
Salt
White pepper to taste

For the rice: I use a rice cooker at home to prepare the rice. Simply place the rice in the cooker with 2 cups water, saffron, currants, and barberries. This marvelous machine will do everything for you and turns itself off when finished cooking. Leave the lid on until ready to use the rice. If you don't have a rice cooker, place the same

ingredients in a wide 3-quart (or more) cooking pot with a lid. Bring to a boil, uncovered, then turn the heat to low and simmer, covered, for about 20 minutes. Keeping the lid on, turn off the heat and let the rice steam for another 10 minutes, then open and fluff with a fork.

For the quinoa: While the rice is cooking, prepare the quinoa. Properly cooked quinoa has a wonderful texture, almost like caviar but without the fish taste. It has a slightly bitter taste, but the commercial milling process usually eliminates most of it. You should wash the grain in a chinois or conical sieve, pushing your hand back and forth in it as the water pours through. Any remaining soapy dust will wash away, and your quinoa will taste its best.

Cook the rinsed quinoa in 2 parts water to 1 part grain. It will take about 12 to 15 minutes, depending on your altitude, far less time than the rice, so begin making it after the rice starts cooking. Don't cook it longer than it takes to soften and swell the little ball-shaped grains. Cooks who leave quinoa unattended will find the grains have gotten too hot and have popped and become flat, not nearly as good to eat.

Empty both the rice and quinoa into a large bowl. Using 2 forks, gently fold in the pine nuts, peppers, and olive oil. Because the peppers are finely diced, the heat of the rice will slightly soften them. Add salt and pepper to taste.

NOTES: Barberries may be found in Middle Eastern groceries. Dried cranberries or dried sour cherries make interesting and flavorful substitutes, and may be easier to find.

At The Fort we use ⅓ cooked quinoa to ⅔ rice. You may want to experiment to see how you like to balance the flavors.

Mushrooms or mushroom stems are an excellent addition. Sauté them and add them along with the peppers.

Basmati Rice with Toasted Coconut and Spices

This recipe makes a delicious side dish to Martha Washington's Chicken Breast with Grains of Paradise (page 130) and Country Captain Chicken (page 104).

Serves 8

2   cups high-quality basmati rice
4   cups water plus enough to dissolve sugar
3   threads saffron
2   teaspoons salt
½   cup shredded or flaked coconut
2   tablespoons peanut or canola oil
1   ground star anise (½ teaspoon; available in the Asian section of grocery stores)
1   teaspoon ground coriander
½   teaspoon ground cardamom
½   teaspoon pure red chile or cayenne pepper
2   tablespoons palm sugar (available at Thai or Filipino groceries, but regular white sugar may be substituted)
Cilantro or parsley sprigs for garnish

Preheat the oven to 400°F.

If you are using a rice cooker, pour in the rice, water, saffron, and salt. Turn on the cooker and let it cook until it turns itself off. If you are cooking rice the old-fashioned way, place the rice, water, saffron, and salt in a deep pot and bring to a boil. Simmer for 5 minutes, then turn the heat to low and cover tightly. Simmer for 12 minutes more, then turn off the heat and allow to stand on the warm burner for 10 minutes before opening.

While the rice is cooking, toast the coconut: Spread it in a pie plate and place in the oven for about 5 minutes, until it browns lightly. Watch carefully!

When the coconut has toasted, combine the oil and spices in a skillet over moderate heat. Do *not* add sugar or coconut yet—only after the spices have cooked 2 to 3 minutes, just enough to bring out their essential flavors. Now add the sugar and toasted coconut, with just enough water to dissolve the sugar. Mix well. After the rice has steamed, the grains should be separate. Gently toss in the spice and coconut mixture using 2 forks. Serve garnished with cilantro or parsley sprigs.

171

Arroz con Huevos Duros

In the summer of 1846, a newly married eighteen-year-old bride named Susan Shelby Magoffin went west with her husband on her honeymoon. It was during those months that General Stephen W. Kearny invaded New Mexico and went on through to Arizona and California, pushing the borders of the United States from coast to coast. Susan's diary has been published several times, first by Yale in 1926, under the title *Down the Santa Fe Trail and into Mexico,* and the original resides at the Bienecke Library at Yale University.

One of her entries described a large bowl of rice with hardboiled eggs, a dish found near Santa Fe. I researched this through Mexican cookbooks of the period and discovered how to make it. It is what is known as a *sopa seca,* or dry soup, but the rice is moister than usual, almost like a risotto. This makes a fine addition to a vegetarian meal.

Serves 6

> 2 **tablespoons oil**
> 1 **tomato, finely diced**
> 1 **onion, finely diced**
> ½ **teaspoon Mexican leaf oregano**
> ½ **teaspoon salt**
> ½ **cup chopped green chiles (canned work well)**
> 1 **cup raw rice**
> 2 **cups low-fat, low-salt chicken broth**
> 3 **or 4 hard-cooked eggs**
> **Dash of red chile powder for garnish (optional)**
> **Parsley or cilantro for garnish**

Heat the oil on high until it smokes, then add the tomato, onion, oregano, salt, and chiles. Stir quickly over high heat until the onions are translucent and the tomatoes have browned a little. Add the rice and chicken broth. Bring it to a boil, stir, turn the heat to low, cover, and don't peek for 25 minutes.

Place on a serving dish and garnish with the eggs, cut in half lengthwise and placed yolk side up. A little dash of red chile dusted across the top makes for a wonderful presentation, with little flowerettes of parsley or cilantro growing from the dish.

Sissy Bear

Longtime residents of Denver still ask me, "Do you have the bear up there?" Although Sissy died in 1982, she had lived at The Fort for nearly twenty years, making many friends with her gentle nature, playful ways, and incurable love of maraschino cherries.

Sissy came to us our first year in the restaurant business through a wonderful character named Tuffy Truesdale, who traveled around the country with a 750-pound gelded black bear named Victor. That summer, Victor gave wrestling demonstrations in the courtyard. Wearing a muzzle, he stood on his hind legs and squared off with all manner of muscled macho men ... varsity football players and the entire Morrison police force. He'd always win and get his bottle of Kool-Aid, which he held between his paws and guzzled down.

Tuffy was a kind man, and when he heard of an abused black bear cub from a Wisconsin game farm who needed a home, he immediately adopted young Sissy and saw that she received the veterinary care she needed. Soon she was healthy and growing fast, but he found that two bears were too much work for him and his wife. So Sissy came to live at The Fort.

Her dearest friend was our German shepherd, Lobo. When Sissy was still smaller than a cocker spaniel, Lobo took on the role of surrogate father. Later, when she approached five hundred pounds and stood over six feet tall, the dog remained respectful but not fearful, and the two played like overgrown kittens at every opportunity.

Sissy lived on the north side of The Fort's courtyard, behind a chain link fence that bore a sign with the warning: PLEASE DO NOT FEED YOUR FINGERS TO SISSY BEAR. HER DIET IS CAREFULLY PLANNED. Sissy decided to make her home at the wide, ruddy base of the giant rock. In her first fall as an adult bear, she began digging a cave for herself in the dirt bank by the rock. For nearly two weeks she dug out her hole. Finally she took refuge in it, and all was well until an early snowstorm put several inches of snow on top of the bank. As it melted, the dirt loosened and the cave collapsed. Sissy emerged disgusted, angry, and very dirty. We decided she needed a real cave. A few days later we blasted a fourteen-foot cave into the red rock for

her hibernation and privacy, and built a wooden house at the cave entrance, with a side door so she could escape from public view.

The stock tank that we'd used for adobe-making became her drinking fountain and swimming pool. Sad was the day that her pink rubber beach ball punctured and became just a lifeless flabby object that she'd lift and whimper at.

Although she had been spayed, that didn't prevent wild bears from visiting her. Son Keith, then a teen, opened the kitchen door one Thanksgiving morning to find himself face-to-face with one of Sissy's beaux. He was a sleek, handsome dandy, but Sissy rebuffed him when he came calling. Her favorite was a scraggly, hippy bear with torn ears and a soulful look. He must have been a poet. How she loved him! She constantly teased and rejected him, teased and rejected, playing the consummate coquette.

Sissy died of a tumor after living a long life for a black bear. She is missed by many, and I cherish my fond memories of her and miss the nice smell and feel of her heavy fur.

Cha-Cha Murpheys

There were many Irish immigrants in the Old West, especially in the U.S. Army. *Cha-Cha Murpheys* are so named because "Murpheys" was the term given in the nineteenth century to Irish potatoes. The "cha-cha" comes from the pepper-hot salsa cruda that is stirred and then baked into the potatoes. We serve this dish on Thanksgiving Day.

Serves 6

    4 8-ounce russet potatoes
½ to ¾ cup light cream
3½ cups Salsa Cruda (page 18)
    6 ounces cheddar cheese, grated (1½ cups)
½ cup grated Parmigiano-Reggiano cheese

Peel and quarter the potatoes. Cover with cold water, bring to a simmer, and cook about 20 to 30 minutes, until a knife can be easily

inserted. When the potatoes are done, drain the water and return the potatoes to the pan placed over very low heat to evaporate the last of the water. This takes just a minute or two and gives you fluffier potatoes.

Preheat the oven to 350°F.

Heat the cream in the microwave (don't boil it) and add to the potatoes. If you really want to build your arm strength, mash the potatoes with an old-fashioned masher and a colander. I prefer to use a potato ricer, which squeezes the potato through small holes.

Add the salsa cruda and cheddar cheese to the mashed potatoes and stir well. Pipe or spoon into individual ramekins or a 9-inch square casserole. You can use the back of a spoon to pull the potatoes up into small peaks that will brown nicely.

Sprinkle with the grated Parmigiano-Reggiano cheese and bake for 20 minutes. Serve immediately.

Fort Potatoes with Corn and Anasazi Beans

Every evening we serve this truly delicious potato dish. The combination of sweet corn, bell pepper, green chile, and a bit of browned onion with small red russet potatoes from the volcanic soil of Colorado's San Luis Valley is unusual and delightful.

Out on buffalo roundups, I add crisp fried bacon and green chiles to this dish for the extra energy needed in winter when driving buffalo at sub-zero temperatures (see Sam's Buffalo Drive Fry Pan, page 180).

Serves 10

 2   cups dried Anasazi beans, soaked for at least 2 hours
 2¾   pounds small red russet potatoes, quartered
 8   tablespoons (1 stick) butter
 ½   cup canola oil
 1   cup finely diced onion
 2   teaspoons seasoned salt
 ½   cup fresh, frozen, or canned white shoepeg corn, drained
 1   fresh green chile, diced (Anaheim chiles are excellent)
 1   red bell pepper, diced
 ¼   cup chopped parsley
 ½   teaspoon toasted canola seeds

Drain the beans and place in a saucepan. Cover with fresh water and boil until soft, about 2 hours. Drain and set aside.

Preheat the oven to 400°F.

Boil the potato quarters in water to cover them for 20 to 30 minutes, or until easily pierced with a knife, then drain and bake on ungreased baking sheets for 15 minutes; the bottoms will brown a bit.

In a large sauté pan, melt the butter with the oil over high heat. When quite hot, add the onion and sauté about 4 minutes, until browned. Add the seasoned salt, corn, green chile, and red pepper. Cook for 2 minutes more, then add the potatoes, beans, and parsley. Mix well to heat thoroughly. Serve with a sprinkle of the canola seeds.

Anasazi Beans

The Navajos gave the name *Anasazi,* or "Old Ones," to the ancient peoples of the cliff dwellings of Mesa Verde in southwest Colorado. Word has it that two archaeologists exploring a cave in the area discovered a clay jar sealed with resin. It contained light gray beans with dark red squiggles. Although the jar had been sealed 850 years before, some of the beans, which the archaeologists named *Anasazi,* were coaxed to germinate. They were found to cook from the dry state without presoaking in only two hours, turning brick red and very sweet. Most unusually, they contained less than 25 percent of the amount of the three chemicals that, in combination, make beans antisocial!

Today, Anasazi beans are grown commercially in ever-increasing numbers. They've been on our menu since 1987.

Fettuccine al Mojo Arriero
(Fettuccine in the Style of the Mule Driver)

Noodles have long been part of Mexico's food heritage. *Fideos,* a kind of spaghetti two to three inches long, were brought from Spain hundreds of years ago and are commonly cooked in broth in wide flat pans.

We found this dish, made with fettuccine instead of fideos, on several menus in Ciudad Juarez, across the river from El Paso, Texas. Our four-year-old grandson, Oren, who liked chiles and loved mules, ordered it at several restaurants. The waiters, being very considerate to the Anglo child, deliberately left the serrano chiles out of his meal! He wasn't very happy. But when we prepare it at home, everyone loves digging into the steaming fettuccine, with golden toasted garlic, cilantro, and lots of chiles.

This makes a great one-dish lunch or dinner. For variety, add grilled chicken, tuna, salmon, or swordfish. It's also terrific made with angel hair pasta instead of fettuccine.

Makes 6 generous entrees or 8 to 10 side dishes

1 **pound dry fettuccine**
3 **to 8 cloves garlic (to taste), minced**

177

⅔ cup olive oil plus oil for sautéing

6 ounces Muenster or other mild, melting cheese, grated (1½ cups)

¾ cup chopped fresh cilantro leaves

1 small red bell pepper, finely diced

1 small green bell pepper, finely diced

8 serrano chile peppers, sliced very thin (remove ribs and seeds before slicing for a milder dish)

In a large quantity of boiling water, cook the fettuccine al dente. While the pasta is boiling, slowly sauté the garlic in just a splash of the oil until golden brown, making sure that it doesn't burn. Add the remaining oil and heat with the garlic. Toss the drained fettuccine in a large bowl with the garlic oil. Add the cheese, cilantro, and peppers. Toss until thoroughly blended and serve.

Fettuccine al Mojo de los Ricos
(Fettuccine in the Style of the Rich)

Serves 6

½ cup dried morel mushrooms or 1 to 1½ cups fresh morel mushrooms (see Note)

⅓ cup canola, safflower, or peanut oil

2 tablespoons extra-virgin olive oil

4 garlic cloves, finely minced

1 pound good, hard durum wheat fettuccine

½ cup heavy (whipping) cream or half-and-half

¼ cup dry vermouth or dry white wine

½ cup canned snails, rinsed in cold water and drained

8 ounces Muenster cheese, grated (2 cups)

Salt

3 serrano peppers, minced (add more if you like!)

¼ cup fresh cilantro leaves

If you are using dried morels, wash them thoroughly and soak in warm water for 30 minutes to soften. If you are using fresh, rinse them quickly but thoroughly under running water to remove the sand. Mushrooms act like sponges, so if you let them sit under water, your finished dish will be watery.

Coarsely chop all but the 4 prettiest morels; these will be used for garnish.

In a large, deep skillet (at least 12 inches in diameter), heat the oils and sauté the garlic over medium heat until light golden. Do not let the garlic get too brown, or it will turn bitter.

Cook the fettuccine al dente according to the directions on the package.

Add the cream, vermouth, and all of the morels to the garlic. Heat for 5 minutes. Remove the whole morels and set aside. Add the snails and heat thoroughly, 3 to 4 minutes.

When the fettuccine is done, drain and add it to the skillet. Toss with the sauce and cheese. Salt to taste. Place on a serving platter and garnish with the peppers, cilantro leaves, and whole morels.

NOTE: If you use dried morels, the water you use to reconstitute them will be wonderfully flavored. Strain it and use it in a soup or gravy.

From the Quartermaster's Storeroom

Sam's Buffalo Drive Fry Pan

To eat this dish as it was originally enjoyed, sit on a horse with below-zero winter winds blowing and five hundred head of buffalo milling around you. Put heavy gloves on and eat it as fast as you can with Buffalo Drive Buffalo Burgers (page 73). Nothing smells better than giant, sizzling fry pans loaded with this dish. It can easily be expanded to fit the size of your frying pans. The huge trail pans hold enough for twenty people.

Serves 6

  8 ounces medium to thickly sliced bacon
1½ large yellow onions, coarsely chopped
  2 pounds unpeeled white potatoes, boiled and sliced
  ½ cup white shoepeg kernel corn (fresh, frozen, or canned)
  ½ cup chopped green chiles (frozen, canned, or fresh), roasted,
      peeled, and stemmed (see page 140)
  1 teaspoon seasoned salt
1½ teaspoons coarsely ground black pepper
      Parsley sprigs for garnish (optional)

Cover the bottom of the frying pans with bacon strips, using all the bacon even if you have to make several layers. Place over a hot fire and turn the bacon when it is well fried on one side. When the bacon is crisp on both sides, add the onions in a layer so that they begin to fry in the bacon grease. Follow with the potatoes, covering the onion-bacon mixture evenly. Fry for about 4 minutes, then turn over the mixture in large portions so that new areas fry. Be sure to scrape the bottom of the pan and be careful not to break up the potatoes too much. When they are half browned, add the corn, chiles, seasoned salt, and pepper, turning to mix and heat thoroughly. If you want to be fancy, add some parsley sprigs on each plate.

Supper for a Bear

Sissy was probably the only bear in America regularly dining on buffalo meat and munching buffalo bones. Part of every new busboy's job was to serve her supper and keep the area clean. Most bussers learned to love her and weren't afraid, for Sissy was a tame bear and enjoyed company. Even children loved to feed her. Large school groups visited often and were especially thrilled when Sissy gently removed maraschino cherries held between the children's lips by the stems. This was the largest entree we ever served at The Fort.

Serves one 500-pound black bear

 8 cups dry dog food (Ralston Purina)
 4 eggs
Outer leaves from 14 to 16 heads lettuce
10 carrots
10 apples
 3 cups meat and bone scraps
½ cup salad oil
 2 cups blackberry or huckleberry syrup
 8 oranges, cut in half (Sissy wouldn't eat oranges unless they were already cut in half!)
Maraschino cherry for garnish (optional)

Pour the dog food into a large tub. Break the eggs over the dog food and add the lettuce, carrots, apples, and scraps. Pour the oil and syrup over, arrange the oranges on top, and garnish with a cherry.

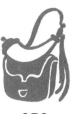

A Historic Menu

1732 Philadelphia Fish-House Punch
Buffalo Tongue with Caper Sauce

Fort Dinner Salad with Creamy Blue Cheese Dressing
Elizabeth Burt's Indian Wars 1870 Potato Bread
Martha Washington's Chicken Breast with Grains of Paradise
Basmati Rice with Toasted Coconut and Spices
Steamed Zucchini

Tocino del Cielo
Coffee and Tisanes

From the Waters

—◆—

WE HAD A HARD TIME JUSTIFYING SEAFOOD ON OUR MENU WITH the foods served at Bent's Fort in the 1830s and '40s. There were some fish in the Arkansas River that were mistakenly called "shad" by eastern visitors; we don't know what they really were. Colorado's lakes are home to trout, but Bent's Fort was miles from mountain lakes. New Mexican workers at Bent's came from a culture where a fried puff or fritter of dried shrimp was part of the diet. But fish was very scarce.

Since many of our customers enjoy seafood, and I cook it a lot at home, we offer oysters, trout, salmon, catfish, and shrimp year-round, and lobster, oysters, and green-lipped mussels according to season.

Trout with Orange Mint Glaze

This recipe makes a marvelous glaze for lamb shanks and pork roasts, too. The oven's heat caramelizes the marmalade to sweeten it wonderfully. Gourmets and the French turn up their noses at mint sauce with lamb, but if it is made this way, the most curmudgeonly gourmet might give it a thumbs-up.

Per serving:
1 12-ounce boneless, butterflied trout with head and tail attached
Vegetable oil to coat
2 to 3 tablespoons Orange Mint Glaze (recipe below)
1 tablespoon coarsely chopped fresh mint leaves

Orange Mint Glaze
Makes about 1½ cups

1½ tablespoons finely chopped fresh mint leaves
2 tablespoons water
1 10-ounce jar orange marmalade
1 tablespoon Dijon mustard

Over heat, stir to combine thoroughly. Keep it warm until ready to use. This can also be prepared ahead of time and reheated just before using.

Preheat the broiler. Rinse the trout and pat dry with a paper towel. Brush the skin with oil and place, skin side down, on a baking sheet. Brush the trout generously with glaze and sprinkle with the chopped mint. Broil 3 to 4 inches from the heat for just a few minutes, until the glaze begins to bubble. The trout will be done.

From the Waters

185

Taos Indian-Style Trout

In Taos, New Mexico, Carl and Mary Schlosser ran Carl's Trading Post for many years, selling very fine Native American goods. Mary, a full-blooded Taos Indian, gave me this recipe for trout. It sounds a bit odd, but it is excellent. The bacon with the mint leaves imparts a delicious herbal taste.

Per person:

1 12- to 16-ounce boneless, butterflied trout with head and tail attached
6 short sprigs fresh mint
Salt
2 tablespoons olive oil
1 teaspoon salt
Freshly ground black pepper
2 long fresh mint runners (if you are fortunate enough to have mint growing in your garden)
2 strips bacon
Lemon slices

Rinse the trout and pat dry with a paper towel. Combine the mint sprigs with the salt and olive oil, and mash them to release their flavor. Fill the cavity of each trout with the oily leaves. Salt and pepper the trout. Wind the trout with the long mint runners. Then, using a toothpick, pin one end of a bacon strip near the tail of the fish and wind it around the fish toward the head. Pin it there with another toothpick. Repeat the process with the second strip of bacon, starting on the other side of the fish. The trout may be covered and refrigerated until ready to broil.

Preheat the oven to broil for about 20 minutes. Place the fish on a broiling pan and broil 5 inches from the heat for about 5 to 7 minutes on each side, until the bacon is well crisped. Remove the toothpicks and mint from both inside and outside the trout. Serve with lemon slices.

Indian Dancers

One of the most memorable evenings in the early days of The Fort was when the Koshares came up from La Junta for a performance. These Boy Scouts had made their own Indian costumes with utmost authenticity and performed a spectacular dance program. Led by the late Buck Burshears, they were famous for years for their fine programs.

For all of us that night, it was magic to see the Indian dancers by firelight in the courtyard of The Fort—Sissy, the big black bear, looking on—and to hear the deep resonant drums with the sonorous chanting. One felt alive in another time and place, back in the 1830s Bent's Fort days. Ghosts of Kit Carson, Ceran St. Vrain, William and Charles Bent, and General Stephen W. Kearny were all there that evening. Maybe even the ghost of the prairie grizzly who had lived in Bent's Fort's courtyard in 1835 was present as well.

Piñon Catfish

Catfish has long been a welcome standard on Texas menus. Today the fish are farmed commercially and have a particularly sweet, delicate flavor. I agree with the general belief that it's the tastiest of all freshwater fish. Perhaps the best way of cooking it is the old-fashioned method of rolling a whole cleaned fish in cornmeal and then deep-frying it. I've eaten many a catfish that way, and love it. But as an alternative to frying, grilling over charcoal or mesquite and sprinkling with pine nuts achieves wonderful results. The marriage of flavors between the delicate fish and the buttery, distinctive nuts results in a taste that is greater than the sum of its parts.

Serves 4

4   8-ounce boneless catfish fillets
Canola oil
Eros (hot) Hungarian paprika (pure New Mexico red chile
    powder and cayenne also work; see page 188)
4   tablespoons toasted pine nuts for garnish
Lemon wedges

From the Waters

187

Brush both sides of the fillets with oil to keep them from sticking to the grate and tearing. Sprinkle the flesh side with paprika. Grill over medium heat, 4 minutes on one side and 3 on the other. Watch carefully, and cook for slightly longer if necessary. The flesh should be lightly browned. Place the fillets on plates and garnish with toasted pine nuts. Serve with a lemon wedge.

Paprika

In Manhattan's Upper East Seventies, at the turn of the century, a Hungarian named Paprikas Weiss sold Hungarian paprikas from a pushcart. Unable to find good Hungarian paprika in this country, he started an importing business on Second Avenue. Although paprika peppers originated in the New World as chiles, they have been bred over the years by Hungarian farmers to produce a wonderful taste. They vary in pepper hotness from the Noble Sweet through seven variations to the hottest, called Eros. You can tell good Hungarian paprika by its deep, rich red color; aging diminishes the color's intensity.

Spain also produces a paprika that has little flavor but is a bright, lighter shade of red and is very decorative. In the event you cannot find good fresh Hungarian or Spanish paprika, substitute pure ground New Mexico red chile. Some consider it a silly restaurant trick to make foods prettier with paprika, but the eye always eats first!

Broiled Salmon with Dill

Salmon is far and away the most popular fish at The Fort. We sell more salmon than any other restaurant in the Rockies, according to the fish purveyors. Grilled over mesquite coals, a salmon steak is pure delight. Following the Scandinavian tradition, it's accompanied by traditional sour cream with cucumbers and dill weed.

Serves 4

Cucumber Dill Sauce:
1 cup sour cream
1 tablespoon peeled, deseeded, and finely diced cucumber
1 teaspoon chopped fresh dill
5 drops Worcestershire sauce
Dash of salt

4 8-ounce unskinned salmon fillets
Canola or vegetable oil
Paprika or cayenne (optional)
Juice of ½ lemon
Melted butter
1 teaspoon dried dill
Lemon halves

At least 8 hours in advance, combine all the sauce ingredients and refrigerate, covered, until serving time.

Preheat the oven to broil or heat your grill to high.

If you purchase a whole salmon instead of 8-ounce fillets, use a boning knife to cut along the backbone on either side and remove the fillets. Check for small bones near the dorsal fin and any leftover bones you may have missed when filleting. A pair of long-nosed tweezers is used by most fish butchers to pull hidden bones. Feel with your fingers and then tweeze them out.

Brush the fillets with oil to keep them from sticking to the grill. Dust the flesh side with paprika. Broil 3 to 4 minutes per side, skin side down first, over low to medium heat. Watch carefully and don't overcook! The skin can be removed from the fillet before serving, but it serves to hold the fish nicely together while it's on the grill. Brush it with lemon juice and butter, and sprinkle it lightly with dried dill.

From the Waters

Serve with lemon halves and cucumber dill sauce on the side.

These days many people like their fish nearly raw. It is fashionable to sear the outside and leave the inside barely warm. If that's what you like, cut down the cooking time and put it closer to the heat. The fish needs to be extremely fresh if you are going to cook it this way.

Salmon

I have always stressed the value of "fresh only" for fin fish served at The Fort. Thus, at the Aspen Food and Wine Festival a few years ago, I was vexed and disbelieving when a Norwegian frozen salmon salesman said that The Fort was using their fish. I did not know that my chef at the time had been using whole frozen Norwegian salmon. The sales rep noted my horror and promised to prove to me that we were serving as good or better a product as we had when buying fresh. We ran some tests, cooking and tasting. The proof was in our mouths. The so-called fresh didn't taste as fresh as the Norwegian frozen, and the texture of both was identical.

I came to learn that the Sekkingstad family in Bergen, Norway, had been chosen to be licensed by a Japanese company that had developed a remarkable new freezing technique. They are the only company in Norway to have this equipment.

So Carrie and I went to Norway to look at their fish-farming operation in the clean water fjords that are sometimes three thousand feet deep. They take the fish back to a processing plant at the water's edge. The fish are all harvested when they are nearly three feet long and are sorted for secondary fish. Then they go through the freezing process within moments of coming out of the water. The result is that in Denver, Colorado, in my walk-in cooler, the thawed fish starts out with less than 3 percent bacteria count, whereas "fresh" fish comes to us with over 30 percent. Thus, the frozen Norwegian salmon has a longer shelf life, which starts only when it is thawed in the cooler, while the others' shelf life begins at least two days before, in Alaska, Canada, or Chile.

When you look at a fish, it's easy to determine how fresh it is. First, look at the eye for clarity. If they are sunken and dull, the fish is old. Next, the gills can be opened with the fingers and inspected. If the gills are bright red, the fish is fresh; if gray, it's old. Lastly, push against the meat of the fish's body with your finger. If the indentation springs back when you remove your finger, it is fresh. If it stays indented, it's not. The thought of eating old fish is unappetizing, but when I studied at La Varenne École de Cuisine in Paris, we were taught this technique of how to determine freshness. The fish we cooked there ... and ate ... didn't pass the test but still tasted pretty good. So I guess there is a little margin for edibility.

Green-Lipped Mussels in Green Broth

One of the great treasures of New Zealand grows beneath the cold waters in the deep fjords of the South Island: the green-lipped mussel. Named for the marvelous deep emerald color that edges the shell and known for its delicious, delicate flavor and fine texture, this mollusk makes its way to us only after a lengthy period of cultivation in mussel beds accessible only by boat.

The farming process begins when tiny young mussels are affixed to the inside of a cotton sleeve about thirty feet long, through which a rope is fed. This rope and many like it are hung from a horizontal cable stretched between two floats that are moored to the bottom. The mussels grow safely within the sleeve for about eight or nine months. By that time they've attached themselves to the ropes, and the cotton sleeve has dissolved.

When the mussels are fully grown, a scow equipped with a huge winch lifts each rope with its burden of mussels. They are scraped from the rope to fill the scow. At the factories at the head of the fjords, some mussels are shipped fresh and kept cold and damp for longer shelf-life. Others are opened and flash frozen.

The day that we toured the mussel farm, I must have eaten over forty mussels—in fritters, with tomato sauce, with chile sauce, garlic, and pesto. The next morning when I woke, I felt as if I was twelve years old again—a rubber man. Nothing ached. Nothing creaked. And all my muscles were at peace.

When I mentioned how good I felt, I learned that for many years green-lipped mussels were harvested mainly for their therapeutic

qualities. They have long been popular in New Zealand, Australia, and East Asian countries as a therapy for arthritis. A few years ago a large American pharmaceutical firm began testing them and felt so strongly about the preliminary evidence that they financed a number of New Zealanders to acquire licenses for growing in certain waters, building processing plants, and buying boats and equipment. When the company stopped work on the project, the new mussel farmers were left deeply in debt and with no American market. Fortunately, since green-lipped mussels were already known as a delicacy in New Zealand and on a limited basis around the world, the consortium wisely decided to market them internationally as a gourmet food. The mussels are simply scrumptious, and they're on the menus of most fine restaurants in the United States these days.

I don't guarantee that this dish will make you feel like a child again, but it's a favorite of mine. And with green-lipped mussels now available fresh or frozen at the seafood counters of most grocery and gourmet stores, it doesn't have to be a once-in-a-lifetime meal.

Serves 4 as an entree (1 dozen per person)
or 10 to 12 as an appetizer (4 or 5 per person)

1 **cup chicken broth (best homemade, but high-quality canned broth or bouillon cubes are also acceptable)**
¼ **cup olive oil**
1 **cup chopped parsley leaves (no stems)**
½ **cup finely diced shallots**
½ **cup chopped cilantro leaves (see Notes)**
2 **to 3 serrano chiles, finely minced (remove ribs and seeds before mincing for a milder dish)**
1 **teaspoon salt (if using an unsalty chicken broth)**
4 **dozen green-lipped mussels, cleaned and debearded (see Notes)**
3 **cups white wine**

Place the chicken broth, olive oil, parsley, shallots, cilantro, serrano chiles, and salt in a blender and blend for about 5 seconds. Place the cleaned mussels in a large roasting pan or deep stockpot. Pour the mixture over the mussels. Add the wine, cover, and bring to a boil. Turn the heat to low and simmer for 4 minutes, stirring occasionally so that when the mussels open, they'll be flooded with sauce. Serve

immediately with the broth in 4 deep dishes. Be sure to accompany this with lots of fresh crusty French bread to sop up the broth.

NOTES: Some people don't like the taste of cilantro. Some interesting alternatives are a combination of fresh tarragon, fresh mint, and mace; or nutmeg and some whole allspice.

To clean mussels, discard any mussels with broken shells or that have opened because they are already dead. Scrub the remaining mussels in cold water. Remove the byssal threads, commonly called "beards," with which the mussels attach themselves to the ropes. Do this by tugging them away from the shells. Using a kitchen towel may help. Do this just before cooking since the mussels die instantly.

White Cheese Shrimp Enchiladas

In Mexico, dishes with cheese or cream are often called *suiza,* Swiss. This *enchilada suiza* is served flat, like a sandwich, in the New Mexican style. It was one of our more modest entrees during The Fort's first years, and one immensely wealthy family ordered it regularly. We were flattered, but in those tight times we always hoped that they'd eat something more expensive! Now, with shrimp prices so high, the dish is no longer cheap. For a scrumptious and more cost-effective meal, use leftover chicken or turkey instead of shrimp.

Serves 6

    2 cups whole milk
    2 pounds Monterey jack cheese, cubed (8 cups)
    1 cup chopped hot green chile
    1 tablespoon Worcestershire sauce
    1 clove garlic, crushed
    Pinch of Mexican leaf oregano
    1 to 2 tablespoons cornstarch dissolved in 1 to 2 tablespoons
       cold water (optional)
   12 large corn tortillas
    Approximately 1 cup chicken broth
    1 to 1¼ pounds Gulf white shrimp, cooked, peeled, and cut into
       bite-size pieces
   12 sprigs whole fresh cilantro
   12 pimento-stuffed green olives, sliced (optional)

Make the enchilada sauce by heating the milk in the top of a double boiler until almost boiling. Turn down heat and keep it as low as possible. Add the cheese. It will melt slowly, but this is better than turning up the heat or overcooking it, which renders it stringy and tough. When the cheese has melted, stir in the green chile, Worcestershire sauce, garlic, and oregano. Keep the mixture warm over warm water until you're ready to use it. If it seems more souplike than saucelike, don't hesitate to thicken it with 1 to 2 tablespoons cornstarch dissolved in 1 to 2 tablespoons cold water.

The easiest way to prepare the enchiladas is to assemble them on ovenproof dinner plates. If you don't use ovenproof plates, place the tortillas on sheet pans covered with aluminum foil or parchment paper, but transferring them can be tricky.

Preheat the oven to 500°F.

Dip the tortillas into the chicken broth to soften them.

For each serving, use 2 tortillas, ⅙ of the shrimp pieces, about ½ cup cheese sauce, and 1 whole shrimp. Place 1 tortilla on each plate, cover with shrimp pieces, and pour half of the sauce on top. Cover with the second tortilla and pour over the rest of the sauce. Place the plates in the oven for 4 minutes so that the cheese browns a little on top. Garnish with sprigs of cilantro and a whole shrimp. An additional garnish we like is a ring of green olive slices.

Shrimp

Shrimp are sized for commercial use by how many headless, raw, in-shell shrimp there are to a pound. U-15, for example, means that there are fifteen or fewer to the pound. The fewer there are to the pound, the larger the shrimp.

Shrimp come in three varieties. Generally, the color of the uncooked shrimp is a good indicator of the quality. White shrimp, sometimes known as Gulf shrimp, are the most expensive and generally come from the Gulf of Mexico. Pinks are less expensive, and brown shrimp are the least expensive. Freshwater-farmed "Tiger" shrimp from Thailand and the Philippines are sometimes very good, but be sure to choose firm ones with a clean smell. At times I've been able to acquire shrimp from Cadiz, Spain, which, at about 4 ounces apiece, almost look like small lobsters. They are good, but once thawed they have an exceedingly short shelf-life.

It's best to buy shrimp whole. Peeled and deveined shrimp may be easier but are often lacking in flavor. Do it yourself.

Shrimp are quite delicate. To thaw frozen shrimp, place them in the refrigerator overnight. Once shrimp are thawed, they should be used quickly. They can be held briefly in water with some lemon squeezed into it, but not longer than two days. If you buy a large quantity of frozen shrimp in a block, run the block under cold water to separate the amount you need, then rewrap and refreeze the rest immediately.

Shrimp en Appolas

Shrimp en Appolas means simply Shrimp on a Stick. These are just skewered shrimp basted with a scrumptious, mildly hot chipotle chile sauce.

Serves 4

4 **bamboo or metal skewers**

Chipotle Sauce:

½ **cup olive oil**

1 **clove garlic, finely minced**

Juice of 1 lemon

3 **dashes Bufalo brand Mexican chipotle sauce or ½ teaspoon mashed chipotle pepper in adobado sauce**

1 **teaspoon honey or sugar (optional)**

20 **jumbo shrimp with tail on, peeled and deveined (see page 195)**

Fort Rice Pilaf (page 169)

Cilantro sprigs for garnish

If you are using bamboo skewers, let them soak in water while you prepare the sauce so they won't burn on the grill.

About 1 hour before cooking, whisk together all the sauce ingredients. Adding a teaspoon of honey or sugar to the sauce will give the shrimp a slight caramelized glaze. Add the shrimp to the sauce and allow it to marinate for 1 hour.

Preheat a charcoal grill to medium. Thread the heads and tails of each shrimp onto a bamboo or metal skewer, 5 per skewer, and grill for 2 minutes, brushing with the sauce while they cook. Serve on a bed of Fort Rice Pilaf. A sprig or two of cilantro makes a nice garnish.

VARIATION: For a zesty change, add 2 tablespoons of passion fruit or mango vinegar to the marinade.

Chicken Shrimp Baja

Serves 4

1 cup chicken broth
4 8-ounce boneless, skinless split chicken breasts, poached in
 chicken broth
2 tablespoons butter
8 raw jumbo shrimp, peeled and deveined
Baja Sauce (recipe below)
8 ounces Monterey jack or Muenster cheese, cut into thin slices
 (2 cups)
Fort Rice Pilaf (page 169)

Bring the chicken broth to a boil in a skillet large enough to hold the chicken breasts in a single layer. Add the chicken and simmer for 1 minute. Remove from the heat, cover, and allow to poach for 12 to 15 minutes, depending on the thickness of the breasts. Remove from the pan and set aside.

Heat the butter in a small skillet and sauté the shrimp just until pink. This will take only a few minutes; don't overcook.

Preheat the broiler. Place the chicken in an ovenproof dish. Top each breast with 2 ounces of Baja Sauce and with 2 shrimp, then cover with slices of cheese. Place under the broiler until the cheese melts. Serve on a bed of Fort Rice Pilaf.

Baja Sauce
Makes 1 cup (4 servings)

6 ounces pure red chile puree (Bueno Foods brand or make
 Red Chile Puree on page 83 but omit the garlic, salt, and
 oregano)
1 clove garlic, pureed
⅛ teaspoon leaf oregano
½ teaspoon cornstarch
2 tablespoons cold water

To make the sauce, combine the chile puree, garlic, and oregano in a saucepan and heat to a slow boil. Dissolve the cornstarch in the cold water, then add to the sauce and bring to a boil again. For an extra-smooth sauce, put it through a sieve.

Shrimp en Globo

When shrimp are broiled over a hot charcoal grill, they lose so much moisture that large, juicy, impressive shrimp become tiny, shriveled, unimpressive specimens. I considered this one evening after watching a glorious grillful of shrimp practically disappear. "Why not cook the shrimp in a contained atmosphere?" I asked myself. Shrimp en Globo is just that—a simple balloon of aluminum foil encasing five or six shrimp with a touch of herb butter. The moisture in the butter and shrimp turns to steam, and the high heat of the grill very quickly cooks the shrimp to moist and tender perfection.

One great thing about this dish is that it's easy to prepare in advance. After making the herb butter, cleaning the shrimp, and sealing them in foil, the packets can be refrigerated until needed.

Serves 4

- 6 fresh basil leaves (pepper basil, often found in Thai groceries, is excellent)
- 8 sprigs parsley
- 2 cloves garlic, crushed
- Juice of ½ lemon
- 4 tablespoons butter
- 2 pounds Gulf white shrimp as large as you can find (at least 12 to the pound), peeled and deveined
- 16 squares aluminum foil, approximately 10 inches square
- 4 cups cooked white rice (optional)

Using a mortar and pestle or food processor, blend the basil, parsley, garlic, lemon juice, and butter. Set aside.

For each serving, lay 1 square of aluminum foil on top of another. Double layering prevents spillage and breaking. Divide the shrimp and herb butter among the 4 foil packets. Cover with 2 additional sheets of foil, fold over the edges, and seal well. Store in the refrigerator for a few hours, until ready to use, or freeze for later use.

When ready to cook, preheat the grill. Turn the heat to medium and place the foil packets over the fire for about 5 minutes, until they puff up, then remove from the fire. If the shrimp were frozen, they will have to cook for another 3 minutes until done.

The shrimp may be removed easily from the packets by snipping with scissors. They're delicious over a bed of rice. Or serve in the closed packets and allow your guests to open them at the table.

Tipsy Shrimp

Many years ago I discovered a manuscript cookbook in the Mexico City library that was written in 1780 by Father Geronimo Pelayo. My wife and I stayed with Mexico City friends Esther and Arturo Campos while Arturo translated the book from ancient Spanish to English. I brought the book back to Denver to try the recipes in my kitchen at home. One of the most wonderful discoveries (although not from Pelayo's cookbook) was Esther's *camarones borrachos*, or tipsy shrimp, which she prepared for our dinner one night. It was so good that we began serving it at the restaurant. The brandy cooks out, but the flavor's superb.

Serves 6

    1 tablespoon cooking oil
    1 tablespoon flour
   16 ounces Salsa Cruda (page 18)
   ¾ cup diced celery
   ½ teaspoon mustard seed
   ¼ cup chicken broth
    1 ounce brandy (cognac preferred)
    2 pounds uncooked white shrimp, peeled and deveined
   Salt
   Freshly ground black pepper
    6 cups cooked white rice
   Parsley or cilantro sprigs for garnish

Heat the oil in a saucepan. Add the flour and stir into a roux. Cook over medium-high heat, stirring, until golden. Turn the heat to high and add the Salsa Cruda, celery, and mustard seeds, stirring for several minutes. Add the broth and brandy, and simmer, uncovered, for several more minutes.

Add the shrimp and cook gently for 2 to 3 minutes, until the shrimp are done. Stir to make sure that the shrimp cook evenly. Adjust the seasoning. Serve over rice and garnish with parsley or cilantro.

From the Waters

Lobster and Shrimp Swiss Enchilada

The Fort was for many years headquarters of the Colorado Chapter of the International Connoisseurs of Green and Red Chile (ICGRC), with several hundred members. One dish I developed for the group was a baked shrimp and lobster casserole, which proved to be so good that Carrie and I served it at our wedding lunch.

Serves 12

 1 quart milk or light cream
 1 pint sour cream
 1 to 2 cloves garlic, crushed
 1 teaspoon salt
 1 tablespoon Mexican leaf oregano
 ½ pound (2 sticks) butter
24 corn tortillas
 1 pound uncooked shrimp, peeled, cleaned, and deveined
 1 pound raw lobster meat
 2 onions, finely diced
 2 to 3 cups chopped mild green chiles (fresh or canned)
 1 cup chopped walnuts
 1 cup sliced ripe olives
 1 pound Monterey jack cheese, grated (4 cups)
 1 pound sharp cheddar cheese, grated (4 cups)
 Avocado wedges, strips of red pimento, black and green olives, or toasted walnuts or pine nuts for garnish (optional)

Preheat the oven to 350°F.

In a saucepan, heat the milk or cream, sour cream, garlic, salt, oregano, and butter until almost boiling. Keep warm on the stove top while you create the enchilada.

Line an 8-quart buttered casserole with half of the corn tortillas. Overlap them to cover the bottom and sides completely. Scatter half of the shrimp and half of the lobster over the tortillas, then half of the onions, chiles, walnuts, and olives. Pour over 2 cups of the hot milk mixture. Combine the cheeses and sprinkle half into the casserole.

Repeat the process with the remaining ingredients, beginning with the corn tortillas and finishing with the cheese.

Bake for about 1½ hours, until well heated. When the cheese bubbles and becomes golden brown, the enchilada is ready to eat. If your casserole is deeper than it is wide, the enchilada may take longer to cook all the way through. In this case, when the cheese has browned, cover the dish with aluminum foil and continue to bake.

Garnish as you like with avocado, pimento, olives, or toasted nuts.

Lobster

There are two divisions of lobster in this world: Maine-type clawed lobsters and spiny (langousta) nonclawed lobsters. The langousta "rock lobsters" come from both warm and cold waters. The best of the rock lobsters are found in cold water off the coasts of Australia and New Zealand, and are considered the world standard.

One company, Beachport Co-op in Australia, offers cold water tails commonly known as "Beachport tails," distinguishable by the tail's pebbled surface. Individual boatmen catch the lobsters in pots and bring them back alive daily to the processing plant where they're sized, cut, and bled. Because these tails are processed and frozen daily, they're the best of the best. Other companies fish from big ships that are far from shore for months. They flash-freeze whole lobsters and hold them on board before returning to the processing plants. At the plants, the lobsters are partially thawed, processed, and refrozen. I like to use Beachport tails because, although they're fiercely expensive now, even frozen they're better tasting than fresh warm-water lobster tails.

Three-Legged Lobster with Lemon Butter

One of the joys of lobster, scallops, and crab is that when they're grill-browned, the slightly burned taste of the outside much improves the flavor. This recipe calls for first browning and then arranging for a unique presentation that your guests will not soon forget. It works best for lobster tails of 8 ounces or larger.

Serves 4

4 lobster tails, 8 ounces or larger
Sprinkle of paprika

Lemon butter:
8 tablespoons butter, melted
Juice of ½ lemon
2 lemons or sweet limes

Preheat a grill to medium.

Place the lobster tail on the counter so that it rests on the shell. Using kitchen scissors, cut along the lower edge of the shell to remove the bottom cover skin. Reach between the meat and the shell to gently loosen the entire tail, leaving the extreme back end attached. With a sharp knife, slit the meat lengthwise up the middle, making two "legs" of the meat. Brush these with lemon butter and a little paprika, then lay the meat on the grill and cook on low to medium heat. When they've browned a bit, turn over and brown the other side.

When the meat is opaque and cooked through, remove the tails to a serving plate. Stand them up to form a tripod of shell and both "legs" of meat. Place a small cup of melted butter combined with lemon juice in front of the lobster tail beside half of a lemon or sweet lime wrapped in a square of cheesecloth twisted at the top and tied with a piece of string.

Trout Stuffed with Corn, Piñones, and Green Chiles

Rosalea Murphy, owner of Santa Fe's marvelous Pink Adobe restaurant and my friend since 1948, has an equally creative daughter, Priscilla Hoback. In the little New Mexican village of Galisteo, Priscilla sculpts pottery art panels that are sought by collectors across the nation. She is also a wonderfully creative cook, and guests lucky enough to be invited to her studio home might be welcomed with pine nut trout. We have adapted her recipe for special occasions at The Fort, for trout is very popular in Colorado where the streams and lakes assure a fresh supply year-round.

Serves 6

1 cup fresh kernel corn (or canned or frozen)
¼ cup toasted pine nuts
¾ cup chopped fresh medium-hot or mild green chiles
½ cup dried bread crumbs
1 egg
½ teaspoon dried dill weed
½ teaspoon dried thyme
Salt
Freshly ground black pepper
6 12-inch rainbow or cutthroat trout, deboned and butterflied with head and tail still attached
3 tablespoons canola oil

Preheat the oven to 350°F.

Mix the corn with the pine nuts, chiles, and bread crumbs. Beat the egg with the dill, thyme, salt, and pepper. Mix the corn and egg mixtures thoroughly and stuff into the cavity of each trout. Brush the fish with oil to coat. Bake for about 30 minutes.

From the Waters

Oysters and Green Chile

In the summer of 1846, traveler Susan Maggoffin and her husband Samuel visited Santa Fe on a covert spy mission in advance of General Stephen W. Kearny's invasion during the Mexican War. In her diary she describes supping on oysters and cold champagne. Since oysters were extremely favored in the nineteenth century, it is no surprise that canned oysters had been part of the merchandise carried west during the previous twenty years.

One of my culinary joys is trying to combine foods I really like. Oysters and green chile go together wonderfully. If you use mild green chile, the shellfish's flavor is enhanced.

Serves 4

- 2 tablespoons butter or vegetable oil
- 3 tablespoons all-purpose flour
- ¾ cup chicken broth (fresh, canned, or from bouillon cubes)
- 1 cup chopped green chile
- 24 freshly shucked oysters in their liquor, or 2 cups jarred fresh oysters (use canned as last resort)
- ½ teaspoon salt
- ¼ teaspoon freshly ground black pepper
- ¼ teaspoon leaf oregano
- 4 pieces white toast
- 4 sprigs cilantro or parsley
- ½ chopped red bell pepper

In a sauté pan, melt the butter, then add the flour and stir until it is absorbed. Cook for 1 minute over medium heat until smooth and bubbling. Add the chicken broth and stir until it thickens a little. Add the green chile and heat until boiling. Add the oysters and seasonings, turn the heat to low, and simmer for 3 to 4 minutes, until the oysters are plump and barely cooked. Serve over toast garnished with a sprig of cilantro or parsley and red pepper.

VARIATION: For a creamier dish substitute ¼ cup heavy cream for ¼ cup broth.

Hangtown Oyster Fry

The origin of this dish seems to be in Placerville, California, which in 1849 was called Hangtown, due to an overzealous judge. The story goes that a miner had been ten months in the hills, slogging through cold waters, eating miserable food, and without the company of ladies, but finally he found gold. He went to town and told the proprietor of a tent restaurant to fix him up with the richest dish he could.

Eggs were a dollar apiece and oysters equally expensive. When the oyster omelet arrived at the table, it was dubbed a "Hangtown Fry." It has survived to this day and is popular in California restaurants. We've prepared this dish at The Fort for historic lunches.

Serves 2

 5 large eggs
 2 tablespoons beer or water
 ½ cup all-purpose flour
 ½ teaspoon cracked black pepper
 ½ teaspoon salt
10 select fresh oysters
 4 tablespoons butter
 4 tablespoons coarsely chopped parsley leaves
 4 pieces hot toast

In a copper bowl, beat or whisk the eggs with the beer until frothy.

In another bowl, combine the flour, pepper, and salt. Dry the oysters on a paper towel, then roll in the flour mixture.

Heat the butter in a large skillet, rotating the skillet to coat the bottom and partway up the sides. Place the floured oysters evenly around the skillet and sauté for 3 minutes, turning with a spatula, until browned.

Pour the egg mixture over the oysters. Lower the heat under the skillet and cook for about 4 minutes, swirling the pan and poking holes in the cooking egg so that all the egg is cooked. Use a spatula to gently loosen the egg from the walls of the pan. Gradually, when the bottom is firm enough and lightly browned, and the center is very moist but not runny, fold the omelet in half.

Slide the omelet onto a serving platter and garnish with parsley. Serve with toast.

From the Waters

A Winemaker's Dinner

One night we held a dinner celebrating Fess Parker's wines. It was a dandy time for all.

First Course
Buffalo Tongue Canapés
Broiled Scallops Wrapped in Applewood Smoked Bacon
1992 Johannisberg Reisling

Second Course
Trout Stuffed with Corn, Piñones, and Green Chiles
1992 Chardonnay

Third Course
Charbroiled Quail Glazed with Red Chile Honey
1990 Merlot

Fourth Course
Mesquite-Grilled Elk Medallions with Shiitake Mushrooms
Vegetable Terrine with Tricolor San Luis Valley Potatoes
Barrel Sample 1992 Syrah

Dessert
Pear Walnut Crepes
1991 Muscat Cannel

From the Bread Oven

W E'VE COME A LONG WAY FROM 1830S FRONTIER BAKING TO today's turbo and steam-injected bread ovens and home bread machines. Wheat flour was a scarce item on the frontier; cornmeal was much more common. The lime-treated hominy called *nixtamal*, finely ground and made into small, thin tortillas with the addition of water and a little salt, was the most common bread eaten on the frontier.

Hopi and Navajo peoples often make little balls of corn dough and roast them right in the ashes among live coals. The Mexican will bake his tortillas on a flat sheet of steel, called a *comal*. In New Mexico, the *horno* beehive oven has been used for centuries.

White settlers of the Old West brought with them Dutch ovens— round, cast-iron, high-walled pots with a lid. Many Dutch ovens have a ridge around the lid to allow hot coals to be placed on top, providing heat from both top and bottom. The Mexicans call this method of cooking *entre dos fuegos,* or cooking between two fires. It's easy enough to bake bread or biscuits, sticky buns and cakes this way, provided you grease the Dutch oven well beforehand.

Reflector ovens, found in historic places, were also used. And should you be caught in the woods with naught but dough, aluminum foil, and a match, build a curved foil reflector behind the fire, skewer the dough on a forked stick between the fire and the reflector, and bake!

Our breads at The Fort are a collection of old and new recipes, old and new techniques, from a simple 1870s potato bread recipe found in an old military fort to a complex white chocolate stollen passed down from our former chef's grandmother.

Leakey Bread

Louis Leakey, the anthropologist who discovered much about the origins of man in Kenya, was an amateur bread maker. He visited The Fort several times and shared a fine bread recipe with us.

Makes 2 loaves

  1 **tablespoon sugar**
  1 **tablespoon (1 package) active dry yeast**
 ¼ **cup lukewarm water (105°F to 115°F)**
  2 **tablespoons butter, softened**
  1 **teaspoon salt**
4½ **to 5 cups flour**
  1 **cup water**

In the bowl of a standing mixer with a dough hook attachment, dissolve the sugar and yeast in the lukewarm water. Let stand until the yeast foams, about 5 minutes.

Mix in the butter and salt, then add the flour and water alternately, mixing until a very smooth dough forms. Place the dough in an oiled bowl, turning once so that the top is oiled. Cover with a damp cloth and let rise until double in size, about 1 hour. (If you don't trust your eyes, simply stick 2 fingers into the dough. If it has doubled, the impressions will remain.)

If you refrigerate the dough overnight, it will develop a delicious yeasty flavor. You may refrigerate it at any point during the rising process.

Preheat the oven to 400°F.

When the dough has doubled in size, punch it down and knead vigorously for at least 5 minutes. Shape into 2 balls and place in greased loaf pans. Let them rise in a warm place for 20 to 30 minutes. Bake for 12 minutes, then lower the heat to 350°F and bake another 24 minutes, or until the tops have browned and the bottoms of the loaves, when turned out of the pans, sound hollow when thumped.

Louis Leakey's Unsolved Mystery

Louis Leakey's last visit to Denver, shortly before he passed away in 1972, was a special treat. I brought a big pot of the Bowl of the Wife of Kit Carson (page 102) to the house of anthropologist Marie Wormington, where about a dozen people had gathered. During the lunch I asked Mr. Leakey if he had ever seen, during his years in mysterious Africa, anything that he couldn't explain.

His answer was yes, and he related an incident that had happened many years before when he was a constable for several of Kenya's native villages. He was asked to help a widow get rid of a poltergeist. The natives believed the ghost to be the spirit of her late husband, for she hadn't performed the proper death rituals when he had died.

Leakey took eight policemen to the village and found the widow, crying, and the other villagers standing around the woman's grass hut. They were afraid to enter, they said, because the poltergeist was throwing objects at anyone who came to the door. Peering inside, Leakey was nearly hit by a barrage of flying pots.

"Come out now, or I'll burn down the hut," he cried. No one came forth, so his men surrounded the hut and set it aflame. When the hut was nothing but ashes, he and his men searched the rubble but found nothing. They checked for a cellar hole or other hiding place and found none.

Leakey never figured it out.

Ranch-Style Pan Bread

Cast-iron frying pans were used on the frontier for making all manner of breads, including this one, a quick, easy baking powder bread with a light, cakey texture.

Serves 9

- 2 cups sifted all-purpose flour
- 3 teaspoons baking powder
- 1 teaspoon salt
- 6 tablespoons vegetable shortening
- 1¼ cups milk

Preheat the oven to 450°F.

Combine the ingredients in a food processor, being careful not to overmix. The dough will be quite sticky. Bake in a greased 9-inch square iron skillet for 25 to 30 minutes, or until dark golden brown. Trust your eyes to tell you when this bread is done, not the clock.

For a crustier bread, bake ranch style, spread thinly in a 9- by 12-inch greased iron skillet and baked until dark golden brown.

NOTE: For more authentic, traditional flavor, use lard or bacon fat instead of vegetable shortening. Bake ranch style.

From the Bread Oven

Indian Horno Bread

Often on summer evenings, guests will encounter a young woman in 1840s garb drawing loaves of fresh, hot bread out of an adobe-and-mud beehive-shaped bread oven in The Fort's courtyard. Pueblo Indians commonly used these ovens, called *hornos*. The Spanish brought them to the Americas, but they originated even farther east and were introduced to Spain by the Moors. These ovens are still found today throughout the Mediterranean countries but are practically forgotten here.

The art of horno building lives on in Taos, New Mexico, where it is historically the work of women, whose traditional title is *enjarradora* (literally, a northern New Mexican term meaning "mud plasterer"). In 1988 an *enjarradora*, Anita Rodriguez, of Taos came to Colorado to build our horno. The oven imparts a slightly smoked taste to foods and produces a beautifully crusty bread. Some people don't have hornos at home. Fortunately, this recipe also works very nicely in the kitchen.

Makes 2 loaves

- 1 **tablespoon (1 package) active dry yeast**
- ¼ **cup lukewarm water (105°F to 115°F)**
- 2 **tablespoons melted lard or shortening, plus extra for brushing on the loaves**
- 4½ **cups sifted all-purpose flour**
- 1 **teaspoon salt**
- 1 **cup water**

In the bowl of a standing mixer with a dough hook attachment, dissolve the yeast in the lukewarm water. Let stand until the yeast foams, about 5 minutes.

Mix in the melted shortening, blending thoroughly. Sift together the flour and salt, then add the flour and water alternately, mixing until a smooth dough forms. Place the dough in an oiled bowl, turning once so that the top is oiled. Cover with a damp cloth and let rise until double in size, about 1 hour. (Two fingers stuck into the dough will leave impressions.)

Preheat the oven to 400°F.

When the dough has doubled, punch it down and knead vigorously on a lightly floured board for at least 5 minutes. Shape into 2 balls and place on a greased baking sheet. Brush the loaves with melted shortening and let them rise in a warm place for 15 minutes. Bake for 50 minutes, or until the loaves are lightly browned.

Horno Baking

The horno at The Fort has both an arched opening in front, with a burlap-covered wood door that has a small handle, and a tiny smoke hole around the side near the top, plugged with a burlap-covered stick.

Because of its long burn time, hard wood is preferable for horno baking, but pine and aspen also work well. Before firing up the oven, the burlap is soaked with water. The wood is lit and the oven allowed to "preheat" for three hours before baking. Rather than use a thermometer, we stoke the fire until it's "pretty damned hot," which means that you can't hold your hand in the door for more than three seconds. In Fahrenheit degrees, it's about 450. The oven will cool when the bread goes in because the coals will come out.

While the horno is heating, the bread dough is made and has ample time to rise. When we're ready to bake, the coals are raked with a long-handled hoe out the door and into a fireproof container. The bread is immediately placed in the oven, and both door and smoke hole are sealed. After twenty minutes it's usually safe to loosen the door and take a peek. If the loaves are quite golden brown, they can be removed and thumped; a good hollow sound means they're ready to eat.

Horno-baked bread is sold at Santa Fe's Palace of the Governors' sidewalk market for $2 a loaf. At Taos Pueblo, tourists pay twice that. But even at the inflated price, it's worth buying.

From the Bread Oven

Herb Bread

Just outside the back door of The Fort's kitchen, by the trapper's cabin, is a little garden where we grow herbs. Over the years, dill, parsley, rosemary, thyme, tarragon, and oregano have served us with their delights. We toast this delicious herb bread and serve it with Broiled Buffalo Marrow Bones (page 33) and Broiled Asadero Cheese (page 27), and make mouth-watering Croutons (page 150) for our salads.

Remember that if you're using fresh herbs, increase the amount three times over dried.

Makes two 2½- × 12-inch loaves

1 tablespoon (1 package) active dry yeast
1 tablespoon sugar
1 cup lukewarm water (105°F to 115°F)
2 tablespoons vegetable oil
3 to 3½ cups all-purpose flour
1 teaspoon salt
1 teaspoon garlic powder
1 teaspoon ground oregano
1 teaspoon dried leaf oregano
1 teaspoon dried thyme
1 teaspoon dried rosemary
1 tablespoon dried dill weed
2 tablespoons dried parsley
Sprinkling of cornmeal

In a large mixing bowl, dissolve the yeast and sugar in the water. Add the oil.

In a separate bowl, stir together the flour, salt, and herbs. Add to the yeast mixture and mix thoroughly to form a soft dough. Place it in an oiled bowl, turning the dough once so that the top is oiled. Cover with a wet cloth and let rise in a warm place until double in size, about 1 hour.

Punch the dough down and let it rise again. (This helps develop the flavor of the yeast.) Turn out onto a floured board. Shape into two 12-inch French loaves and place them on a greased cookie sheet that has been sprinkled with cornmeal. Slash the tops diagonally. Cover and let rise again until double.

Preheat the oven to 375°F.

Bake for 25 to 30 minutes, until golden.

Yeast

The really good yeasty flavor of professional loaves comes from letting the dough age at least a day or two, to let the bacteria develop. Simply take a couple of cups of bread dough and place it in a large covered bowl in the refrigerator. Let it rest in the refrigerator for two days, then knead in a bit more flour plus some lukewarm water to reactivate the yeast. When you're ready to bake, let the dough rise and bake as usual. Your loaves will have a nice nutty flavor.

Elizabeth Burt's Indian Wars 1870 Potato Bread

Fort Laramie in the southeast corner of Wyoming was originally a fur trade center like Bent's Fort. It later became a military base and a major stopping point on the California Oregon Trail. It remained a military center for the rest of the nineteenth century and is now operated as a national historic site by the National Park Service.

The wife of the second-in-command in the 1870s, a lady named Elizabeth Burt, kept a cookbook that is a treasure trove of foods from the Indian Wars period. Her recipe for potato bread is hearty and good. If you visit Fort Laramie today, you'll find her cookbook in the fort's library.

Sometimes I like to sprinkle this bread with green za'atar before it's baked. This Middle Eastern ingredient is a combination of thyme, sesame seeds, and powdered sumac.

Makes 24 dinner rolls or 3 loaves

4 medium white potatoes
Dash of salt
1 tablespoon sugar
2 tablespoons (2 packages) active dry yeast
½ cup lukewarm water (105°F to 115°F)
3 cups all-purpose flour
1 tablespoon salt
4 tablespoons butter
2 cups scalded milk, cooled to lukewarm
1 egg

From the Bread Oven

215

1 tablespoon water
Thyme (optional)
Sesame seeds (optional)
Powdered sumac (available in Middle East grocery stores;
    optional)

Peel the potatoes and place them in boiling water with the salt. Boil until very soft, about 25 minutes. Drain, reserving the water, and mash them thoroughly by putting them through a potato ricer or using an electric mixer. If you use an electric mixer, be sure not to beat too long. Do not use a food processor; it breaks down the cells and you will end up with a gluelike substance that has very little resemblance to mashed potatoes.

In the bowl of a standing mixer with a dough hook attachment, dissolve the sugar and yeast in the lukewarm water. Let stand while the yeast foams, about 5 minutes. Add the flour, salt, butter, potatoes, and milk, blending continuously with the dough hook attachment. Knead in enough of the potato water to make a good bread dough.

Place the dough in an oiled bowl, turning once so that the top is oiled. Cover with a damp cloth and let rise until double in size, about 1 hour.

If you refrigerate the dough overnight, it will develop a delicious yeasty flavor. You may refrigerate it at any point during the rising process.

Preheat the oven to 400°F.

Punch down the dough and form it into 3 loaves on greased baking sheets or cut into rolls. Let rise again in a warm place for 20 to 30 minutes.

Beat the egg with the water and brush the tops of the loaves with the egg wash. While they are still wet, sprinkle the loaves or rolls with a dusting of thyme, sesame seeds, and powdered sumac.

For rolls, bake for 5 minutes and then lower the heat to 350°F and bake for 15 minutes more. For loaves, lower the heat to 350°F after 5 minutes and bake for 35 minutes more.

Lakota Indian Fry Bread

It's not known exactly when or how fry bread came to the Plains Indians. It was certainly not until they had metal kettles for frying, and that was after trade began with whites. There is no indication that frying in pottery or on a hot rock was part of the pre-Columbian culture. It was probably introduced to the Indians in the form of German or Dutch settlers' doughnuts, called "oily cakes."

This recipe was first prepared for me in 1969 by a woman of the Brulé tribe, a branch of Sioux Indians in South Dakota, when I visited the Rosebud Sioux Indian Reservation to film traditional American Indian dishes for my PBS series *Fryingpans West.*

The woman prepared the dough by hand, mixing dry ingredients in a bowl and then beating in small amounts of water with a long wooden spoon until a moist but firm dough had formed. After kneading it well, she rolled out a grapefruit-size ball of dough with a piece of broom handle to about ½ inch thick and cut it into 4- by 5-inch pieces. (Pueblo Indians traditionally make disks with approximately ¾-inch holes punched in the center. The hole serves two purposes: It allows the hot fat to flow through to cook the top surface of the bread, and it allows for easy removal when done.)

Then she dropped the dough into an iron kettle filled with melted pork lard that had been heated to near the smoke point and immediately began spooning hot fat over the dough. The resulting steam inside the dough puffed it up beautifully. We ate some of the fry bread with honey and some sprinkled with cinnamon sugar, both traditional toppings.

This recipe is a basic white flour bread dough that is leavened with baking powder, formed into flat rectangles or disks, and cooked in hot lard. The procedure is quick and uncomplicated, and the crispy, light bread makes a marvelous treat.

Makes about 20 pieces

    1 **quart tallow, lard, or canola oil**
    1 **pound (approximately 3½ cups) flour, plus more for rolling out**
    1 **tablespoon baking powder**
 1½ **teaspoons salt**
      Approximately 1½ cups water
      Honey or cinnamon sugar, for serving

Heat the oil in a deep pot to 380°F. The best flavor comes from either beef tallow (rendered beef fat) or lard, but with today's food fascism, health-conscious people use canola oil.

The easiest way to make fry bread is with a dough hook attachment on an electric mixer. Thoroughly mix the dry ingredients together. Add water and mix until a uniform dough forms. Add more water if needed to achieve a dough the consistency of normal bread dough: not too sticky but not too dry. Roll out on a floured surface to a thickness of ¼ to ½ inch and cut into either 4- by 5-inch rectangles or 8-inch disks.

If you'd like to try Pueblo-style fry bread, use your finger to make a ¾-inch hole in the center of each piece of dough.

If you don't have a thermometer to check the heat of your oil, carefully put in a small piece of dough. It should blister and puff up instantly. In the first few seconds of frying, use a spoon to pour fat over the bread to make sure all surfaces fry immediately. Remove and drain on a paper towel. Allow a full minute between batches to bring the oil back up to temperature.

Many people dip fry bread in honey or bite a hole in the side and squeeze honey into the center. Others sprinkle cinnamon sugar on it. Whatever your pleasure, the most important thing about fry bread is that it *must* be eaten hot immediately after it's cooked.

Variation

Fry Bread with Brown Sugar and Cheese

We found an interesting variation of fry bread at Pancho's Number Two in El Paso, Texas, where the chefs pressed together two thin pieces of dough encasing a tablespoon each of brown sugar and coarsely grated cheddar. They then moistened the edges and squeezed them together to seal totally, like a giant ravioli, and fried as usual. The melted brown sugar and cheese are delectable.

Variation

Fry Bread with Beer

Beer makes a splendid leavening agent and lends the bread a nice nutlike flavor. Use 1½ cups of beer instead of water and baking powder.

Pumpkin Walnut Muffins

A 1975 Fort menu reads, "The pumpkin nut muffins are a closely guarded secret; the recipe is asked for nightly but never revealed." The secret ingredient is no secret at all: It's the pumpkin. These muffins contain about twice as much as other recipes. Because of that, they're cooked for a long time at an unusually low temperature and turn out especially dense, moist, and flavorful.

Makes about 4 dozen

  5 cups flour
  1 cup sugar
2½ cups dry powdered milk
  4 tablespoons baking powder
  3 tablespoons cinnamon
  1 tablespoon salt
1½ cups brown sugar
1½ cups chopped walnuts
  4 large eggs (size does make a difference!)
1¼ cups vegetable oil
1¼ cups water
  2 29-ounce cans pumpkin (not pie filling)

Preheat the oven to 325°F. Grease 3-inch muffin tins or line with paper.

Mix all the ingredients together. The batter should be easily scoopable. If it is too thick, add a little more water. Fill the tins three-quarters full and bake for 40 to 45 minutes. Let the muffins cool before removing them from the pan.

Because they are so moist, these reheat beautifully.

From the Bread Oven

Pumpkins in the West

The bright orange pumpkins dotting the fields throughout Colorado played a great role in Colorado history. The first domesticated pumpkin was grown in 7000 B.C. in Mexico's northeastern Tamaulipas region. Seeds were traded to other tribes, and by 3000 B.C. pumpkins had traveled to Puebla, Mexico. Within another five hundred years, pumpkins had journeyed as far as Peru.

Pumpkins went north, too. The basket makers in the Durango and Mesa Verde areas of Colorado grew them before A.D. 400. The staple Indian diet consisted of corn, beans, and various squashes, including our common pumpkin. When the fur trappers came west in the early 1800s, pumpkin became a major part of the diet of mountain men such as Kit Carson, Uncle Dick Wootton, and others who frequented the original Bent's Fort.

On an 1842 visit to Fort Lupton, Rufus Sage tells of a trading party of Mexicans from Taos who brought with them packhorses and mules laden with corn, bread, beans, onions, and dried pumpkin to barter for buffalo robes, furs, guns, and tobacco sold at Fort Lancaster (later known as Fort Lupton).

Today thousands of pumpkins are grown near Fort Lupton. But the pumpkin in North America has lost its many uses, and only pumpkin pies and jack-o'-lanterns remain popular. At The Fort we keep the tradition of this noble squash alive in our Pumpkin Walnut Muffins, probably our most sought after recipe.

Blue Corn Blueberry Muffins

One evening in Santa Fe a few years ago, a transplanted New Englander showed me how to make Rhode Island white corn cakes, or johnnycakes, using his own stone-ground meal. While the origin of the name is uncertain—some say they were first called *journeycakes,* others *Shawneecake*—I found that there is no debate on how to prepare them.

"First," I was told, "since this is flint corn, you have to throw boiling water on the meal and let it sit for forty-five minutes or more to soften the corn." Instead of having a gritty texture, the johnnycakes were soft and delicious. Later, when we were developing a blue corn muffin at The Fort, I remembered that trick. Sure enough, our muffins have a wonderful texture every time.

Makes 2 dozen

    3 cups blue cornmeal (available at Mexican markets or natural
       food stores)
    3 cups water
    4 cups all-purpose flour
    1 cup plus 1 tablespoon sugar
 1½ tablespoons baking powder
  ⅛ teaspoon salt
    4 eggs
  ¾ cup vegetable oil
    1 cup blueberries (fresh, canned, or frozen; see Note)

Place the cornmeal in a large bowl. Bring the water to a boil and pour it over the cornmeal. Set aside for 1½ hours.

Preheat the oven to 325°F. Grease 3-inch muffin tins or line them with paper.

In another large bowl, combine the flour, sugar, baking powder, and salt, mixing well. Beat the eggs with the oil and add to the dry mixture. Add the damp cornmeal and stir in well. Gently fold in the blueberries. Spoon into the muffin tins to three-quarters full. Bake for 30 to 35 minutes. Serve with sweet butter.

NOTE: If using canned blueberries, drain first; if using frozen, do not thaw.

If fresh blueberries are unavailable, try to find wild blueberries (usually available canned). They are smaller and have a more intense flavor than regular blueberries, canned or frozen.)

From the Bread Oven

Charlotte's Swedish Pancakes

Charlotte Green ran the kitchen at Bent's Fort in the 1840s and called herself "de onlee lady in de dam Injun country" (Ruxton, *Life in the Far West,* 180). Contemporary reports by British author George F. Ruxton tell of the marvelous fandangos at the fort when Charlotte waltzed with Indians, French and American mountain men, and German and Mexican visitors. Although a slave, Charlotte lived in a remarkably democratic society on the frontier and, according to contemporary journals, was "celebrated from Longs Peak to the Cumbres Espanolas for slapjacks and pumpkin pie" (Ruxton, 180).

We're sure that if Charlotte lived today, these are the "slapjacks" she'd make. They're actually a delicate Swedish pancake like those served with lingonberry jam in our first years at The Fort. The recipe comes from our dear friend Vivian Hansson Phillips, who learned it in Sweden from her mother. They take a little practice to master, but even the ugly ones are so delicious that you'll find willing victims to sample the products of your learning process.

Serves 6

   3 **eggs**
   ¼ **cup sugar**
   1 **cup all-purpose flour**
   2 **cups milk**
   Dash of salt
   About ½ pound (2 sticks) butter (for coating the skillet)
   Preserves for filling (optional)
   Confectioners' sugar (optional)

Beat the eggs just until the yolks have broken. Add the sugar and stir a few times, then add ⅔ cup flour and beat until a paste forms. Gently beat in ¼ cup milk to liquefy the mixture, then add the remaining ⅓ cup flour. Beat slowly, constantly adding the remaining milk until it's all incorporated. The batter will be thin like crepe batter; don't overbeat. Add the dash of salt.

Heat a 10-inch skillet over medium heat. Add about 1 tablespoon butter to the pan, enough to coat the bottom and partway up the sides. Pour in about ⅛ cup batter and swirl the pan to cover the bottom with batter. Let it sit for about 1 minute. Then, using a spatula, lift

the edges of the pancake all around to keep it loose enough to turn it. When it has browned lightly on the bottom, slide the spatula all the way under it. Lift it completely from the pan and turn it over to cook the underside until lightly browned. Slide onto a plate and serve immediately or keep warm in a 200°F oven. Repeat the process with the rest of the batter, adding butter to the skillet as needed.

Roll your favorite preserves up inside or drizzle with melted butter, then sprinkle with confectioners' sugar.

From the Bread Oven

Stollen with White Chocolate

This holiday bread was brought to The Fort by Nigel Richardson, a chef at The Fort several years ago. It was inspired by his German grandmother's stollen recipe, and he generously gave us permission to use it.

Serves 10

Filling:

1 cup toasted almonds

1 tablespoon flour

6 ounces white chocolate (a good brand such as Lindt; do not use a coating chocolate)

1 teaspoon pure almond extract

Stollen:

1 tablespoon (1 package) active dry yeast

⅔ cup beer, at room temperature

3⅔ cups plus ½ cup all-purpose flour

½ pound (2 sticks) butter

½ cup sugar

1 egg

1 teaspoon salt

2 teaspoons almond extract

1⅓ cup raisins, soaked in warm water for several minutes to plump, then drained

⅓ cup mixed candied fruit (a combination of dried papaya and dried mango is great!)

1 cup chopped almonds

Milk for sealing dough (if necessary)

Pearl sugar for topping

2 tablespoons butter, melted, for topping

Confectioners' sugar for topping

Grind the almonds when cool by placing them in a food processor with the flour and turning the processor on and off until they're ground.

Melt the white chocolate in the top of a double boiler. Remove from the heat and add the ground almonds and almond extract. Mix well.

Place 2 pieces of waxed paper on the counter. When the mixture has cooled slightly, divide it in half, placing each portion about 3 inches from the lower edge of the paper. Fold the waxed paper over the nut mixture and use your hands to form each one into a 10-inch log. The waxed paper will keep the mixture from sticking to your hands. Refrigerate.

For the stollen, dissolve the yeast in the beer. Add 1 cup flour. Set aside in a warm place to rise, about 1½ hours.

In a large mixing bowl, cream the butter and sugar together, then add the egg and beat well. Add the salt and combine this batter with the yeast mixture. Add the 2⅔ cups flour and the almond extract, and mix well.

Knead the dough on a floured surface until smooth and elastic, about 10 minutes. Combine the ½ cup flour with the raisins, candied fruit, and almonds, then mix into the dough. Place the dough in a floured bowl, cover with a damp towel, and let rise in a warm place until double in bulk, about 1 hour.

Preheat the oven to 350°F.

Punch down the dough and roll into a 12-inch square. Place the 2 rolls of chocolate parallel to each other, 2 inches from the upper and lower edges of the dough. Fold both upper and lower edges over the chocolate and toward the middle, then fold in half and pinch the edges together. (Seal with milk if necessary.) Place on a greased baking sheet and allow to rise for 20 minutes.

Sprinkle with pearl sugar and bake for about 45 minutes, or until lightly browned. When it's slightly cool, brush gently with melted butter and sprinkle with confectioners' sugar.

Jalapeño Corn Bread

In the days of the early West, *Indian meal*, as cornmeal was called, was commonly used all over America. In Texas, the Mexican population added jalapeño chiles to their corn bread. It's a wonderful combination, and for large parties we often make giant pans full of this pungent bread. It's moist enough to bake in greased corn stick pans without crumbling.

Serves 9

 1 cup cornmeal
 1 cup all purpose flour
 ¼ cup sugar
 1 teaspoon salt
 2½ teaspoons baking powder
 2 eggs
 2 cups coconut milk (available in the Asian section of the supermarket; see Note)
 1 tablespoon plus 1½ teaspoons vegetable oil
 ⅓ cup diced fresh jalapeños, seeds and ribs removed
 ½ cup well-drained canned golden corn kernels

Preheat oven to 350°F. Grease a 9-inch square cast-iron skillet or baking pan with vegetable shortening.

Mix together the dry ingredients. In a separate bowl, combine the liquid ingredients, jalapeños, and corn kernels. Pour this mixture into the dry ingredients and stir just until blended. Pour into the prepared skillet or baking pan and place on a rack in the center of the oven for about 45 minutes, or until pale golden brown. Do not overbake. Serve with sweet butter.

NOTE: Do not use sweetened cream of coconut, which is used to make drinks. You may substitute regular milk, but the bread won't be as sweet.

Making Coconut Milk

To make fresh coconut milk from a coconut, pierce the shell's eyes, found at one end of the coconut, with an ice pick. Drain the coconut water and place the coconut in an oven that has been preheated to 500°F, for 15 minutes, then crack the shell with a sharp blow from a hammer or cleaver. It should crack easily. Pry the meat from the shell and peel off the dark skin with a potato peeler.

Using a food processor or a handheld grater, grate the coconut to a fine consistency and place it loosely in a cheesecloth bag. Place the bag in the bowl with the liquid from the coconut. Pour 1 quart of boiling water over the bag. When it has cooled some, squeeze the bag while it's in the water, working it in your hands for a few minutes. Allow to stand at least 3 hours. Skim off the cream that rises to the top. (It's great in piña coladas.)

Strain the remaining liquid and use.

Quinoa Muffins

When guests' salads are brought to the table, we also bring baskets filled with two breads made that morning in The Fort's kitchen. Among the perennial favorites that we vary nightly are Pumpkin Walnut Muffins (page 219), Elizabeth Burt's Indian Wars 1870 Potato Bread (page 215), and Quinoa Muffins.

Because quinoa contains more usable protein than any other grain, it's said that a man can easily work a twelve-hour day on one cup of it. So far this claim has gone unproven at The Fort. I have an accommodating and faithful waitstaff, but none of them has volunteered to test it.

Makes about 2 dozen

- 3 eggs
- 1 cup vegetable oil
- ¾ cup honey
- ¾ cup brown sugar
- 2 teaspoons baking soda

From the Bread Oven

227

1   teaspoon orange oil (see Suppliers, page 303) or 2 teaspoons
    grated orange peel
1   cup all-purpose flour
1¼ cups quinoa flour (see Suppliers, page 303, and below)
¼   cup yellow cornmeal
½   cup wheat germ
1½ teaspoons baking powder
2   teaspoons salt
½   cup canola seeds (poppyseeds make a dandy substitute)
1   cup coarsely chopped walnuts, toasted
½   to ¾ cup milk

Preheat the oven to 375°F.

Combine the eggs, oil, honey, sugar, baking soda, and orange oil, and blend well. Add both flours and the cornmeal, wheat germ, baking powder, salt, canola seeds, and walnuts. Mix well and add ½ cup milk. If the batter seems too dry, add the additional ¼ cup milk. The batter should be thick but pourable. Pour to fill greased or paper-lined 3-inch tins to three-quarters full and bake for 20 minutes.

Quinoa

In the mid 1970s on a trip to Peru, I learned of the grain called quinoa (pronounced KEEN-wah). The individual grains are like tiny balls and have a texture similar to black lumpfish caviar. Quinoa takes on the flavors of the foods with which it's mixed. But its most significant feature is that it contains more usable protein than any other grain in the world—including amaranth, rice, and spelt. Dr. John McCamant, a professor at Denver University and one of the country's experts on quinoa, says that it is close to being the perfect food.

Archaeological evidence shows that quinoa was cultivated as early as around 5000 B.C. in the Ayacucho basin in Peru. It was a staple of the Andean peoples and was held sacred by the Incas, who called it the "mother grain."

I was so excited about it that I wanted to begin importing the grain to the United States. I discovered that a man named Stephen

Gorad, in Boulder, Colorado, was already importing and selling it to specialty groceries. Eventually he sold the company to a conglomerate in California, and today quinoa enjoys sales nationwide. It will never compete with grains like wheat and barley because it lacks gluten for making yeast bread and because it is very difficult to grow domestically.

Quinoa's native environment is near the equator—which means a long growing season—and high in the Andes, from seven thousand to thirteen thousand feet above sea level—which means cool temperatures. After many years of research and experimentation, quinoa was finally cultivated successfully in the Rocky Mountains in the 1980s. Today, White Mountain Farms, high in Colorado's San Luis Valley, grows (in addition to excellent potatoes) several strains of what has been dubbed the "supergrain of the future." White, tan, and black varieties are available, but the black—the original grain from which the others have derived—is by far the best. In Peru it's called *coital quinoa,* but I haven't been able to find out why.

Preparation of quinoa is easy. The plant grows to about six feet and has a big seed-covered top coated with natural soap to discourage animals and insects from eating it. This is rinsed off in the commercial milling process, but the grain should be rinsed again at home before using. It's important not to overcook quinoa, for the moisture inside the tiny balls will cause them to explode, and then the grain becomes an uninteresting, flat shell. It's cooked like rice, with a grain-to-liquid ratio of 1 to 2. Usually, depending on altitude, it's cooked for twelve to fifteen minutes.

1988 Governor's Award for Excellence Dinner Menu

When The Fort was presented with the State of Colorado Governor's Award for Excellence in 1988, we held a special dinner featuring historic Colorado foods.

Libation: Bent's Fort Hailstorm Juleps

Mountain Man Boudies
Buffalo Eggs
Fort Bean Dip with Fresh Tortilla Chips
Rocky Mountain Oysters
Fresh Greens with Roasted Pepitas
Parker Longhorn Beefsteak or High Meadow Buffalo Steak
Broiled au Natural or Gonzales Style with Green Chiles
San Luis Valley Little Red Russets in Fort Potatoes
Pumpkin Walnut Muffins
Blue Corn Blueberry Muffins

Peaches Flamed in Scotch with Pine Nuts
Coffee and Tisanes

From the
Dessert Cupboard

For the More Adventurous Palate

OUR MOUNTAIN MAN MINSTREL, DAN McCRIMMON, OFTEN TELLS guests that at The Fort there are four basic food groups: whiskey, buffler, caffeine, and sugar. For the fur trappers of the early West this statement was fairly accurate, and food and drink were always appreciated—if not exciting—parts of the mountain man's life.

One of Carrie's and my favorite parts of the restaurant business is that food is not only for sustenance but also for celebrating. We get to be a part of special events in our guests' lives. Over the years we have developed many traditions of our own and take great pleasure in sharing them. Always there is food, and often, when the event is not a sit-down dinner, the food is a dessert-type item. One of my favorite traditions is our annual lighting of the *farolitos*.

As the days grow shorter in November and the air gets a nip in it, we look forward to the Christmas season. Late in November we deck The Fort for the holidays by lining the ramparts with *farolitos*. In Spanish a *farola* is a lantern, and *farolitos* are the little lanterns consisting of a candle inside a paper bag. (In Albuquerque these are called *luminarios*, an alteration of *luminaria*, which actually is a pitch pine bonfire.) For safety's sake, ours are electric lights placed in nonflammable weatherproof bags, but they look just like the real thing.

At dusk on the Sunday after Thanksgiving, we gather friends and the public by a bonfire in the courtyard to honor a person who has done good things for our community. Each guest brings with him one pinecone with a small piece of paper entwined in it bearing the name of a loved one who is no longer with us. There is fresh cider and biscochitos for all, and a little speech is made for the guest of honor. He or she turns on the power to the hundreds of *farolitos* high up on the walls, and the entire Fort lights up in its holiday finery. Then we gather around the fire. All is still and quiet except for the crackle of orange flames licking at the chill night air. Each guest places his resinous pinecone on the flames. In moments the blaze becomes a pillar of fire, taking each person's good wishes high into the sky. The holiday season has begun.

From the Dessert Cupboard

233

Cajeta Sundae

Cajeta is a sweet, dark, thick caramel, originally made from goat's milk in Mexico and stored in little boxes, called *cajetas*. Today it is usually found in bottles in Mexican markets. If you can't find it in your grocery store, you can make it at home from regular Eagle Brand condensed milk. It is simple and inexplicably delicious.

Makes 14 ounces

1 14-ounce can Eagle Brand sweetened condensed milk

Many people (including me) simply submerge the can in water, boil slowly for 4 to 6 hours (it always takes longer at high altitudes), and *voila!* . . . cajeta! There is a chance, however, of the can's bursting open and your getting spritzed, so it's probably best to remove the milk from the can and pour it into the top of a double boiler. (This way you can monitor it and tell when it's done.) Cook over a slow boil, stirring occasionally, about 4 to 5 hours, until it is medium brown. Perhaps the simplest way to cook it is to boil the can for 3 hours, then remove it to a double boiler for the last hour or two, stirring occasionally. This can easily be started one day and finished the next—but be sure to mark the can!

Spoon the warm cajeta over your favorite ice cream. A really high-quality vanilla or butter pecan ice cream is wonderful with it. Traditionally, you should sprinkle a few roasted peanuts on top.

Beatriz's Flan

Flans are probably the most popular dessert in every region of Mexico. They are an inheritance from Spain, where their tradition goes back centuries. Milk, eggs, and sugar, slowly cooked with vanilla, make a fine, delicately flavored custard. You can tell immediately by its smoothness and bubble-free texture that it has been made by a professional. Flans cooked in too hot an oven develop tiny bubbles in them, which makes for an undesirable spongy texture. The secret is slow cooking at low heat over a long period of time.

We used to get the best flan in the city at a fun neighborhood restaurant called Gringo's, opened by Marc Casas, an Argentine Basque who really knew foods. His dessert maker was an Argentinean woman named Beatriz Molina, and one of the restaurant's best dishes was Beatriz's flan.

As time passed, so did this little restaurant, and Beatriz and her husband came to work for The Fort. They have been with us for over ten years, and we never tire of her flans.

Serves 8

6 egg yolks
1 tablespoon vanilla extract
1 14-ounce can sweetened condensed milk
1 12-ounce can evaporated milk
1 cup fresh milk
1½ cups sugar

Preheat the oven to 350°F.

Mix together the egg yolks and vanilla, then add the condensed, evaporated, and fresh milk. Stir, don't beat, because beating will add air and result in a spongy flan.

Melt the sugar in a nonstick skillet, stirring almost constantly, until it becomes liquid and medium caramel in color. Watch it carefully! It will clump at first, then begin to melt. As the sugar melts, fill flan cups with very hot water. As soon as the sugar has caramelized, pour out the water from each cup one at a time and coat with caramel. Do this quickly—the syrup will harden almost instantly, and if it heats for even 30 seconds too long, it will turn to candy. Fill the cups with the flan mixture and place them in a bain-marie to cook. The easiest way

From the Dessert Cupboard

235

to do this is to place the cups in a large empty pan, put the pan in the oven, and then pour water into the pan so that it rises to a level just below the rims of the flan cups. Bake for 45 minutes.

Remove the cups of flan from the oven and the bain-marie and refrigerate, preferably overnight, to allow the caramel to liquefy. When you're ready to serve, run a knife around the edge of the cup, place a plate upside down on top of it, and flip it over so that the flan falls onto the plate topped with caramel.

Fur and Fringes: Mountain man Arnie Buchtel in buckskins and a pipeholder with beads and quillwork. Rolled fringes are authentic to the 1830s.

Tocino del Cielo

My wife and I spent several days in Andalucia, Spain, researching in the Seville Archives of the Indies for early information on Santa Fe. Every evening we drove out of Seville to spend the night at nearby Carmona Parador. This ancient castle is one of several important old buildings that the Spanish government has helped turn into excellent hotels, called *paradors*. It was at the Carmona Parador's restaurant that we first tasted Tocino del Cielo and fell in love with it. Tocino del Cielo translates as the "bacon of heaven." The name probably comes from the dark reddish brown color of the dish. It is an extraordinarily rich flan made with egg yolks and served in tiny portions.

Serves approximately 12

Topping:
2 **cups sugar**
1 **cup water**
1 **teaspoon lemon juice**

Flan:
9 **egg yolks (see Note)**
3 **whole eggs**
1 **teaspoon almond liqueur (optional)**
2¼ **cups water**
1½ **cups sugar**
   Peel of 1 lemon, grated

For the topping, combine the sugar, water, and lemon juice in a skillet and boil over medium heat without stirring (swirl the pan gently to blend) until the mixture turns dark brown. Don't let it brown too much, or it will taste bitter. Pour this into an 8-inch square pan. Tilt from side to side to coat the bottom, then set aside.

To make the custard, mix the egg yolks, eggs, and liqueur well and set aside.

In a saucepan or skillet, bring to a boil the water, sugar, and lemon peel. Allow to boil without stirring (swirl the pan gently to blend) for about 20 minutes, or until its color is a very light caramel. Pour the sugar mixture into the eggs very slowly, whisking constantly to avoid cooking the eggs instantly and scrambling them. Strain through a chi-

From the Dessert Cupboard

237

nois or fine-meshed sieve into the caramel-coated pan. Place the pan in a bain-marie filled with enough water to come three-quarters up the sides of the smaller pan. Use one sheet of aluminum foil to cover the top of both pans securely, crimping tightly to the edge. Don't tuck the foil underneath the pan, or the water will boil up into the flan, making it watery.

Preheat the oven to 350°F.

Place the bain-marie on a burner and cook over medium heat for 12 minutes, then move it to the oven and cook for 15 minutes. Remove from the oven and leave the flan in the bain-marie until cool, then chill in the refrigerator for at least 1 hour. Invert on a pretty platter to serve.

NOTE: Egg whites can be used for meringues or macaroons, or they can be frozen individually in ice cube trays and then placed in sealed plastic bags to be used as needed.

Queso Napolitano (Neapolitan Cheese)

In the early 1950s, *Gourmet* magazine published a story about a Yucatecan restaurant called Circulo del Sureste, or Club Mayan, in the working-class area of Mexico City. On our first trip to the restaurant we arrived to find young women patting out corn tortillas and chopping fresh roast chickens for soft tacos. We feasted on big steaming roasts of young pork, mounds of shrimp salad in huge *cazuelas,* wonderful cold *congrejos moros* (stone crabs) with claws bulging with meat, and water-based hot chocolate, served in little *porrones,* that you sweetened to taste. For dessert there was queso napolitano, a type of firm flan. It reposed on the counter like a great circular caramel-colored wedding cake. It cut and tasted like a soft cheese: sweet, rich, and glorious.

I sought the recipe for many years, and when I finally found it in *Chile Pepper* magazine, I discovered it was nothing more than a very large flan with cream cheese added to make it firm and creamy. Use a flan pan, or springform pan covered on the outside with aluminum foil to prevent leaking.

Serves 12

⅔ cup sugar

¼ cup water

1 14-ounce can sweetened condensed milk

1 12-ounce can evaporated milk

6 eggs

1 tablespoon vanilla extract

8 ounces cream cheese

Preheat the oven to 350°F.

Combine the sugar and water in a saucepan and cook on high heat, stirring several times to dissolve the sugar. When it comes to a boil, lower the heat to medium and simmer for about 30 minutes, swirling the pan often, until the sugar turns golden and caramelizes. Once the sugar begins to caramelize, the process will continue rapidly, so don't answer the phone or you may have to start over. Immediately pour the caramelized sugar into the flan mold and tilt so that it covers the bottom of the mold.

Combine the remaining ingredients and beat until smooth. Pour into the mold and cover with foil. Place the mold in a pan of water

From the Dessert Cupboard

239

that reaches to within an inch of the top. Place it in the center of the oven and bake for 40 to 50 minutes, or until a knife inserted in the center comes out clean.

This is best when well chilled, so allow the flan to cool overnight before unmolding and serving.

Leche Quemada

Father Geronimo Pelayo was a Mexican priest who wrote a cookbook in 1780 of recipes served to monastery priests of the late eighteenth century. I had the book translated from Old Spanish into contemporary Spanish and then into English. Then I set to work converting ingredients and methods into recipes for use in the home kitchen. They are, with only a few exceptions (such as lung with cloves), imaginative and wonderful. One of my favorites is this flan. Easy to make, it holds well because it is cooked slowly.

Serves 8

1 quart milk
½ cup sugar
6 eggs
1 teaspoon cinnamon
1 teaspoon cornstarch
½ teaspoon salt
Cinnamon and sugar for garnish

Preheat the oven to 325°F. Butter a 1½- or 2-quart ovenproof pottery or china serving bowl.

Mix—but do not beat—the milk, sugar, and eggs with the cinnamon, cornstarch, and salt. Cover the bowl tightly with aluminum foil. (Don't wrap the foil under the bowl, or it will transfer water and make the custard soggy.) Place the bowl in a bain-marie with enough water to come halfway up the sides of the serving bowl. Bake for 1½ hours. Remove the bain-marie from the oven and the bowl from the bain-marie, and allow to cool at room temperature before refrigerating. Serve cold with cinnamon and sugar sprinkled on top. Spoon into individual bowls at tableside.

Cider-Cooked Trapper's Fruit

During the fur trade days of the early nineteenth century, the trappers and the military relied heavily on dried fruits. Apples, apricots, peaches, and other dried fruits were often stewed to accompany meat or to serve as dessert. In The Fort's recipe, a compote of dried apples, spices, hazelnuts, and rum gets darker and darker, and more and more delicious, as it boils down. Serve it with Thanksgiving Buffalo Hump Roast (page 91) or Prime Rib Roast or as a dessert with a dollop of ice cream or a generous splash of heavy cream.

Serves 8

½ cup coarsely chopped hazelnuts, toasted
4 quarts apple cider
2 pounds dried apples
2 cups applesauce
3 tablespoons brown sugar or honey
½ cup fresh lemon juice
1 tablespoon coriander seeds
½ teaspoon ground cinnamon
½ teaspoon ground cloves
½ teaspoon grated nutmeg
½ cup golden raisins
1 tablespoon vanilla extract
1 cup Myers's rum

Combine all the ingredients except the rum in a large pot and bring to a boil over high heat. Lower the heat and simmer for at least 1 hour to reduce the liquid. Trapper's Fruit will be ready to eat whenever you're ready to eat it. At The Fort we like to cook it, covered, for several hours, stirring frequently to prevent burning. Just before serving, add the rum.

NOTE: My sister Mary adds fresh quinces to this dish. She cores them and cuts them into large chunks, then adds them along with all the other ingredients. They hold up well and add a nice flavor.

From the Dessert Cupboard

Bee-nanas

In 1954 I took my wife and daughter to a sleepy village on the coast of Mexico that a friend had told me would someday be a major resort. We debarked from one of three Aeronaves Convair flights per week onto a grassy airfield to see only a grass shack with a radio. A broken-down taxi bore us to the Paraiso Hotel, where we paid $5.60 daily for a room with a beautiful oceanfront view and all meals. It was hard to believe that Puerto Vallarta would ever change.

It was there that I had my first honeyed bananas flambé. Each night after dinner we watched with anticipation as our waiter brought out his chafing dish and simmered the local bananas in melted butter, dark honey, sweet limes, and rum. These were so wonderfully good that years later when we opened The Fort, I was pleased to find I could recreate the dish's intense sweet and sour flavors by cleverly injecting bananas with honey and lime juice and broiling them in their skins. One night I found the syringe, broken, in a kitchen drawer and asked the chef how he made do without it. "We stopped injecting the bananas weeks ago," he said. "And they taste exactly the same!" He was right; I'd been eating them all along and never noticed. The juices of the broiled bananas are sweet and flavorful all by themselves.

Serves 4

4 **bananas**
4 **tablespoons butter**
2 **tablespoons dark honey**
Juice of 1 small lime
Dash of ground cinnamon
¼ **cup dark rum**

Cut the bananas in half lengthwise, then in half crosswise, yielding 4 pieces per banana.

In a chafing dish, cook the butter, honey, lime juice, and cinnamon over high heat to boiling. Gently place the bananas in the chafing dish, flat side down. Lower the heat and simmer for 3 minutes, then add the rum. Light a match and carefully flame the dish.

Coat the banana pieces well with sauce and serve 4 pieces to a plate. These may also be arranged around a scoop of vanilla ice cream.

Variation

Bee-nanas Without the Bee

Here is my delicious, easy alternative to flambéed bananas.

Serves 8

   8 **bananas, unpeeled**

    Preheat a grill to high. If you're using an oven, set it to broil. Place the bananas on the grill and cook 5 minutes on each side, or until black on both sides. If cooking under the broiler, place the bananas on a foil-lined pan and broil 5 minutes on each side, or until black. Slit the peel and serve with an entree or as a dessert. The sweet, softened, warm bananas are wonderful with a scoop of vanilla ice cream.

From the Dessert Cupboard

Peaches Flamed in Scotch

When we first opened, we had a group of waiters who loved to do tableside cooking, so we took advantage of their skills. After they left, I learned that they moved from new restaurant to new restaurant, making off with the profits of poorly organized novice operations. Still, I wasn't sorry they'd passed through The Fort; it was hard to find truly professional servers, and they did an excellent job.

One night when we were serving peaches flamed with kirschwasser over ice cream, one of these waiters picked up a half cup of Scotch whiskey instead of the cherry brandy. Only after he had dramatically prepared the dessert at tableside and returned to the bar did he discover his mistake. I made my way to the table to apologize and was welcomed with exclamations about how delicious and unique the dessert was. I tasted it, and have flamed peaches in Scotch whiskey ever since.

Serves 6

   6 fresh peaches (or 3 if very large), preferably Freestone
   8 tablespoons (1 stick) sweet butter
   2 cups sugar
Juice of 2 lemons
Juice of 4 oranges
   3 ounces Cointreau or triple sec
   3 ounces Scotch whiskey
  ½ teaspoon ground cinnamon
   1 quart vanilla ice cream
Mint sprigs for garnish

Blanch the peaches by boiling them for 1 to 2 minutes. Plunge them into cold water, remove the skins, and then cut them in half.

In a skillet or chafing dish, melt the butter with the sugar and cook over medium heat, stirring, until the sugar begins to melt. Add the lemon and orange juice, and bring to a boil. Add the Cointreau and Scotch. Flame it with a match and when burning, add the peach halves. Coat with sauce and sprinkle with cinnamon.

Place the peach halves and sauce over the ice cream in dessert bowls. Garnish with a sprig of mint.

Vera's Caramel Canola Brownies

One day in 1988 a woman called asking if I'd ever consider hiring a baker who was eighty years old. "You bet I would. She probably knows more than all the rest of us!" I said. Vera Dahlquist, who had emigrated from Finland as a youngster, was a gifted baker. We and our guests enjoyed her banana cream pies and fragrant rolls, but our very favorite was a caramel canola brownie she invented. Instead of the usual cakey texture, these have a nice chewiness halfway between candy and brownies.

Do not use an electric mixer for this recipe, because you don't want too much air beaten into the batter. Hand-stirring will yield a chewier brownie.

Makes 15 large brownies

2½ **cups all-purpose flour**
3 **cups brown sugar**
3 **teaspoons baking powder**
¼ **teaspoon salt**
4 **eggs**
1¼ **cup (2½ sticks) butter or margarine, melted**
1 **teaspoon vanilla extract**
1 **cup chopped walnuts or pecans**
¼ **cup toasted canola seeds, poppy seeds, or sesame seeds**

Preheat the oven to 350°F. Grease and line a 9- by 13-inch baking pan with parchment paper.

In a large bowl, blend together the flour, brown sugar, baking powder, and salt. In a small bowl, beat the eggs slightly. Stir in the butter and vanilla extract. Add the egg mixture to the dry ingredients and blend well. Stir in the nuts and seeds.

Spread the batter in the prepared pan. Bake for 25 to 30 minutes, or until the center can be touched without leaving an indentation. *Do not overbake!*

From the Dessert Cupboard

Canola

In the 1970s, Canadian genetic engineers analyzed rape seed oil, a common lubricating oil for steam engines. Like many cruciform plants such as mustard, rape contained erucic acid, inedible to humans. The engineers worked to develop a genetically low-erucic rape seed. This accomplished, they named the oil "canola," for Canada and oil. Because it is so low in saturated fats, it is now the cooking oil of choice in North America.

Portugal Cakes

One evening we had the pleasure of serving Marie C. Meseroll, a fellow food historian who researched and compiled *A Pennsbury Manor Cookbook* with family recipes of William Penn provided by the Historical Society of Pennsylvania. One of the seventeenth-century recipes was for "Portugal Cakes." We found them so wonderfully tasty that we began to make them on special occasions as a dessert cake, without changing the recipe a bit. They have a texture somewhere between a cake, a cookie, and a scone, and are delicious served with coffee or tea.

Makes 18 cakes

1¼ cups sugar

2 cups all-purpose flour

½ pound (2 sticks) butter

1 tablespoon rose water (available at larger liquor stores) or sherry

Dash of mace

2 eggs

1 egg yolk

1 cup fresh or dried zante currants, blueberries, or cranberries (see Note)

⅓ cup water

Preheat the oven to 350°F.

Combine 1 cup sugar with the flour. Cream the butter and add half the sugar and flour mixture, the rose water or sherry, and the

mace. Add the eggs, egg yolk, and the rest of the flour mixture. Mix to form a thick dough. Stir in the fruit.

Grease a cupcake pan or spray with nonstick cooking oil. Fill with batter to three-quarters full. In a small pot, heat the water and ¼ cup sugar until the sugar is dissolved. Pour a small amount of syrup over each cake and bake for 20 minutes, or until light brown and the center can be touched without leaving an indentation. Be careful not to overbake or the sugar syrup will burn.

NOTE: If you are using dried fruit, plump them in hot water for several minutes and drain before adding to the batter.

VARIATION: For variety you can separate the plain dough into 3 bowls before adding the fruit and then add ⅓ cup of each fruit to the individual bowls.

From the Dessert Cupboard

247

Biscochitos

Christmas time in Santa Fe is delightful, with the cool, crisp winter air perfumed with smoke from cedar and pine nut fires. On Christmas Eve many Santa Feans travel south about forty miles to a Native American prayer ceremony and midnight Mass at a pueblo called San Felipe. It was there in 1948 that I ate my first biscochito.

These days my family holds an annual Christmas Eve street party in Santa Fe, building pitch pine fires along the roadside and giving traditional anise-cinnamon cookies to friends and passersby, along with hot cider to warm our bellies. The chile powder sprinkled on top enhances the cinnamon and adds a mild zip. It's fun to quiz your guests to see if anyone can name the elusive flavor!

Makes 6 to 8 dozen cookies

6 eggs
1 cup lard or vegetable shortening
4 cups sifted all-purpose flour, plus more if necessary
2 cups sugar
2 tablespoons anise seed
Rum or bourbon
Cinnamon to taste
Pinch of chile powder (optional)

Beat the eggs. In another bowl, combine the shortening and flour. Cream the sugar into the flour-shortening mixture. Add the anise seed to the eggs and enough flour to make a firm dough. Chill for about 1 hour.

Preheat the oven to 350°F.

Roll out the dough on a floured board until it is very thin, no thicker than ¼ inch. Cut it into your favorite cookie shapes. Brush the tops of the cookies with rum or bourbon, then sprinkle with cinnamon and chile powder. Bake on regular or insulated baking sheets for 3 to 5 minutes, or until barely brown. (They may take a few minutes longer on insulated baking sheets.) These are perfect with hot cider, steaming coffee, or cocoa.

Katze's Oatmeal Crackers

On December 13 of each year we enact the charming Swedish holiday ceremony of Santa Lucia, Queen of Light. Originally representing a blind Sicilian saint, Santa Lucia offers gifts of light and cookies to promise relief from the dark days and long nights of winter. A young woman dressed all in white and wearing a crown of evergreens and lighted candles walks slowly through the restaurant, offering cookies to guests. She is accompanied by several other young women in traditional Swedish dress singing "Santa Lucia." Everyone enjoys glögg, a drink of hot red wine and aquavit, and these cookies, a crisp, barely sweet cracker that my mother, Katze, learned from her grandmother.

Makes about 7 dozen crackers

2½ **cups oats**
  3 **cups all-purpose flour**
  1 **cup sugar**
  8 **tablespoons (1 stick) butter, softened**
  1 **teaspoon baking soda**
½ **cup warm water**
   Zest and juice of 1 lemon or orange

Preheat the oven to 325°F.

Combine all the ingredients and mix well. Divide into thirds and roll each third onto an oiled baking sheet to about an ⅛-inch thickness. Cut with a rolling cutter or knife into 30 crackers that are 2 by 4 inches and bake for 15 minutes.

In the unlikely event that these aren't gobbled up immediately, they keep well in an airtight container and freeze beautifully.

Margaret's Pumpkin Pie

For years after we opened The Fort we'd have lunch up in Indian Hills a few miles away. The Indian Hills Café was run by Don and Margaret Weiss. She was one super cook! Her pies were so good that instead of wedding cake, Carrie and I ordered eighteen pies to serve our guests. She made dandy strawberry and raspberry chiffon pies, great peach and rhubarb pies, but primo of all were her pumpkin pies. This is Margaret's recipe, a delightful mild pie that we serve each Thanksgiving.

1½ cups sugar
2 eggs
1¼ teaspoons cinnamon
¼ teaspoon salt
1 15-ounce can pumpkin (*not* pumpkin pie filling)
1¼ cups milk
1 uncooked 10-inch deep-dish pie shell or 2 uncooked 9-inch pie shells

Preheat the oven to 350°F.

Gently whisk together the sugar, eggs, cinnamon, and salt. Fold in the pumpkin and gradually fold in the milk. Pour into the 10-inch pie shell and bake for 1 hour and 45 minutes to 2 hours, or until a knife inserted in the center comes out clean. For a thinner pie, pour into two 9-inch pie shells and bake for approximately 1 hour and 25 minutes.

Bobbie's Cheesecake

At Christmastime, longtime friend Bobbie Chaim always presents me with one of her cheesecakes. It's about five inches tall, and is the creamiest, lightest, moistest, most delicious slice of heaven ever. Kept sealed in the refrigerator, it invites sinful snacking. The crust contains vanilla sugar, an easy-to-make preparation that Bobbie claims is the secret of Viennese baking. A tablespoon of it in a recipe or sprinkled over a pastry just before baking makes all the difference in the world.

We've made thousands of these wonderful cheesecakes. In spite of repeated requests to sell them wholesale, we simply don't have the kitchen space. Instead, we concentrate on maintaining the high quality of the ones we serve.

The recipe is simple enough, but *don't deviate*! And always use only Kraft Philadelphia Brand cream cheese. Other packaged cream cheeses are too salty, and fresh cream cheese doesn't contain necessary stabilizers.

Serves 12

German Mürbteig Crust:
1½ cups all-purpose flour
¾ teaspoon baking powder
⅓ cup sugar
Pinch of salt
1 tablespoon vanilla sugar (see Notes)
1 egg
8 tablespoons (1 stick) margarine or butter, softened

Filling:
4 egg whites, beaten until fairly stiff (½ cup to a scant ¾ cup)
1 cup sugar
¼ teaspoon vanilla extract (the highest quality available; we use Neillsen Massey; see Suppliers, page 303)
24 ounces Kraft Philadelphia Brand cream cheese

Topping:
1 pint sour cream
2 tablespoons sugar
½ teaspoon vanilla extract

From the Dessert Cupboard

251

Preheat the oven to 350°F (see Notes).

For the crust, combine the dry ingredients. Add the egg and softened butter, and mix until the dough forms a ball. This is easiest to do in a standing mixer with a dough hook attachment. Pat the dough in an 8-inch springform pan, lining the bottom and sides all the way to the top. Try to achieve a uniform thickness.

For the filling, beat the egg whites until fairly stiff but not dry. Add the sugar slowly and then add the vanilla. Slowly, in small amounts, add the cream cheese. Mix to smooth the major lumps, but be careful not to overbeat. Pour into the crust-lined pan and bake for 25 minutes. Remove from the oven and set aside.

Raise the oven temperature to 500°F. While the oven is heating, prepare the topping: Combine the sour cream, sugar, and vanilla. Spread very gently on the top of the cheesecake and bake for 5 minutes. Let cool at room temperature and then refrigerate. Remove the springform pan and keep tightly covered with plastic wrap. Serve well chilled.

NOTES: To make vanilla sugar, place several vanilla beans in a tall jar (the kind that olives come in). Pour sugar over the beans to nearly fill the jar. Shake it up a bit, then put the jar in your spice cabinet. After a week you'll have lovely vanilla sugar! Simply replace the sugar with fresh as you use it.

The time and temperature for this recipe work perfectly at Denver's mile-high altitude. At sea level, bake for 22 minutes at 350°F and 4 minutes at 500°F.

President Andrew Jackson's Trifle

A year before Bent's Fort was built in 1833, President Andrew Jackson completed his four-year term as head of the nation. Known as "Old Hickory" because he'd bend but not break, Jackson had a sweet tooth and favored this dessert. It's an almond custard over sherry-soaked macaroons and topped with orange marmalade, sherry-flavored whipped cream, and almonds.

We serve it on special occasions commemorating historic events. In 1996 we made it for the 150th anniversary celebration of Charles Bent's appointment as governor of New Mexico. As the mountain men would say, "It war some!" Today we'd probably say, "Awesome!"

Serves 8 to 10

2 cups milk
⅓ cup sugar
Dash of salt
1½ tablespoons cornstarch
2 eggs
½ teaspoon almond extract
½ pound soft almond macaroons
½ cup sweet sherry
1 cup orange or grapefruit marmalade

Topping:
½ pint heavy (whipping) cream
2 teaspoons sugar
1 teaspoon sweet sherry

½ cup toasted slivered almonds

In a saucepan, heat the milk until it almost boils. Place the sugar, salt, cornstarch, and eggs in the top of a double boiler over medium heat. Beat until smooth, then add the milk a little at a time. Whisk well. Stir until the custard has the consistency of mayonnaise, then flavor with almond extract and allow to cool.

Lay the macaroons on the bottom of a glass serving bowl. Pour the sherry over them, then cover with the custard. Spread the marmalade on the top.

To make the topping, beat the heavy cream, sugar, and sherry until the cream holds its shape. Top the trifle with the whipped cream and garnish with the almond slivers. Chill before serving.

From the Dessert Cupboard

Bird's Nest Pudding

Easter wasn't Easter at our house when I was a child without Bird's Nest Pudding. I have no idea where my mother learned the dish. It probably came from her mother's English Quaker ancestors, the Fox family. I found a similar recipe with the same name in *Brigg's Cookery,* published in London in 1788.

It's basically a flavored blancmange molded in the shape of eggs and laid in a nest of candied orange and grapefruit strips on a bed of tasty wine gelatin. It's lots of fun for guests to choose which color egg they want. As a boy, I loved all of them—especially the green mint, blue almond, and pale vanilla.

Because the recipe calls for a dozen empty eggshells to use as molds, I accumulate shells over a period of several weeks, storing them in an egg carton until I have enough. Otherwise, when you make this dish, plan on omelets for dinner!

Makes 12 custard eggs

1 dozen egg shells (see Note)

Wine gelatin for nest:
2 tablespoons plain gelatin
½ cup cold water
1⅔ cups boiling water
1 cup sugar
⅓ cup orange juice
1 cup wine (sherry or Madeira is best, but not cooking sherry)
3 tablespoons lemon juice

Blancmange for eggs:
2½ cups milk, scalded
1⅓ cups sugar
1 tablespoon cornstarch
1 teaspoon vanilla extract
Salt
2 tablespoons plain gelatin
½ cup cold water
½ teaspoon concentrated vanilla flavoring
2 drops yellow food coloring (optional)
½ teaspoon concentrated mint flavoring

2 drops green food coloring (optional)
½ teaspoon concentrated almond flavoring
2 drops blue food coloring (optional)

Candied orange peel nest:
2 cups orange or grapefruit peel (no white pith), to use as straw
Water
1 cup sugar

1 pint heavy cream for serving

To make the wine gelatin, sprinkle the gelatin on the cold water and let it soften according to the package instructions. Add the boiling water, sugar, orange juice, wine, and lemon juice. Stir until the sugar is dissolved. Fill a bowl ½ to ⅔ full with the wine gelatin and chill for 3 to 5 hours, until set.

To make the blancmange, combine the milk, sugar, cornstarch, vanilla, and salt to taste in a double boiler until the mixture thickens.

Sprinkle the gelatin on the cold water and let it soften according to the package instructions. Add to the custard and stir well.

Divide the custard equally among 3 bowls. To make different-flavored eggs, add vanilla flavoring and yellow food coloring to one bowl, mint flavoring and green food coloring to the second, and almond flavoring and blue food coloring to the third. Stir to combine.

Rinse the eggshells with cold water to moisten and carefully pour in the custard. Return the eggshells to the carton with the open end up and chill until set, at least 3 hours.

While the eggs and gelatin are chilling, prepare the candied peel. Place the peel in a saucepan with 1⅓ cups cold water and bring to a boil. Simmer for 15 minutes, drain, and set aside. Bring ½ cup water and ¼ cup sugar to a boil and add the citrus strips. Boil until the syrup reaches the soft ball stage. (Use a candy thermometer if you're not sure.) Remove the citrus strips and allow to cool, then roll them in the ¾ cup sugar.

When the gelatin has set, build a "nest" of citrus strips around the edge of the wine gelatin.

When you're ready to serve, carefully crack and peel the custard eggs and set them on the wine gelatin so that they look as if they're in a nest.

Let each guest request the flavor egg he or she prefers. Spoon a portion of gelatin, candied peel, and 1 or 2 eggs into a small bowl and serve with heavy cream.

NOTE: Using the point of a knife, open the eggs at the large end, carefully breaking a hole ½ to ¾ inch in diameter. Gently pour the contents of the egg into a bowl. After removing the egg, rinse the shells well with cold water and let dry.

Winter Quarters at Bent's Fort

It was a zinger of a first night! Carrie and I had slept on a buffalo robe, covered by Rio Grande blankets, on the floor of William Bent's room at Bent's Fort in La Junta, Colorado. Morning crept slowly upon us with the mooing of the milk cow. At 6 A.M. the watchtower bell announced the beginning of the day—the beginning of a day in March 1846. Shivering in the cold, we donned our nineteenth-century clothes and signed for "employment" with the Bent, St. Vrain Company, agreeing to various conditions and to submit to "whatever disciplines The Company might meet [sic] out."

One hundred and twenty-seven years after its destruction in 1849, Bent's Fort rose again in 1976. Western historians across the nation cheered when the National Park Service spent several million dollars rebuilding it from bare ground during the American bicentennial year. Sometimes called the "Sturbridge Village of the West," this famed mud-and-straw adobe brick citadel stands proudly some 160 miles southeast of Denver.

We had joined a group of twenty-two men and women, a mix of interpretive historians and buckskinners, for a three-day reenactment of wintering at Bent's Fort, organized by the National Park Service. We had no idea it would be more than just an easy adventure.

Participants were divided into three groups: hunters, trappers, and outfitters; tradesmen; and domestics. Carrie and I signed on with the domestics and the captain sparingly offered us twenty-five cents per day. (I accepted it, but what he didn't know about was my store of good, French St. Julian Medoc wines, including a bottle of 1847 Madeira!) It was time to inspect the kitchen.

A great open stone fireplace dominated the kitchen area. There were two work tables, a water barrel with gourd, several dull "Greens" (Green River skinning knives), an ax, and round birch boxes of various spices used at that time: oregano, dry coriander (called *cilantro* by the fort's Mexican employees), ginger, clove, cinnamon, black pepper, and ground red chile pepper. An adjacent cellar boasted hanging hams, bacon, and barrels of staples such as rice, pinto and red beans, pilot bread, pearl barley, and green coffee.

Some of the other male participants assigned to be tradespeople learned the blacksmith's skills, while others in the carpenter's shop learned to make wagon spokes with a drawknife. The "trappers" actually learned to set and bait traps with castorium (beaver sex scent). Black powder rifle repair, horse and mule packing, sinew sewing, wagon wheel repair, and other nineteenth-century frontier skills were learned and practiced.

With the domestics, my first chore was to make lots of coffee. Pan-roasting green coffee and grinding came first, then brewing. Our next job was making breakfast for twenty-five cold, hungry trappers, tradesmen, and domestics. Scrambled eggs, thick bacon, red chile sauce, and singed biscuits were cooked over the open fireplace. The blacksmiths had made a crane from which swung the coffeepot, griddle, or the fat, cast teapot over a blazing fire. Pots and Dutch ovens on spiders acted as bakers, roasters, and boilers.

Clouds of smoke regularly filled the kitchen, and there was only enough light when the doors were opened. But then, while the smoke and darkness departed, the bitter winter winds came in.

After breakfast at ten and a hitching demonstration, an eleven-month-old buffalo was killed quickly with a rifle and the carcass elevated and skinned by the trappers. They used special care to keep the paunch (stomach) intact so that I might use it for a cooking demonstration the next day.

Then it was time to start preparing supper, to be ready at three. We domestics soon discovered that it was a tremendous job. We had to milk the cow, strain the milk, churn the butter, carry the wood and water, make the candles, kill and pluck the chickens, mix and knead the bread, pat the tortillas, grind the chiles, cut the meat, wash the multitude of dishes and glasses, stoke the horno beehive oven, and bake the bread and roasts. Five of us were exhausted providing food every day for twenty-five people.

Just before dinner "Mr. Bent" arrived. With a stern patrician look he designated who would sit at the first table and who at the second. Much as in medieval England, the American West observed the custom of "first table," "second table," and so on. Important personages and guests sat at first table and were served first and got the very best food and drink.

Sometime long after midnight Saturday we were awakened by musket shots, shouting, and an Indian attack alarm. It was very realistic, and you wondered how Bent had felt with some six thousand lodges of Cheyennes camped just outside these walls!

Before it seemed possible, it was time to prepare Sunday dinner. It consisted of Hailstorm 1840-style mint juleps and appetizers of pickled oysters and fresh buffalo tongue in a vinaigrette sauce. Next came beaver tail soup, cooked the old way with red-hot rocks placed with the broth in the suspended buffalo paunch. As a main course we served horno-roasted haunch of fresh buffalo with posole corn and red chile. Wines were homemade chokecherry and the French Medoc red bordeaux. Hot Trapper's Fruit made a fine, sweet ending to the feast.

After dinner most of the men retired upstairs to a special bar and billiard room. We drank a bottle of 1847 Madeira. It infused our mouths with a rich, complex, intense, and almost burned grape sweetness. Those who had transformed the grapes into wine when Bent's Fort was bustling with activity in 1847 were now long forgotten; six generations had passed. But the wine was a fine way to celebrate those who had gone before us.

(Information about living history activities at Bent's Fort may be obtained by writing to Bent's Fort National Historic Site, 35110 Highway 194 East, La Junta, CO 81050.)

Capirotada

It is quite likely that the many apple orchards of New Mexico grew from seeds brought from Europe in the very early days by French and Spanish priests, when a supply wagon train came from Mexico to the missions every two years. Later, more frequent wagon trains continued to bring wines, fruit, grape shoots, chocolate, cheeses, and delicacies north to New Mexico.

A dessert mentioned by many travelers along the Mexican part of the Santa Fe Trail after 1825 was *capirotada,* a bread pudding dating back at least to medieval days. Capirotada is a Lenten dish and one of the things that makes the season of sorrow a pleasant time in Mexico.

Diego Granado's cookbook, *Libro del Arte Cozina,* published in 1599, lists three capirotada recipes. They are entrees that use baked layers of toasted bread, onion, and cheese with various additions of meat, quail, or partridge, wine, and a topping of sweet meringue. From this unusual recipe has evolved today's capirotada, or *sopa,* as it's now called in New Mexico. Onions in a dessert may seem strange, but when cooked, they add to the pleasing applelike flavor. This dish was often called "Spotted Dog" because of the raisins and because the mountain men had little patience with the Spanish language.

Serves 6

1½ cups crushed piloncillo or brown sugar
1 cup water
½ medium onion, finely chopped
3 eggs
1½ cups milk
4 cups toasted bread, cut or torn into approximately 1½-inch pieces
¾ cup sultana raisins (plumped in hot water if too dry)
½ cup sliced apples
4 tablespoons butter or margarine
1½ teaspoons ground cinnamon
½ teaspoon grated nutmeg
4 ounces yellow cheddar cheese, grated (1 cup)
Heavy cream for pouring on top

Preheat the oven to 350°F.

Boil the sugar and water to make a syrup approximately the consistency of maple syrup. Add the onion and continue boiling for 5 minutes.

In a separate bowl, stir together the eggs and milk. Don't beat them!

In a 3-quart baking dish, layer the bread, raisins, apples, butter, cinnamon, and nutmeg. Pour the syrup-onion mixture on top, then the egg-milk mixture. Push down the filling with a spoon to make sure all the ingredients become moist. Bake for approximately 40 minutes, remove from the oven, and spread the cheese on top. Return it to the oven for 5 minutes, or until the cheese is melted and well browned. The pudding should absorb all the liquid and be very moist, with a well-browned top. If it seems to be getting too brown, cover with foil for the remainder of the cooking time. Serve hot with a bit of cold heavy cream poured over each serving.

NOTE: Capirotada may be baked ahead of time, except for the cheese topping. Thirty minutes before serving, preheat the oven to 350°F. Cover the capirotada and heat for 20 minutes. Top with the cheese and return to the oven for 5 minutes to allow the cheese to melt and begin to brown.

Negrita

Named "best chocolate dessert in Denver" by *Westword* newspaper, Denver's equivalent of New York City's *Village Voice*, the *negrita*, or "little black one," originated in the Vera Cruz region of Mexico. While it bears a resemblance to chocolate mousse, its texture is very different—firmer, like a slightly soft chocolate bar. Unlike many highly concentrated chocolate desserts, of which a few bites are enough, this one begs for the dish to be scraped (or licked) clean. A spoonful on the tip of the tongue followed by hot coffee is luscious. This recipe can be halved.

Serves 10

1¼ pounds Ghirardelli sweet dark chocolate (see Note)
6 eggs
1 tablespoon vanilla extract
¼ cup dark rum (preferably Myer's, but any high-quality dark rum will do)
½ pint heavy cream, whipped for topping

To melt the chocolate, place it in a double boiler over simmering water. Do not let the water touch the bottom of the bowl holding the chocolate. Stir the chocolate periodically. When it is about half melted, turn off the heat and leave it over the warm water to finish melting and to keep it warm.

Separate the eggs. In a dry, clean bowl, beat the egg whites until stiff. In a separate bowl, beat the egg yolks until they're pale yellow.

Carefully add the chocolate, vanilla, and rum to the egg yolks, then fold in the beaten whites. Stir until thoroughly blended. Ladle into 2½-ounce ramekins or wineglasses and chill. Serve topped with whipped cream.

NOTE: Don't use chocolate chips for this recipe. They don't contain as much cocoa butter as whole bars do, and they don't melt as well or taste as rich.

It is important not to let the chocolate cool too much before blending with the other ingredients, or it will become grainy. If you think it has become too cool by the time you're ready to use it, turn on the heat to warm it slightly.

VARIATIONS: Vary this according to your own taste by using liqueurs other than rum. Kahlua makes for an unforgettable coffee-chocolate dessert, and Grand Marnier is also a delicious substitute.

From the Dessert Cupboard

Charlotte's Strawberry Surprise

The kitchen at Bent's Fort in the 1840s was run by Charlotte Green, who was known far and wide for her cooking. We named this wonderful strawberry sorbet, or *granita,* for her, although it's actually an invention of Marian Cunningham, author of the revised *Fannie Farmer Cookbook.*

If you use a sugar substitute, this dish contains no fat, no sugar, no cholesterol, and only eighteen calories per serving—six in each strawberry. It's ideal for diabetics and dieters or those who simply prefer a terrific light end to a heavy meal. The same recipe works deliciously with other fruits: blueberries, peaches, mangos, papayas, and so forth.

Serves 6

18 large strawberries, stemmed, cut in half, and frozen hard (Driscolls are my favorite)

3 egg whites

6 teaspoons (or packets) sugar or artificial sweetener such as NutraSweet

2 tablespoons almond extract

2 tablespoons fresh lemon juice

6 mint leaves for garnish

Place everything except the mint in a food processor and whirl. The mixture will first break into ice crystals. Let the machine keep running until the mixture homogenizes and turns creamy. Stop the processor periodically to scrape the sides. Don't try to prepare more than 6 servings at a time. Spoon the sorbet into pretty bowls or wineglasses and garnish with a mint leaf.

This may be made ahead of time and frozen. Remove from the freezer about 15 minutes before serving. The fresher it is, though, the creamier it will be.

Oatmeal Ice Cream

A Denver friend who emigrated to Scotland sent me a Scottish cookbook. One of the recipes called for toasted oatmeal sprinkled over ice cream. We found that actually mixing the oatmeal into the ice cream was best. It's simple to make using store-bought ice cream.

    1 **quart French vanilla ice cream**
    1 **cup regular or instant oatmeal flakes (whole regular flakes are best)**

Place the ice cream in the refrigerator to soften.

Toast the oatmeal by stirring it constantly in a skillet over medium heat until golden brown. Combine the ice cream and oatmeal in a large bowl and stir quickly to mix, then return it to the original ice cream container and freeze.

Give it at least a few hours to set before serving with a truly good hot fudge sauce. The best one I know is called Narsai's Chocolate Decadence, made by Narsai David in Berkeley, California (see Suppliers, page 303). When poured warm over ice cream, it hardens into a rich chocolate shell.

A Historic Scottish Explorer and a Modern Bear

Sissy, our tamed black bear, lived at The Fort for twenty years, and perhaps her most trying experience was with Scottish bagpipes.

I had always dreamed of having my own piper to pipe me and my guests to dinner in the style of Sir William Drummond Stewart, a famous early nineteenth-century noble Scottish visitor to the American West. On my fortieth birthday my wife arranged this esoteric delight. Piper Roy Hess came out for a special dinner and walked the ramparts of The Fort playing "The Blue Bells of Scotland" and "Scotland the Brave." Then there was a Grand Procession to the dining hall. Our piper in full regalia led the way. My wife and I followed in historic western dress, my knee-high black drover's boots striding in time with the piper's music. Behind us came the manager and Sissy Bear, all five hundred pounds of her, solemnly marching in cadence. A party of friends took up the rear.

What a dream of glory had come true! 'Twas like being king of your own castle. All went perfectly until the piper turned and walked toward the bear in the dining room. "Oh, no . . . not me!" you could see Sissy thinking. She bolted, dragging the manager at the end of the chain back out of the restaurant to safety. *Sic transit gloria!*

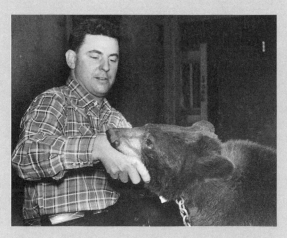

Joseph A Jancar, who helped build The Fort and is now eighty-six, wrote to me recently about Sissy, "A bear feels like a big quilt rolled into a bundle." That's the best description of Sissy Bear I've heard. Sometimes, though, a bear just feels like a big thumb.

Chocolate Hazelnut Ice Cream Pie

For many years we served a scrumptious chocolate ice cream pie with a gingersnap crust. The bottom layer was dark chocolate ice cream. The second layer was light chocolate ice cream separated from the dark with a lusty squirt of Tia Maria and a layer of vanilla praline ice cream.

    1   pint French vanilla ice cream
    ½   cup granulated sugar
    ½   cup toasted hazelnuts
    ½   pound gingersnaps
    5½ tablespoons butter, softened
    1   pint dark chocolate fudge ice cream
    1   pint light chocolate ice cream
    2   tablespoons Tia Maria or Kahlua coffee liqueur
        Hot fudge (optional)
        Whipped cream (optional)

Soften the French vanilla ice cream in the refrigerator for about 1 hour.

In a heavy skillet, preferably cast iron, heat the sugar until melted and golden. Stir in the hazelnuts. Spread buttered aluminum foil on a flat surface and pour the nut-caramel mixture onto it. Allow it to cool, then coarsely crush it with a rolling pin. Mix these pieces into the ice cream and return it to the freezer.

Preheat the oven to 375°F.

Whirl the gingersnaps in a food processor with the butter, turning the processor on and off intermittently until the crumbs have a coarse consistency. Press the mixture into a 9-inch pie plate, carefully working it up the edges. Place another pie plate on top to hold it in place. Bake for 20 minutes, or until the crust is solid. Allow to cool completely.

Soften the ice creams by keeping them in the refrigerator for about 1 hour.

To construct the pie, use a large spatula to spread the dark chocolate ice cream on the shell, then the coffee liqueur, followed by a layer of the light chocolate, then a layer of the vanilla praline. Cover and refreeze until ready to serve.

Pour good hot fudge on the top of each slice or serve with whipped cream, as you prefer. (My favorite hot fudge sauce is Narsai's; see Suppliers, page 303.)

From the Dessert Cupboard

Schwartzwald Mexican Ice Cream Pie

Our newest ice cream pie is a masterpiece of sinful delight. We start with a Famous Chocolate Wafer crust, douse it with Kahlua coffee liqueur, add dried cherries and a thick filling of light Mexican chocolate ice cream, and then top with Enstrom's chocolate almond toffee candy made in Grand Junction, Colorado. We buy our ice cream from Liks, a maker of fine custom ice creams right here in Denver. They make wonderful ice creams for The Fort, among them ginger, toasted oatmeal, and Mexican chocolate. Variations on these are easy to make at home.

Serves 12

- 2 quarts chocolate or light chocolate ice cream
- 1 cup dried cherries (check for pits; see Notes)
- 1 9-ounce box Nabisco Famous Chocolate Wafers, crushed (2 cups; see Notes)
- 8 tablespoons (1 stick) butter, softened
- 2 ounces Kahlua or other coffee liqueur
- 2 tablespoons cinnamon
- 1 cup crushed chocolate almond toffee candy (for Enstrom's, see Suppliers, page 303)

Let the ice cream soften in the refrigerator for about 1 hour, until just soft enough to blend with the cinnamon.

Refresh the dry cherries by soaking them in hot water for about 30 minutes.

Mix the chocolate wafer crumbs with the butter. With a spatula, press the mixture evenly into a 10-inch springform pan, lining the bottom and sides. Chill. When the crust has set, sprinkle the cherries on the bottom and then sprinkle with the coffee liqueur.

When the ice cream has softened just enough to stir in a standing mixer, make Mexican chocolate ice cream by blending in the cinnamon. It's best to do this in a mixer because the ice cream won't have to soften too much. When the cinnamon is thoroughly incorporated into the ice cream, spoon it into the crust and pour the crushed almond toffee on the top. Freeze and allow a day before eating (if you can!) so that the flavors blend and it freezes thoroughly.

NOTES: Crushing the chocolate wafers is most easily done in a food processor.

For a real treat, refresh the cherries in Cherry Heering, a Danish liqueur.

Remy Dessert in a Glass

Years ago, just for fun, I put three ounces of Remy Martin VSOP cognac in a blender with three scoops of vanilla ice cream, and whipped it up. Oooh! So good! Serve it as we do at The Fort, in a snifter.

Holly's Adobe Sundae

During our first years of business, my family lived on the second floor of The Fort. One day I caught my nine-year-old daughter, Holly, sneaking ice cream out of the kitchen for her friends. At that time we were serving squares of French vanilla ice cream with different toppings. Holly had sprinkled a few blocks with powdered Mexican hot chocolate mix. They were reddish brown and looked just like a miniature version of the adobe bricks of The Fort. The simple dish went on the menu. Today, a gummy rattlesnake candy lurks atop each serving.

  1 **16-ounce can Nestlé Quik or other sweetened hot chocolate
     mix**
½ **cup granulated sugar**
  2 **tablespoons powdered cinnamon**
Vanilla ice cream

Thoroughly combine the hot chocolate mix, sugar, and cinnamon. Sprinkle over the ice cream.

Wild Huckleberry Sundae

In 1965 I took a motorcycle trip through the Canadian Rockies, then south through western Montana. I stopped one day at the north end of Flathead Lake, just south of Kalispell. There I discovered an interesting enterprise. My memory is that Eva Gates and her husband had converted the garage of their small home into a little factory.

Inside the garage a few women worked in whites over eight little gas burners on which rested six-pint oval cooking pans. Using the traditional formula of equal parts sugar and fruit, Mrs. Gates was making the finest preserves I had ever tasted. While she made other preserves—strawberries and cherry, as I recall—the blackcap raspberry and the blueberrylike wild huckleberry preserves were to dream about. When I returned to Colorado, I ordered her syrups and preserves and sold them at The Fort.

Then I lost track of Eva Gates until I was called to do the promotion for a gourmet marketplace in Littleton, a suburb of Denver. There on the shelves were jars of Eva's huckleberries! I rushed home and wrote a radio commercial telling about how good these were. The shelves emptied, for it seems that the very word "huckleberry" has a magical appeal.

In 1986 I sought the Gateses again. I found that Eva had passed away but her granddaughter was running the company, still producing superb preserves.

The recipe is simple—just serve high-quality vanilla ice cream topped with either huckleberry preserves or syrup.

If huckleberry products aren't available at a local grocery, Eva Gates's products are available by mail order (see Suppliers, page 303).

Jolly Rancher Watermelon Sundae

The Jolly Rancher candy company is located near Golden, Colorado, just north of The Fort. One of their best products is a hard candy that is watermelon in both color and flavor. Years ago I approached the factory and asked if they'd concoct a sundae topping of unsellable broken pieces of candy. They agreed, and produced a syrup that poured at room temperature and yet hardened atop cold ice cream. The combination of brittle watermelon over soft vanilla ice cream is superb.

Makes about 2 pints

2 cups Jolly Rancher watermelon candy pieces
2 cups corn syrup
¾ cup water

Place the candy in an airtight plastic bag, then place this inside a second plastic bag. With a rolling pin or mallet break the candy into small pieces. Pour them into a saucepan along with the corn syrup and water. Heat over medium heat, stirring occasionally, until the candy has melted and a uniform syrup has formed. Don't boil! Bottle and use it over ice cream.

Chocolate Chile Cake

In the early 1500s, Montezuma in his Mexico City palace drank chocolate daily, usually with red chile in it. Apparently the king knew that chile, in small amounts, amplifies and enriches the taste of chocolate. This is also known by Jane Butel, the noted cookbook author and specialist in Mexican cookery, who generously provided the recipe from which this cake was adapted. At The Fort it's the centerpiece of a birthday and anniversary ritual from which good-natured celebrants emerge with a photo of themselves in a horned buffalo or coyote hat.

Serves 12

Chocolate chile cake:
- 2 tablespoons New Mexico medium-ground red chile powder (Dixon is the best)
- 2 cups water
- 1 tablespoon vanilla extract
- 1 cup plus 2 tablespoons all-purpose flour
- 1 cup plus 2 tablespoons cake flour (not self-rising)
- 2 cups granulated sugar
- 1 teaspoon baking soda
- ½ teaspoon salt
- ½ cup unsweetened, nonalkalized cocoa powder, such as Hershey, Nestlé, or Ghirardelli (do *not* use Dutch process)
- ½ pound (2 sticks) unsalted butter, cut into pieces and softened
- ½ cup buttermilk
- 2 large eggs, at room temperature

Chocolate frosting:
- ¾ cup unsalted butter
- ¾ cup unsweetened nonalkalized cocoa powder
- ¼ cup plus 2 tablespoons buttermilk
- 1½ pounds (5 to 6 cups unpacked) confectioners' sugar
- 1½ tablespoons bourbon
- 3 tablespoons vanilla extract

- 1½ cups chopped walnuts

For the cake, preheat the oven to 350°F and place a rack in the center of the oven. Butter two 9-inch round cake pans. Lightly dust the sides of the pans with flour, tapping out the excess, and line the bottoms with circles of parchment or waxed paper.

In a medium saucepan, cook the chile powder in 1 cup of the water over medium heat until simmering. Remove the pan from the heat, stir in the vanilla, and set aside.

Using a mixer with a wire whip attachment for best results, combine the flours, sugar, baking soda, salt, and cocoa, and beat on low speed until well mixed. Add the softened butter to the dry mixture and beat thoroughly on medium-low speed. The mixture should be a uniform, grainy texture. Raise the speed to medium and gradually add the remaining cup of water and the buttermilk. Add the eggs one at a time, beating well after each addition.

Slowly add the hot water–chile mixture and continue to beat just until well combined; be sure not to overbeat. Pour the mixture equally into the pans and bake for 35 to 40 minutes, or until a toothpick inserted in the center of each layer comes out clean.

To cool, set the pans on a wire rack for 15 minutes. Then turn the cakes out onto the rack, remove the paper from the bottom, and immediately reinvert so that the risen tops don't flatten. Let sit until completely cool before frosting.

For the frosting, combine the butter and cocoa in a large saucepan and melt over medium heat. Stir in the buttermilk. Add the confectioners' sugar a little at a time, stirring with a wire whisk between additions. Stir in the bourbon and vanilla. The frosting should stiffen as it cools. (In warm weather you may need to refrigerate it.) When it has reached a spreadable consistency, you can assemble the cake.

If necessary, trim the tops of the cakes so that they are level. Place one of the cake layers on a 9-inch round cardboard cake circle. Spread 1 cup of the frosting over the cake layer. Sprinkle 1 cup of the chopped walnuts evenly over the frosting. Place the second layer of cake on the frosted base. Use the remaining frosting to cover the top and sides of the cake. Finish the top of the cake by holding the spatula at a slight angle and making several strokes to smooth the top. To decorate the cake, press the remaining walnuts against the lower half of the sides and on top of the cake.

Pink Cherry Blossom Ginger Ice Cream

While visiting Tokyo, I loved exploring the food halls in the basements of the major department stores. There, among all manner of exciting foods, I was particularly enticed by the soft pink color of a little plastic bag. Noticing my questioning look, an older Japanese man explained it was preserved cherry blossoms, used for coloring foods such as sushi yo shoga (gari), the sweet, pickled ginger chips traditionally served with sushi. I'm immensely fond of pickled ginger, and when I returned home, I chopped some of it into a fine consistency and stirred it into vanilla ice cream. I've always liked ginger ice cream, but the ginger ice cream I'd had was made with candied ginger and lacked the zingy zest of pickled ginger. This is excitingly delicious.

1 quart softened high-quality vanilla ice cream (Häagen-Dazs is my favorite national brand)

¾ to 1 cup very finely chopped sushi yo shoga (gari) (pickled sweet pink ginger; see Note)

Red food coloring (optional)

Soften the ice cream in the refrigerator for about 1 hour, then blend in the ginger. The easiest way to do this is in a standing mixer. To give ice cream a very light pink color, add a few drops of red food coloring. Replace in the original container and refreeze for at least 2 hours.

NOTE: Be sure to use the right kind of ginger. Sushi yo shoga (or gari) is a different, sweeter ginger than the salty, bright red julienned beni-shoga (or kizami-shoga), used in the Fort Dinner Salad.

Green Chile Ice Cream

Over thirty years ago I was given a membership in the International Connoisseurs of Green and Red Chile, better known as the ICGRC. We met in church social rooms and restaurants, including The Fort. While it was great fun to taste unusual chile dishes at Moroccan and Thai restaurants, my favorite meetings were the potluck evenings. On these nights members began arriving at 7 P.M., each couple bearing a dish to feed at least eight. My secretary, Leili Olsen, and her husband, Rei, checked them in, and the food was arranged on two long serving tables. Often eighty people or more would come, bringing thirty or forty dishes—everything from appetizers and salads to tamales, burritos, enchiladas, and casseroles, to breads and desserts—all made with chiles. A signal was given, and people moved down both sides of the tables, serving themselves. Plates piled high soon meant an empty table, and woe to anyone who arrived twenty minutes late!

One day, with a potluck drawing near, my daughter, Holly, challenged me to produce a green chile ice cream. It turned out so well that a local ice cream purveyor sold it at his shop for several years. It's one of those really great taste surprises that make you wish you'd left more room for dessert.

 1   quart French vanilla ice cream
 ½ avocado, pitted, peeled, and pureed
 Juice of ½ large lime
 ¼ cup canned diced mild green chiles
 ¼ cup coarsely chopped salted roasted mixed nuts (no peanuts)
 2   to 3 drops green food coloring

Soften the ice cream in the refrigerator for at least 1 hour.

Add the lime juice to the pureed avocado and mix thoroughly. Place the green chiles in a sieve and rinse with cold water.

Place the ice cream in a large bowl and combine all the ingredients, blending well. Return to the ice cream container, placing the extra in an additional bowl, and refreeze for at least 2 hours.

From the Dessert Cupboard

Green on Green Avocado Dessert

Avocados, long ago called "alligator pears," were hardly known in this country in the 1930s. They were a splendid treat when I was a child, and I was thrilled when a young engineer from Brazil stayed with my family and taught me how to make this scrumptious dish. Years later it made its way onto the menu. It's a chilled, sometimes frozen, avocado dessert that is simply delicious. Don't tell your guests it's made from avocados, because lots of people are nervous about eating avocados for dessert, however good it may be!

Serves 4 to 6

1 large ripe avocado, pitted and peeled (black-skinned Haas avocados from California are delicious)
Juice of 3 large limes
¾ cup confectioners' sugar
½ pint heavy cream

Puree the avocado in a food processor.

Combine the lime juice and sugar, stirring to dissolve the sugar. Add the lime juice–sugar mixture to the avocado puree and blend thoroughly.

In a separate bowl, whip the cream until firm. Fold the avocado mixture into the cream and blend gently and well. Pipe or spoon into individual ramekins or pretty glasses and refrigerate. These will hold well, covered with plastic wrap, for 2 days. You may freeze them, too, removing them from the freezer 30 minutes prior to serving.

Guava Paste with Cream Cheese

This easy dessert, brought to us by The Fort's first manager, a Cuban gentleman named Luis Bonachea, is a combination of tart, sweet fruit paste and smooth, rich cream cheese, which simply delights the soul. And it's likely none of your guests has ever had it before. It consists of alternate slices of guava paste and cream cheese.

Buy Pasta de Guayaba, a long rectangular stick of guava paste, available at South American groceries or natural food stores. It is guava fruit that has been boiled down into a thick jelly. Both Goya and Ancel make it.

For each guest, simply cut two ½-inch-thick slices of guava paste, lay them nicely on a dessert plate, and alternate with 2 similar cuts of Kraft Philadelphia Brand cream cheese. Garnish with a sprig of fresh mint and eat with a fork, making sure each bite contains equal amounts of guava paste and cream cheese.

Guava Cream Pie with Chocolate Curls

Inspired by Key Lime Pie, I experimented with a variety of fruit concentrates to come up with other flavors: papaya, tangerine, mango, and my favorite, guava. To ensure that the pie firms up and to offset the natural sweetness of guava and other tropical fruits, I squeeze in a fresh lime. A French *confiseur* taught me that a touch of liqueur or alcohol in some form is a must in pastry desserts, so I added a dash of Cointreau to the pie shell, which moistens it and adds a nice touch to this light summer dessert.

Serves 12

1 large dry sponge cake shell (like Bahlsen)
⅓ cup Cointreau plus water to make ½ cup
1 cup frozen guava puree or concentrate
1 can Eagle Brand sweetened condensed milk
Drops of red food coloring
Juice of 1 lime
1 4-ounce or larger bar Ghirardelli sweet dark chocolate or equivalent high-quality chocolate

Place the sponge cake shell on a pie pedestal or a large plate. Pour the Cointreau-water mix over the shell evenly. Place the guava puree and condensed milk in a blender with a few drops of red coloring. Beat until thoroughly mixed, adding the lime juice while beating. Pour into the pie shell and spread evenly with a spatula. Refrigerate.

Place the chocolate bar on a microwaveable plate. Using the lowest setting, heat the chocolate for about 10 seconds, until it is less firm but not soft. You may want to rotate it halfway through if your microwave heats unevenly. The chocolate must be just soft enough that when you run a blade against it at a 90-degree angle, the chocolate will curl upward against the blade. Or you may run the softened chocolate against the slicing blade of a mandoline or grater. Garnish the pie with chocolate curls. Chill well and serve.

Dusty Road Sundae

My daughter, Holly, married Jeremy Kinney in February 1996. Jeremy's favorite dessert is a sundae that he calls a "Dusty." It's very simply malted milk powder sprinkled over coffee ice cream. I remember relishing "Dusty Roads" back in New England in the 1940s. The coffee ice cream was the road, the hot fudge sauce was the tar, and malted milk powder was the dust.

In Jeremy's honor we added The Fort's version of the Dusty Road Sundae to the menu, using Promez mesquite powder, which tastes like the insides of malted milk balls. It's an old Native American food, high in protein and with a sweet deliciousness.

Per sundae:

2 large scoops coffee ice cream
3 tablespoons hot fudge sauce (my favorite is Narsai's Chocolate Decadence; see Suppliers, page 303)
1 heaping tablespoon Promez mesquite powder (see Suppliers, page 303) or Horlicks or Carnation malted milk powder
Whipped cream
Chocolate-covered coffee bean for garnish

Place the ice cream in a dish, pour the sauce over it, sprinkle on the mesquite powder, and top with whipped cream and a coffee bean.

Mesquite Powder

I grew up on malted milk. I drank it for breakfast on Pullman railroad dining cars, had it at home whenever I was sick, and chewed on Horlicks plain or chocolate malted milk tablets going to school. During Prohibition many breweries converted their malting operations to making malted milk. Soda fountains everywhere whipped up "malts" or "malted milk shakes," combining ice cream, milk, chocolate syrup, and a few spoons of malted milk powder. Chocolate-covered malted milk balls have been a favorite of moviegoers for over a half century.

Horlicks malted milk, originally an American company, now is produced in England in bulk, then sent to Hong Kong for bottling and distribution to Asia and the United States. I buy my bottles of Horlicks here in Denver at an Asian grocery store.

This spring, dear friend Teresa McCrimmon brought me a zippered bag of a different malty powder called mesquite powder. It tastes just like the inside of a malted milk ball and is derived from the pods and seeds of the mesquite plant, familiar to most Americans as a wood used for a delicious flavor when grilling. They are hammer-milled and filtered, and the resulting powder is useful and wonderfully tasty.

When the Spanish arrived in Peru over three hundred years ago, they thought the mesquite pods were carob, or *garroba* in Spanish, and the plants were so named. In Peru they make and sell a molasses-like sweet syrup made from the powder, called *algarrobina*. A popular Peruvian drink is made with algarrobina syrup, canned milk, and Pisco brandy over ice.

Friends of Pronatura, a Tucson, Arizona, environmental company, is marketing the Promez mesquite powder, which is approved by the Food and Drug Administration, as a non-sucrose sweetener useful for diabetics.

Red Chile Dinner Menu

Finger Fajitas with Buffalo and Red Chile Sauce
Posole with Pork and Chipotles
Chimayo Chicken in the New Mexican Style

Chile Chocolate Cake
Coffee or Tea

In a Lakota war shirt and buffalo-horn helmet, Sam Arnold "tomahawks" a bottle of champagne, much as French soldiers once did with bayonets. The blade hits the glass ring at the top of the bottle, and the cork and glass ring shoot off under the pressure of the bubbly.

From the Bar

In a second-story room at Bent's Fort was a huge slate billiard table. Across one end of the room ran a counter or bar over which drinkables were served. Although we don't boast a billiard table, we do serve concoctions of the nineteenth century as well as modern-day libations. It's a standing offer at The Fort that anyone who gives the Mountain Man Toast from memory has his drink on the house.

THE MOUNTAIN MAN TOAST

In 1990 the meeting hall of the United Nations' International Atomic Energy Agency (IAEA) in Vienna, Austria, rang with a toast. More than one hundred Atomic Energy Conference delegates from fifty nations raised their glasses high and repeated lustily after me the "Mountain Man Toast." I had been invited to Vienna as a media consultant by the IAEA for a conference on exploring ways to make atomic plants more user-friendly. At the final session I was asked to lead the toast. The Mountain Man Toast evokes the Old West, with 1830s fur trade–period jargon.

The toast requires motions as well as words and is the sort of ritual that warms the soul and brings smiles to the faces of hearty eaters and drinkers everywhere.

"Here's to the childs what's come afore (Glass in right hand, held at shoulder)

And here's to the pilgrims, what's come arter. (Glass in right hand, arm extended)

May yer trails be free of griz, (Left hand over glass, making clawing motion with fingers)

Yer packs filled with plews, (Left and right arms extend out, making a circle)

And fat buffler in yer pot! (Glass extended, left hand rubs/points at your belly)

WAUGH!" (Extend hand with glass)

The toast was created in 1988 when Dr. Peter Olch and his wife, Mary, and I and my wife, Carrie, were invited to Bent's Fort to give talks. Peter gave his famous speech on "Bleeding, Purging, and Puking," or medicine on the western frontier. I gave a talk on the culinary delicacies of the mountain man (dried buffalo lung with congealed blood pudding among them). After the hot day was over, we retired to a Mexican restaurant for dinner.

All four of us were authors with a good command of early nineteenth-century words and phrases. It was only a matter of adding a very large pitcher of margaritas, and the Mountain Man Toast was born. The toast has since traveled the world over, been printed and reprinted, and has gained a life of its own.

Childs:	What the mountain men called one another.
Pilgrim:	Lightly derisive term used by mountain men for the "sod-busting" covered wagon emigrants coming west.
Arter:	After.
Griz:	Grizzly bear, a major cause of death for mountain men.
Plews:	Large beaver pelts, originating from the French word *plus*, pronounced "plew." The extra-large pelts were marked with a plus sign, so big beaver skins were called "plews" by Americans.
Fat buffler in yer pot:	Fat, tasty buffalo in your belly.
Waugh:	Historic Sioux exclamation, meaning "cheers" or "right on" (see page 294).

Bent's Fort Hailstorm Julep

Back in the 1830s at Bent's Fort in southeastern Colorado, the favorite hot-weather drink, especially on the Fourth of July, was the Hailstorm. Enjoyed by trappers, voyageurs (traveling men employed by fur trade companies), Mexicans, and Native Americans alike, it is the earliest known mixed drink in Colorado and was described in a number of journals of the early West. The Hailstorm was originally made with either Monongahela whiskey from Pittsburgh or a wheat whiskey from Taos, three hundred miles to the south of Old Bent's Fort. At The Fort we use a variety of whiskeys or cognac for this bestselling drink.

Per serving:

3 ounces bourbon, scotch, or cognac

2 teaspoons sugar (confectioners' sugar is best because it dissolves easily)

2 sprigs fresh mint leaves

Crushed ice to fill one widemouthed pint Mason jar or julep cup

Place the alcohol, sugar, and mint in the jar and fill with ice. Secure the lid and shake vigorously 50 times. If using a julep cup, just muddle it with a silver spoon, crushing the mint against the ice and the walls of the jar. (I like to do a little chant to the god of mint during this process.) The ice will bruise the mint, releasing its flavor, and begin to melt to dilute the drink. When well shaken, remove the lid and drink from the jar.

NOTE: If you are preparing these for a party, fill jars with sugar, mint, and ice, and set them out for guests to add their own choice of liquor. French canning jars work well, because the tops are attached and you don't have to scavenge for lids at the end of the evening.

Real Georgia Mint Julep

In the pre–Civil War south, mint juleps identified a distinct way of life. Business was done out on the verandah with a julep or two. Courting involved juleps, too, again usually on the verandah. Thomas Jefferson even designed a special julep cup that is still made. There are still many rules for how fine the ice has to be crushed; how much sugar should be added; how big the silver goblet should be or if a cup is used instead; how many mint leaves to add. Should one use normal spearmint leaves or peppermint? Should spirits other than cognac or bourbon be added? Every southern colonel has his favorite recipe, but this Real Georgia Mint Julep, served in Mason jars in a tradition begun at the Kentucky horse races, is so good that you'll feel like a hog in hickory nuts. The perfume of peach makes it especially wonderful.

Per serving:
- 1 teaspoon cold water
- 1 teaspoon confectioners' sugar
- 12 sprigs fresh mint leaves
- 3 ounces cognac
- 3 ounces peach brandy or whiskey
- Crushed ice to fill a widemouthed pint Mason jar or julep cup

Place the water in the jar. Add the sugar and dissolve it. Add the mint, cognac, and peach brandy, and fill the jar with ice. Stir with a spoon but do not crush the mint.

Jim Bridger

We created this drink in 1964 and named it for the great frontiersman. Jim Bridger was a fur trapper who made a name for himself in the Wind River, Wyoming, area and throughout the West. He never came as far south as Bent's Fort, we believe, but Alfred Jacob Miller painted Ol' Gabe Bridger (his real name was Gabriel) on horseback in Wyoming wearing a British armored breastplate, a gift from the western-sojourning Scottish lord Sir William Drummond Stewart.

One hundred fifty years later, a descendant of his visited us and enjoyed the concoction. But she disclosed that Jim had been a teetotaler and would not have added the rum!

Per serving:
1 ounce apple juice concentrate
1 ounce fresh orange juice
1 ounce sweet and sour syrup (available at liquor stores)
1 ounce lime juice
½ ounce grenadine
1 dash orgeat syrup or Falernum (almond syrup)
3 ounces Jamaica golden rum
Crushed ice to almost fill a widemouthed pint Mason jar
Orange slice and maraschino cherry for garnish

Combine all the ingredients except the garnish in the jar. Top with the orange slice and maraschino cherry.

Bear's Blood

This was a favorite while we were experimenting with original creations in the early days of The Fort. We soon discovered, however, that it did not work to have the waiters serve as judges. They were soon smashed.

Per serving:
3 ounces orange juice
3 ounces light rum
½ ounce grenadine
Juice of ½ lime
Dash of orange flower water
Dash of sweet and sour syrup (available at liquor stores)
Crushed ice to half-fill a widemouthed pint Mason jar
Carbonated water to top
Mint leaf for garnish

Combine all the ingredients except the carbonated water and mint leaf in a widemouthed pint Mason jar. Top with carbonated water and a mint leaf.

How to Teach a Bear to Drink

How do you teach a bear to drink from a bottle? You take a bottle of the bear's favorite drink—root beer or Kool-Aid, in Sissy's case. Hammer a nail through the bottle cap in three places to make small holes, then give the bottle to the bear. She'll worry it and worry it, first licking the cap, and when she realizes where the sweet bubbly liquid is coming from, she'll suck at the cap. Soon you can give her an open bottle, and she'll hold it up and guzzle the sweet stuff down.

It was great fun to take Sissy into the barroom. Hermann, the bartender, filled up a bottle with fountain cola, and Sissy would belly up to the bar, standing up like a man, to swill it down just like anyone else. Some bar patrons were sure they had reached their drinking limit when Sissy showed up!

From the Bar

Father Pelayo's Pinto Colada

I first had this drink at the Inn at Loretto hotel bar in Santa Fe. I thought I'd died and gone to heaven. It was served in a tiny glass, leaving me wanting more. So at The Fort we've increased the drink to 12 ounces and serve it in a pint Mason jar. I am just sure that my favorite Mexican cook, Father Geronimo Pelayo, would have loved it back in 1780. If one can drink in heaven, he'll be enjoying this—and in pint jars, too.

Per serving:
4 ounces pineapple juice
4 ounces coconut milk
3 ounces gold Jamaica rum
1½ ounces Frangelico liqueur
Crushed ice to fill a widemouthed pint Mason jar

Stir and serve in a widemouthed pint Mason jar.

St. Vrain's Mule

Ginger was a major spice in nineteenth-century America. Gingerbread and ginger cookies were commonly eaten. Bars served ginger beer and ginger brandy. Every kitchen cabinet contained dried ginger to use with meats, birds, sauces, and all manner of desserts.

The Wayside Inn in East Sudbury, Massachusetts, serves a historic drink of half ginger brandy and half white rum. It's called the "OO-AH!" because that's what you say when you drink it!

St. Vrain's Mule is even simpler but no less delicious. Named for the partner of the Bent brothers, Ceran St. Vrain, who was known to ride a crazy mule, it is a large iced cup or stein filled with a combination of ginger beer and ginger brandy.

Bee-Bite

Per serving:
2 ounces gin
2 ounces light cream or half-and-half
1 rounded tablespoon honey
Juice of ½ lemon
¼ cup ice

Blend in a blender and serve in a sour glass.

The Last Roundup

Our drink menu warns that we restrict guests to two of these per person unless he's riding a horse who knows his way home!

Per serving:
1 ounce Demerara rum
1 ounce white rum
1 ounce Puerto Rican gold rum
1 ounce Jamaica Mount Gay rum
4 ounces orange juice
3 ounces sweet and sour syrup (available at liquor stores)
1 ounce Falernum (almond syrup)
½ ounce grenadine
Carbonated water to top
Orange slice and maraschino cherry for garnish

Combine all liquid ingredients except the soda with ice in a wide-mouthed pint Mason jar. Top with carbonated water and garnish with an orange slice and cherry.

From the Bar

289

New Orleans Sazerac Cocktail

In mid-nineteenth-century newspapers, long advertisements proclaimed the merits of bitters, among them Hostetters and Peychaud. During the days of Bent's Fort, a few drops of bitters were commonly added to a small glass of spirits, often cognac. Peychaud is still in business today, produced by the Sazerac company in New Orleans.

The story is that Antoine Peychaud, a French apothecary on the West Indies isle of San Domingo, fled during a native uprising in the 1790s with naught but his clothes and his bitters recipe. He arrived in New Orleans where he began making and selling his delicious potion. Quite unlike Angostura, Peychaud's reddish bitters has a slight taste of fresh fennel or anise, and makes this a delightful drink.

Per serving:
½ ounce Pernod or other pastis
3 ounces cognac or bourbon
2 teaspoons fine sugar
8 drops Peychaud bitters
Orange slice and maraschino cherry for garnish

Pour the pastis into a large rocks glass and roll the glass to coat the inner walls. Pour out any that remains. Pour in the cognac, sugar, and bitters. Stir, add ice cubes, and stir again. Garnish with an orange slice and cherry.

Caipirinha (or Kaipirinha)

Over a decade ago a young German fellow named Jörg Fischer stayed with us for a year to get restaurant experience in America. He fell in love with the American West, especially its wonderful food. He now operates the Santa Fe New Mexican Restaurant and Bar in Kiel, Germany, and has succeeded in making margaritas immensely popular there. He also serves this drink, well known among the German student population. We have adopted the Caipirinha (pronounced ky-per-AIN-ya) at The Fort. The alcohol is a clear Brazilian brandy distilled from sugarcane, quite different from rum. Basically, this is a fresh lime sour.

Per serving:
1 lime
3 ounces Pitu cachaça (Brazilian brandy)
2 teaspoons brown sugar
Dash of simple syrup
Crushed ice to fill a short bar glass

Cut the lime in half and deeply cross-hatch both halves with a sharp knife, cutting through the peel but not all the way through so that each half remains in 1 piece. Place them, cut side up, in the glass and crush to squeeze out the juices. Add the cachaça, brown sugar, and simple syrup, and fill the glass with crushed ice. Serve with a swizzle stick and continue to prod the lime and stir as the ice melts.

1732 Philadelphia Fish-House Punch

As a young man in Pennsylvania, I drank this punch at many weddings. It goes down easily but can be truly lethal. I came across it in one of my favorite books of nineteenth-century libations, *Jerry Thomas' Bar-Tender's Guide,* published in 1887, and added it to our menu in 1994 because it is indeed a historic drink.

According to N. E. Beveridge's *Cups of Valor,* Fish-House Punch may be the oldest punch still in use in America. Word has it that it originated in London as Farmers' Club Punch late in the 1600s. It then traveled to the famous tavern Fishhouse of the State, believed to be in Schuylkill near Philadelphia. Because of an association with Norfolk and the navy yard in the early 1800s, the National Trust for Historic Preservation serves it today under the name Decatur Punch.

Makes about 2 quarts

1½ pints sweet and sour syrup (available at liquor stores)
¾ pound white sugar dissolved in a little water
½ pint cognac
¼ pint peach brandy
¼ pint Jamaica rum
1 pint cold water

Combine all the ingredients with ice and serve. It tastes so smooth that some guests may not be aware of its power. If you serve it from an unattended punch bowl, post a warning sign.

Jersey Sour

Toward the end of the 1700s, a group of farmers near Pittsburgh, Pennsylvania, refused to pay tax on the whiskey they produced. They attempted to form a separate country, but President George Washington came among them, accompanied by the New Jersey National Guard, and put down the Whiskey Rebellion. The New Jersey guardsmen were often portly and wore long, dark green great-coats left open to reveal a red vest with black buttons. The defeated Pennsylvanians derisively termed these men "watermelon soldiers." This historic sour is a memorial to those heroes.

Per serving:
1 large teaspoon confectioners' sugar dissolved in a little water
2 or 3 dashes lemon juice
4 ounces applejack
Fresh berries for garnish

Fill the glass with crushed ice and all the ingredients except the berries. Shake, strain, and garnish with the berries.

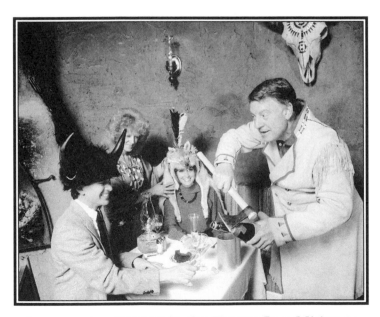

Anniversary Dinner in the Tower: In addition to tomahawked champagne, victims receive a photograph taken of them in buffalo helmet and coyote hat.

Good Evening! Good Cheer! Welcome! Or . . . Waugh!

Anyone who has visited The Fort or read the Mountain Man Toast no doubt has encountered the word "waugh." *Waugh!* is our watchword at The Fort, and we often say it instead of the more traditional "Good evening!"

The first recorded use of the word "waugh" that I've found was by a newspaper reporter in 1811 at a meeting of Sioux Indian chiefs in western Wisconsin. He wrote that at the meeting, when the big chief gave a lengthy speech and said something that the others liked or agreed with, they'd rock back and forth and exclaim, "Waugh!" The closest English equivalent is "Right on!" In the 1830s mountain men were often quoted as saying "Waugh!" and all modern mountain men use it today.

When pronounced correctly (exuberantly, from the belly), the word sounds more like "*hoooowah!*" And since it's the sound of the word that counts, it can be spelled many ways: waugh, wagh, wa, wah, hwa, ouaaa, waw, roi, roy. In 1993 we hosted our first "Wa" dinner, inviting anyone with the name to attend the special evening. Carrie and I have been made honorary Waughs by the group and always enjoy these memorable evenings.

Waugh!

1809 Stone Fence

In early nineteenth-century America, drunkenness was rife. Congress passed many laws trying to limit the manufacture and sale of spirits. Rum and whiskey were two major offenders, but the biggest problem was applejack, which nearly everybody could make. Apple cider, once fermented, can be frozen and the alcohol poured off; you don't even need a still. One food historian suggested that the famed Johnny Appleseed who traveled the countryside planting apple trees might well have been the publicity man for the distiller's league! Temperance groups literally decimated the apple orchards of early America in an effort to slow alcohol consumption. Fortunately, they didn't succeed in wiping them out. This drink, from *Jerry Thomas' Bar-Tender's Guide,* published in 1887, is a Fort favorite.

Per serving:
1 wineglass of bourbon or rye whiskey
2 or 3 small lumps of ice
Apple cider

Combine the bourbon and ice in a small bar glass and fill with sweet cider.

Original Santa Fe 1848 Gin Cocktail

At the United States Hotel on San Francisco Street in Santa Fe, travelers in 1848 found that their host was a New Englander by the name of "Long Eben" (short for Ebenezer). He served a concoction called a Gin Cocktail. This slightly sweet but powerful gin drink is a dandy!

Per serving:
3 ounces gin
Dash of Peychaud bitters
2 dashes maraschino liqueur
2 dashes white vermouth
2 small lumps of ice
Small lemon slice for garnish

Stir all the ingredients together with the ice, strain, and serve garnished with a lemon slice.

From the Bar

295

Strawberry Sangaree

Fruit sangarees were popular in the days of Bent's Fort. Fruit syrups were combined with red wine and ice for a cool, refreshing drink. Made the same way today at The Fort, they're very popular during the hot summer months.

Per serving:
- 6 ounces red wine
- ½ cup frozen strawberries in syrup
- ⅓ cup cracked ice

Blend in a blender and serve in a tall glass.

Virgin Strawberry Sangaree

Per serving:
- ⅔ cup frozen strawberries in syrup
- 2 ounces sweet and sour syrup (available at liquor stores)
- 4 ounces sparkling mineral water

Blend in a blender and serve in a tall glass. Nonalcoholic red wine may be substituted for the mineral water.

Pilot's Cocktail

Since airplane pilots may not drink alcohol for many hours before flying, we developed the Pilot's Cocktail, which is close to an alcoholic drink in taste but without the alcohol. We simply fill a wide-mouthed Mason jar with ice and our favorite mineral water, then add a good squirt or two of Peychaud bitters. The tiny amount of alcohol in the bitters is insignificant, yet the bitters' flavor provides a wonderfully refreshing drink that's not sweetened with sugar. It's excellent for diabetics, calorie counters, and restaurant owners.

Hot Buttered Rum

In Colonial America, rum was plentiful due to trade with the West Indies. Newly made rum was often shipped from Jamaica and other British colonial islands to the London docks where it rested to age. Some of it, though, was shipped to America, where it was often drunk pretty raw, with just a bit of sugar and water to ease its way down.

Even today, nothing in the world tastes better when you've been out on a cold, snowy day than a real hot buttered rum. I like the taste of heavier Jamaica Mount Gay or Demerara rum in this drink, though not the really dark ones like Myers's.

Per serving:
6 ounces water
1 rounded teaspoon Hot Buttered Rum Batter (recipe below)
2 ounces dark rum
Cinnamon stick
Pat of butter

Bring a bar mug of water to a boil in the microwave. Stir in the batter and the rum. Garnish with a cinnamon stick and top with the butter.

Hot Buttered Rum Batter
Makes enough for about 30 drinks

½ pound (2 sticks) butter
1 cup dark brown sugar
1 teaspoon ground cinnamon
¼ teaspoon grated nutmeg

Soften the butter. Whip all the ingredients together and store, covered, in the refrigerator.

From the Bar

297

Yard of Flannel

A fine colonial winter specialty in taverns, this hot ale drink takes its name from its lovely soft texture. The Yard of Flannel is a wonderful holiday drink that used to be a favorite among the coachmen, outriders, and wagoneers. Coming out of the tavern, bartenders would hand up a yard-long glass of this to freezing coach drivers perched high above. The recipe sounds far more complicated than it is, and is worth the effort in the resulting warmth of body and soul.

Serves 4

1 quart good ale
4 eggs
4 tablespoons sugar
1 teaspoon powdered ginger
½ cup Jamaica dark rum
Grated nutmeg for sprinkling

Heat the ale in a saucepan.

Beat the eggs with the sugar in a blender. Add the ginger, then the rum, and blend well. When the ale is almost boiling, slowly combine the two mixtures, alternately pouring the hot ale a bit at a time into the egg mixture and blending well, to prevent curdling. Pour back and forth between the saucepan and the blender until it is silky, or as soft as flannel. Serve in a large glass sprinkled with nutmeg.

Trade Whiskey

The alcohol that came west, despite federal efforts to limit or eliminate it, was plentiful. It was referred to by many names, among them "Great Father's Milk," "belly wash," and "whistle-belly vengeance." Traders often watered it down to as little as 3 percent to extend its profitability. Many strange additives were used to give an interesting taste—red chile, tobacco, or even a liberal pinch of black gunpowder (sulfur, charcoal, and saltpeter). Some said the sulfur was good for a spring tonic, the charcoal kept teeth bright, and the saltpeter preserved your meat. It was said that when ordinary whiskey was later made available to the Indians, they rejected it because it "didn't have that good old-fashioned flavor."

Having read about this concoction in early trappers' journals, I tried it and found it surprisingly good. We began serving it in 1964, and it has remained on the menu ever since. Modern consumers of this libation find it both tasty and smooth, and many prefer it to regular raw whiskey.

Makes 36 shots

1 cup water
2 tablespoons cut tobacco (Virginia Burley is best)
4 small dried red peppers (piquines)
1 liter Old Crow or similar bourbon whiskey
½ teaspoon black gunpowder (*do not use modern high-speed powder; it is poisonous!*)

Make a tea by boiling the water, tobacco, and red peppers together for 5 minutes. Strain and add the tea to the whiskey, little by little, to taste. Then add the gunpowder. It should have a gentle nip from the peppers and an herbal taste from the tobacco. The small amount of saltpeter in the black powder will have no effect. Damn!

From the Bar

Prickly Pear Margarita

Stubby prickly pear cacti with their flat, pear-shaped lobes, are a familiar sight throughout the Southwest. Prickly pear syrups and jellies have recently popped up in gourmet food stores across the country, but their use is nothing new to the inhabitants of the West. In the days of Bent's Fort, traders sometimes came up from New Mexico bearing a syrup made from prickly pear juice. In the 1830s, references were made to cold prickly pear drinks at the south Platte River fur trade forts: Lupton, Jackson, Vasquez, and St. Vrain.

The cactus's fruit has tiny spines on it, and these are best burned off over an open fire. Hold with a fork, not fingers. Cut and ream out the meat and then press through a sieve, expressing the wonderfully scarlet juice. Cook this with sugar to make a syrup. Or you may prefer to buy Cahill's Prickly Pear Syrup or frozen prickly pear puree (see Suppliers, page 303).

Per serving:
2 ounces white tequila (preferably Herradura)
Juice of ½ large lime
1 teaspoon confectioners' sugar
1½ ounces triple sec
1½ ounces prickly pear syrup
½ cup cracked ice
Salt for the rim of the glass
Slice of lime for garnish

Shake all the ingredients except the salt and lime slice with a little ice in a mixing glass. Strain and serve straight up in a salt-rimmed glass garnished with a slice of lime.

Blue Blazer

According to *The American Heritage Cookbook*, Professor Jerry Thomas, author of *Jerry Thomas' Bar-Tender's Guide*, printed in 1887, was the inventor of the Blue Blazer.

It originated when a miner came into Professor Thomas's El Dorado Bar in Sacramento carrying a poke of gold dust. The miner told how he'd been up to his waist in cold mountain water and snow to find his gold strike, and now his greatest desire was a truly warming drink. He was directed to come back in twenty minutes. Returning to the dimly lit bar, he saw Professor Thomas with a cup in each hand, pouring a living stream of fire back and forth through the air. The cups held what we today call a whiskey toddy, containing alcohol strong enough to make it flame brilliantly.

When I read about this, I had to have the Blue Blazer at The Fort. I set about practicing, wearing heavy leather gloves and using 151 proof rum. Surprisingly, it doesn't take long to develop a style that looks very dramatic but is safe enough to do bare-handed. Our bartenders became accustomed to making it without harming either guests or themselves, but it does take practice and a good pair of gloves!

Per serving:
3 ounces high-proof whiskey
2 ounces boiling water
Dash of simple syrup
Sliver of lemon peel

Combine the ingredients in a mug and heat in a microwave until hot enough to ignite when a match is held to it. Immediately pour it into a second mug, then back into the first, and back again several times, gradually stretching the distance between the mugs. It is indeed a "blue blazer" and heartwarming as well as impressive looking. But don't burn your lips when the drinking begins! Warn your guests that the rim may be hot.

Lemonade with Chia

In Mexico, street vendors at stands filled with ten-gallon glass jars of *refrescos* offer refreshing cold drinks. They are delicious: tamarind, rice water, horchata, and my favorite, fresh lemonade with chia seeds. Chia, whose botanical name is salvia, has long been used as a food by the Native Americans of California, Arizona, New Mexico, Nevada, and Old Mexico. Chia seeds were so highly prized in Montezuma's day that they were accepted as payment for taxes. Today it's grown in Mexico and south Texas, and is available in most herb or natural food stores. Sometimes the seeds are sold as a novelty on a clay pot shaped like a head or an animal. You sprinkle the seeds on it, water it, and in a few days, *voilà!* Green chia sprout hair or fur.

Our chia laced lemonade is a summertime favorite. Somewhat like tapioca, chia seeds are fun to nibble on as you drink your lemonade.

Makes about 1 quart

½   **teaspoon chia seeds**
½   **cup hot water**
1   **quart very cold freshly made lemonade**

Stir the chia seeds into the hot water, then add to the lemonade.

Suppliers of Hard-to-Find Ingredients

BEANS: ANASAZI AND OTHERS
Native Seed/SEARCH
2509 N. Campbell Avenue, #325
Tucson, AZ 85719
Fax: (520) 327-5821

BUFFALO
Rocky Mountain Natural Meats
P.O. Box 16668
Denver, CO 80216
(303) 838-7005

CAHILL'S PRICKLY PEAR SYRUP
Sunrise Desert Foods
490 E. Pima Street
Phoenix, AZ 85004
(888) 224-4457

CANOLA SEEDS
West Star Farms
5430 West Road, 9 North
Del Norte, CO 81132
(719) 754-9161

CAVIAR
Boyajian, Inc.
349 Lenox Street
Newtonville, MA 02062
(800) 419-4677

CHESTNUTS, WHOLE, ROASTED, PEELED
Williams-Sonoma
(800) 541-2233

CHILE: DIXON PURE GROUND NEW MEXICAN RED CHILE; CHILE RISTRAS
The Chile Shop
109 E. Water Street
Santa Fe, NM 87501
(505) 983-6080

CHUTNEY
Geetha's Gourmet Products
India-West Enterprises, Inc.
1589 Imperial Ridge
Las Cruces, NM 88001
(800) 274-0475

ENSTROM'S CHOCOLATE ALMOND TOFFEE
Enstrom's Candies
P.O. Box 1088
Grand Junction, CO 81502
(800) 367-8766

HUCKLEBERRY PRESERVES
Eva Gates Homemade Preserves
P.O. Box 696
Bigfork, MT 59911
(406) 837-4356

MUSHROOMS
Rocky Mountain Shiitake
572 Holmes Gulch Road
Bailey, CO 80421
(303) 838-7005

NARSAI'S CHOCOLATE DECADENCE AND OTHER GOURMET DESSERT SAUCES
350 Berkeley Park Boulevard
Kensington, CA 94707
(510) 527-7900

NIELSEN-MASSEY VANILLA
Nielsen-Massey Vanillas, Inc.
1550 Shields Drive
Waukegan, IL 60085-8307
(800) 525-7873

ORANGE OIL
Boyajian, Inc.
349 Lenox Street
Newtonville, MA 02062
(800) 419-4677

POTATOES
White Mountain Farms
8890 Lane 4 North
Mosca, CO 81146
(719) 378-2436

PROMEZ MESQUITE POWDER
Friends of Pronatura
240 E. Limberlost
Tucson, AZ 85705
(520) 887-1188

QUAIL
Manchester Farms
P.O. Box 97
Dalzell, SC 29040
(803) 469-2588

QUINOA
White Mountain Farms
8890 Lane 4 North
Mosca, CO 81146
(719) 378-2436

RATTLESNAKE
Colorado Mountain Game
12556 Weld County Road
P.O. Box 568
Brighton, CO 80601
(303) 659-9219
Fax: (303) 659-1090

RED CHILE HONEY
Santa Fe Olé
P.O. Box 2433
Santa Fe, NM 87504
(505) 473-0724

VERJUICE
Bonnie Doone Vineyards
P.O. Box 8376
Santa Cruz, CA 99506
(408) 425-3625

Bibliography

Abert, Lieutenant James W. *Through the Country of the Comanche Indians in the Fall of the Year 1845*. Edited by John Galvin. San Francisco: John Howell Books, 1970.

American Heritage Cookbook, The. The American Heritage Publishing Company, Inc., 1964; distributed by Simon and Schuster, New York.

Arnold, Sam. *Fryingpans West*. Denver: Arnold and Company, 1985.

———. *Eating Up the Santa Fe Trail*. Niwot, Colo.: University Press of Colorado, 1990.

Barclay, Alexander. Letter dated October 15, 1838. Bancroft Library, University of California, Berkeley.

Beveridge, N. E. *Cups of Valor*. Harrisburg, Pa.: Stackpole Books, 1968.

Ervin, Janet Halliday, ed. *The White House Cookbook*. Chicago: Follett Publishing, 1964.

Foster, Nelson, and Linda S. Cordell, eds. *Chilies to Chocolate:* Food the Americas Gave the World, Tucson, Ariz.: University of Arizona Press, 1992.

Granado, Diego. *Libro del Arte Cozina*, 1599. Owned by the Hispanic Society of America, New York City. Microfilm.

Magoffin, Susan Shelby. *Down the Santa Fe Trail and into Mexico: The Diary of Susan Shelby Magoffin, 1846-1847*. Edited by Stella M. Drumm. New Haven, Conn.: Yale University Press, 1926.

Meseroll, Marie C., ed. *A Pennsbury Manor Cookbook*. Historical Society of Pennsylvania and The Pennsbury Society, 1986.

Ruxton, George Frederick. *Life in the Far West*. Edited by Leroy R. Hafen. Norman, Okla.: University of Oklahoma Press, 1951.

Thomas, Jerry. *Jerry Thomas' Bar-Tender's Guide*. New York: Fitzgerald Publishing Corporation, 1887.

Whitman, Arthur. *Walter B. Jetton's LBJ Ranch Cookbook*. New York: Pocket Books, 1965.

Index

Index

Index